The FAIR Reader

Critical Studies in Communication and in the Cultural Industries

Herbert I. Schiller, Series Editor

The FAIR Reader: An EXTRA! Review of Press and Politics in the '90s, edited by Jim Naureckas and Janine Jackson
Communication and the Transformation of Economics: Essays in Information, Public Policy, and Political Economy, Robert E. Babe
A Different Road Taken: Profiles in Critical Communication, edited by John A. Lent
Consumer Culture and TV Programming, Robin Andersen
Marketing Madness: A Survival Guide for a Consumer Society, Michael F. Jacobson and Laurie Anne Mazur
Public Television for Sale: Media, the Market, and the Public Sphere, William Hoynes
Counterclockwise: Perspectives on Communication, Dallas Smythe (edited by Thomas Guback)
The Panoptic Sort: A Political Economy of Personal Information, Oscar H. Gandy, Jr.
Triumph of the Image: The Media's War in the Persian Gulf—A Global Perspective, edited by Hamid Mowlana, George Gerbner, and Herbert I. Schiller
The Persian Gulf TV War, Douglas Kellner
Mass Communications and American Empire, Second Edition, Updated, Herbert I. Schiller

FORTHCOMING

Monopoly Television: MTV's Quest to Control the Music, Jack Banks
Invisible Crises, edited by George Gerbner, Hamid Mowlana, and Herbert I. Schiller
Introduction to Media Studies, edited by Stuart Ewen, Elizabeth Ewen, Serafina Bathrick, and Andrew Mattson
The Communications Industry in the American Economy, Thomas Guback
The Social Uses of Photography: Images in the Age of Reproducibility, Hanno Hardt
Ideology, Government Broadcasting, and Global Change, Laurien Alexandre
Hot Shots: An Alternative Video Production Handbook, Tami Gold and Kelly Anderson

The F·A·I·R Reader

An *Extra!* Review of
Press and Politics
in the '90s

edited by
**Jim Naureckas and
Janine Jackson**

Critical Studies in Communication and in the Cultural Industries

All rights reserved. Printed in the United States of America. No part of this publication may be reproduced or transmitted in any form or by any means, electronic or mechanical, including photocopy, recording, or any information storage and retrieval system, without permission in writing from the publisher.

Copyright © 1996 by Westview Press, Inc., A Division of HarperCollins Publishers, Inc.

Published in 1996 in the United States of America by Westview Press, Inc., 5500 Central Avenue, Boulder, Colorado 80301-2877, and in the United Kingdom by Westview Press, 12 Hid's Copse Road, Cumnor Hill, Oxford OX2 9JJ

Library of Congress Cataloging-in-Publication Data
The FAIR reader : an Extra! review of press and politics in the '90s / edited by Jim Naureckas and Janine Jackson.
    p. cm. — (Critical studies in communication and in the cultural industries)
  Articles appeared originally in Extra! or Extra! update.
  Includes bibliographical references and index.
  ISBN 0-8133-2802-0.(hc) — ISBN 0-8133-2803-9 (pbk .)
  1. Press and politics—United States. 2. Mass media—United States —Objectivity. 3. Reporters and reporting— United States. 4. United States—Politics and government —1989– I. Naureckas, Jim. II. Jackson, Janine. III. Extra! (New York, N.Y. : 1987) IV. Series.
PN4888.P6F35 1996
302.23'0973—dc20   95-45758
                                                                                          CIP

The paper used in this publication meets the requirements of the American National Standard for Permanence of Paper for Printed Library Materials Z39.48-1984.

10   9   8   7   6   5   4   3   2   1

*To Lauren, Sean, Caitlin, and Patrick:
Don't believe
everything you read.
—J.N.*

*To my parents
—J.J.*

Contents

Acknowledgments xiii
Introduction: The Media Agenda
JIM NAURECKAS AND JANINE JACKSON   XV

PART ONE
The Bush Years

1 Bending Over Bushwards
George Bush: Not a Wimp, but a Rough Rider   WILLIAM GIBSON   3
Peter Pan-omics: Happy-Talk on the Recession   DOUG HENWOOD   4
Clarence the Credible: Media Delusions
    on the Thomas Story   6
Iran-Contra: "Sweep It Away"   8

2 Rallying 'Round the Flag: The Panama Invasion
The Media Go to War: How Television Sold
    the Panama Invasion   MARK COOK & JEFF COHEN   11

3 Creating the New Hitler: The Gulf War
Media on the March: Journalism in the Gulf   JIM NAURECKAS   20
Gulf War Coverage: The Worst Censorship Was at Home
    JIM NAURECKAS   28
The Polling Game   42
"Slaughter" Is Something Other Countries Do   43
Back to Iraq: News Reporting Echoes Bias of Desert Storm
    SAM HUSSEINI   45

PART TWO
The '92 Election

4 The Primaries: Limiting Choice
On the Campaign Trail: Public Logic Versus Press Logic
    JOSHUA MEYROWITZ   55

Sex, Polls, and Campaign Strategy: How the Press Missed
    the Issues of the '92 Election   JANINE JACKSON   57
Media Campaign to Limit Voters' Choices   66
The Philandering Front-Runner and the Mad Monk   68
Buchanan and Duke: Playing the Same Hand   70

5 The Presidential Campaign: Unfair to Voters

Democracy Versus Punditocracy: The Handful of Insiders
    Who Shaped Campaign News   LAWRENCE SOLEY   77
The Anti-Democratic Convention: Corporations, the Real
    "Special Interests," Got Little Play   JIM NAURECKAS   81
Conventional Wisdom: How the Press Rewrites Democratic
    Party History Every Four Years   JIM NAURECKAS   83
Issues, Images, and Impact: A FAIR Survey of Voters' Knowledge
    in the 1992 Campaign   JUSTIN LEWIS & MICHAEL MORGAN   87
Unfair to Bush? Unfair to Clinton? Campaign Coverage
    Was Unfair to Voters   JIM NAURECKAS   94

6 Race and Gender in the '92 Election

Press Finds "New Candor" in Old Stereotypes   JANINE JACKSON   103
A Short Walk on the Wilder Side   STEVE COBBLE   106
Clinton's Willie Horton?   107
Women Candidates in 1992 Election Coverage
    TIFFANY DEVITT & JANINE JACKSON   108
The Media Factor Behind the "Hillary Factor"   DOROTHEE BENZ   112
Playing Games with Rape and Sexual Harassment   115

PART THREE
Clinton and the Media Agenda

7 Promises to Break: The New Administration

Pundits to Clinton: Break Campaign Promises,
    Ignore "Liberal Interests," Join Washington Insiders
    JIM NAURECKAS   121
Media Litmus Test on Clinton's Cabinet   JIM NAURECKAS   123
Ask Not What Gays Will Do to the Military—
    Ask What the Military Is Doing to Gays   JIM NAURECKAS   126
When Clinton "Soaks the Rich," Pundits Drip
    JEFF COHEN & NORMAN SOLOMON   128
New York Times on Immigrants: Give Us Your Healthy,
    Wealthy, and 24-Hour Nannies
    VEENA CABREROS-SUD & FARAH KATHWARI   130

Lani Guinier: Quota Queen or Misquoted Queen?
ROB RICHIE & JIM NAURECKAS   132

8   **The Scandal Beat**
Whitewater Under the Bridge: How the Press
   Missed the Story   JEFF COHEN & NORMAN SOLOMON   137
Koppel Covers for Limbaugh's Rumor-Mongering   139
Paula Jones and Sexual Harassment: The World Stayed
   Right Side Up   LAURA FLANDERS   141

9   **Trade: NAFTA's Manifest Destiny**
Free Trade Fever Induces Media Delusions
   JOHN SUMMA & PATRICE GREANVILLE   145
Happily Ever NAFTA?   149
NAFTA's Knee-Jerk Press   151
NAFTA Lockout at the *New York Times*   152
Trade Reporting's Information Deficit   DEAN BAKER   153

10 **Health Care Reform: The Single-Payer Taboo**
America's Health Care Crisis: A Case of Media Malpractice
   ROBERT DREYFUSS   157
When "Both Sides" Aren't Enough: The Restricted Debate
   over Health Care Reform   JOHN CANHAM-CLYNE   161
Health Care Reform: Not Journalistically Viable?   165
NPR Health Reform "Debate" Needed Second Opinion   167

11 **War and "Peacekeeping": Intervention in the Clinton Era**
Media on the Somalia Intervention: Tragedy Made Simple
   JIM NAURECKAS   171
Somalia: Shifting Stereotypes   176
Enemy Ally: The Demonization of Jean-Bertrand Aristide
   JIM NAURECKAS   177
Haiti: The Crisis Is Not Over   180

PART FOUR
In Search of Scapegoats

12 **Teen Mothers and Other Young Monsters**
The "Crisis" of Teen Pregnancy: Teenage Girls Pay the Price
   for Media Distortion   JANINE JACKSON   187

Too Many Kids and Too Much Money: The Media's Persistent
    Welfare Stereotypes   RENU NAHATA   191
"Sexually Incorrect"—Or Just Inaccurate?   194
Bashing Youth: Media Myths About Teenagers   MIKE MALES   195

13 The Crime Scam
New York Post: Militant White Daily   205
Crime Contradictions: *U.S. News* Illustrates Flaws
    in Crime Coverage   JANINE JACKSON & JIM NAURECKAS   206
Crime Hysteria's Illogical Conclusion   212
Hearing What They Want to Hear: Media on Jesse Jackson
    on Crime   JANINE JACKSON   213

14 Economic Losers
No Hope for the Homeless at the *New York Times*
    JIM NAURECKAS   217
Geezer-Bashing: Media Attacks on the Elderly
    JOHN HESS   218
Alarming Drops in Unemployment! Why the *New York Times*
    Wants Your Job   DOUG HENWOOD   221

PART FIVE
Beyond Clinton

15 Contracting the American Spectrum: The '94 Election
Wines's World: The Tie-Dyed Clinton   227
Want to Cast an Informed Vote for Congress? Don't Look
    to Major Dailies   DAN SHADOAN   228
Drafting Students into the "War on Immigration": *Channel One*'s
    Anti-Immigrant Propaganda Has a Captive Audience
    KIM DETERLINE   232
"Move to the Right": Pundits' Tried-and-Failed Advice
    JIM NAURECKAS   235

Appendix: The Media's Corporate Connections   239
About the Book and Editors   243
About the Contributors   244
Index   246

Acknowledgments

Thanks are due to all the contributors to *Extra!* and to the staff and interns of FAIR. Among those who provided invaluable help were Jim Levendos, Gabi Meja, and especially Angela Littwin and Rebecca Brown.

We are grateful to all who helped us review the manuscript, especially Geralyn Byers, Jeff Cohen, Carolyn Francis, Doug Henwood, Sam Husseini, Mike Males, Kathleen Naureckas, Steven Rendall, and Norman Solomon.

EDITORS' NOTE

These articles originally appeared in the magazine *Extra!* (or in *Extra! Update,* its companion newsletter). They have been edited for publication in this book, with some minor corrections and style changes. Tenses have been changed to reflect the passage of time.

Introduction:

The Media Agenda

JIM NAURECKAS AND JANINE JACKSON

THINGS WERE SIMPLER in the '80s. Throughout most of that decade, the view of the world presented in mass media accounts closely resembled the vision of reality put forward by official Washington. Books like Edward Herman and Noam Chomsky's *Manufacturing Consent,* Martin Lee and Norman Solomon's *Unreliable Sources,* and Michael Parenti's *Inventing Reality* documented a press corps that was more than willing to bend the facts to suit the reigning ideology of the Reagan and Bush administrations.[1] With a couple of exceptional periods—during the depths of the 1982–1983 recession, and immediately after the revelation of the unconstitutional Iran-contra arms deals—the attitude of journalists toward the White House was summed up in the title of Mark Hertsgaard's book on the Washington press elite: *On Bended Knee.*[2]

In the 1990s, the relationship between press and state has gotten more complicated. George Bush, lionized by the media during the Gulf War, ended up a year later bashing the press—promoting bumper stickers that read, "Annoy the Media/Vote Bush." Journalists singled out Bill Clinton as destined for victory in the race for the 1992 Democratic presidential nomination, and they shaped primary coverage to make this a self-fulfilling prophecy—but they also singled out Clinton for unprecedented focus on personal scandal, dredging up decades-old allegations of sexual infidelity and draft-dodging.

The love-hate relationship between Clinton and the media continued into his term in office. Pundits praised his leadership on issues like deficit reduction and trade, while savaging him on his attempt to lift the military ban on gays and on several of his high-level nominations. His health care reform proposals were first praised, then savaged. Whereas the press had rallied around Reagan-Bush era interventions in Grenada, Panama, and Iraq, Clinton's use of military force in Somalia and Haiti became the focus of intense scrutiny and debate.

What's the explanation for these seeming paradoxes? The essays, studies, and investigative reports in this book—articles that originally appeared in *Extra!* and *Extra! Update,* the publications of the media watch group FAIR (Fairness & Accuracy In Reporting)—attempt to provide an answer.

FAIR is an independent, nonprofit group founded in 1986 to provide progressive criticism of mainstream news media. At the time, media criticism came overwhelmingly from the right, attacking the "liberal bias" of journalists. FAIR emerged to make a structural critique of the news industry—drawing attention to patterns of ownership and sponsorship that limit and direct the content of news.

FAIR points out that the major media in this country are almost exclusively owned by for-profit Fortune 500 companies and that revenues for both print and broadcast journalism come overwhelmingly from corporate advertisers. While the primary goals of both media owners and advertisers is to make a profit, such corporations are also aware of the power of media to shape opinions, and they frequently make use of that power to further a corporate agenda.

It is FAIR's argument that the dominant ideology of the press can be traced back to this corporate agenda. The agenda can be seen in the underlying assumptions of news reports (known as the "conventional wisdom") in the range of viewpoints that are considered "mainstream," in the kinds of sources that are considered credible and legitimate, and in the very definitions of what constituents "news."

It's important to stress that media bias is not a monolithic phenomenon. (If it were, you would not be reading this book, which is published by a subsidiary of a company owned by conservative media mogul Rupert Murdoch.) Corporate board members generally do not send instructions to reporters on how to cover events, and journalists sometimes have a great deal of flexibility about how they cover an individual story. The viewpoints of individual reporters can and do affect their reporting on particular topics.

But the opinions of reporters on the beat are ultimately not as important as the interests of the organizations for which they work. It is the management of news outlets that decides what goes into the paper or out over the airwaves; journalists will rise through the ranks into positions of decisionmaking power to the extent that they serve the needs of the company.

The editors and producers who have the power to decide what's news are disproportionately white males from upper-middle-class backgrounds. At the most powerful, agenda-setting news outlets—like the *New York Times,* the *Washington Post,* the major newsweeklies, and the TV networks—top journalists tend to socialize and identify with governmental and political elites.[3] The ideology of these news managers and pundits can be broadly described as "centrism"—an allegiance to the status quo and to establishment institutions, and a resistance to reforms that would challenge those in power. These individual biases reinforce rather than offset the biases produced by corporate ownership.

The chapters that follow look at how mainstream media have covered the major political issues of the 1990s. They reveal a fairly consistent media agenda behind the transient shifts of who's up and who's down in the press's day-to-day scorecard.

During the Reagan and Bush administrations, corporate leaders closely identified with the White House. As Thomas Ferguson and Joel Rogers argued in their book *Right Turn,* the "Reagan Revolution" did not reflect so much a change in public opinion as it did a turn by business leaders toward a low-wage, low-tax, anti-union strategy.[4] In the 1980s, corporate media owners and sponsors generally allowed the Reagan administration to set the media agenda, in large part because the Reagan message closely matched the interests of news owners and advertisers.

The 1990s present a more complex picture. Bill Clinton was elected president with substantial business support, and his administration has been dominated by appointees with corporate ties. Nearly all of the policies of the Clinton administration have been designed to win corporate support. But the ideology of corporate America has moved far to the right over the past two decades, to the point where a moderately conservative Democrat like Clinton begins to seem dangerously liberal. And unlike the Republican Party, Clinton is dependent to a certain extent on constituencies—like labor and urban minorities—whose interests openly conflict with big business. Many business leaders do not trust him to consistently follow a corporate agenda.

In the Reagan era, manipulation and attacks from the White House helped keep the media within the ideological limits preferred by their owners; in the 1990s, it is more often media that are used by corporate America to keep the White House on track. The establishment press acts as a sort of political sheepdog, barking when the administration strays past acceptable boundaries and wagging its tail at approved policies.

When Clinton followed a corporate-friendly line on issues like health care and trade, he was rewarded with enthusiastic media support. Although a majority of the public and a strong minority in Congress favored a Canadian-style single-payer health care plan and opposed the North American Free Trade Agreement (NAFTA), these positions were often barely visible in media coverage. Press discussions on these issues reflected the corporate consensus, not the public or governmental debate.

When Clinton threatened to pursue policies that were of less interest to the business community—for example, putting job creation ahead of deficit reduction—the media response was sharply critical, and often was instrumental in persuading Clinton to alter course. Meanwhile, the obsessive coverage of allegations about Clinton's private life helped to keep the president weak and malleable. The scandal-mongering avoided serious questions about how Clinton's public decisionmaking was influenced by private interests, while creating the impression that a hard-hitting press was fearlessly investigating the powers that be.

Mainstream media's embrace of the perspective of their owners and sponsors can also be seen in the journalistic approach of blaming social and economic ills on relatively powerless groups like racial and ethnic minorities, the poor, immigrants, women, and the elderly. As corporate America increasingly retreats from the high-growth, high-wage economics that characterized the 1950s and 1960s, scapegoats must be found to explain away the failure of the economic pie to grow. The media spotlight on street crime and welfare as the defining issues of our era helps focus mainstream resentment against the poor, not the wealthy and powerful.

What does the future hold for the relationship between media and politics? Speaker of the House Newt Gingrich (R.–Ga.) has called for a new era of increased corporate domination over the media. In a *Washington Post* interview, he approvingly pointed to the vast power of advertisers: "If they believe in free markets and a newspaper editorializes against free markets, they're under no obligation to continue to advertise. If they think a particular news outlet is not helpful, they're not obligated to continue advertising."[5] Gingrich later attacked media outlets as "irresponsible" if they do not consistently promote their own corporate interests in their editorials.[6]

Gingrich's brand of conservatism has much to offer media conglomerates, with Republicans leading the charge in 1995 to junk virtually all regulations on the telecommunications industry. In return, Gingrich asked a gathering of the most powerful media chief executives to exercise more direct control over news content and over journalists: "Get your children to behave," he reportedly said.[7]

Gingrich's vision is a departure from the traditional lip service paid to journalistic objectivity. But it only makes more obvious what was already clear to anyone who studies the dynamics of the newsroom: In the media, as anywhere else, it's those who pay the bills who have ultimate control.

Notes

1. Edward S. Herman and Noam Chomsky, *Manufacturing Consent: The Political Economy of the Mass Media* (New York: Pantheon Books, 1988); Martin A. Lee and Norman Solomon, *Unreliable Sources: A Guide to Detecting Bias in News Media* (New York: Lyle Stuart, 1990); Michael Parenti, *Inventing Reality: The Politics of the Mass Media* (New York: St. Martin's Press, 1986).

2. Mark Hertsgaard, *On Bended Knee: The Press and the Reagan Presidency* (New York: Farrar, Straus and Giroux, 1989).

3. Robert Parry, *Fooling America: How Washington Insiders Twist the Truth and Manufacture the Conventional Wisdom* (New York: W. Morrow, 1992).

4. Thomas Ferguson and Joel Rogers, *Right Turn: The Decline of the Democrats and the Future of American Politics* (New York: Hill and Wang, 1986).

5. *Washington Post*, March 8, 1995. See also Jim Naureckas, "Brave Newt World," *Extra!*, May/June 1995, p. 2.

6. Kim McAvoy and Don West, "Newt Gingrich: The Great Liberator for Cybercom," *Broadcasting & Cable,* March 20, 1995, p. 6.

7. *Washington Post*, January 21, 1995.

PART ONE

The Bush Years

1 Bending Over Bushwards

George Bush: Not a Wimp, but a Rough Rider
March/April 1989

WILLIAM GIBSON

For years George Bush suffered the reputation of being one of the great wimps in American politics. Richard Nixon told dirty jokes about his subservience; Garry Trudeau mocked him relentlessly for months in "Doonesbury." For a while, the nation's newspaper columnists even discussed "the wimp factor" in evaluating the 1988 presidential primaries and the possible outcome of the election. Then Bush went on the offensive, grabbed the flag, enlisted Willie Horton as a campaign aide, and learned to speak like Clint Eastwood ("Make My Day"), with his very own "Read My Lips, No New Taxes."

For those Americans still clueless that a virile, active president had replaced an aging, enfeebled one, the Bush administration kindly and gently choreographed a remarkable outdoors routine for the nation's press photographers: See George Bush standing chest-deep in the foaming surf of Florida, casting his lure in search of a big one! See George Bush trout fishing in Maine! See George quail hunting in the thick cactus-filled brush of south Texas!

Bush was not the first surf-and-turf president. That honor goes to Theodore Roosevelt, president from 1901 to 1909. Roosevelt had campaigned for office as a war hero, the legendary "Rough Rider" from the Spanish-American War. The legend of San Juan Hill was itself carefully cultivated by Roosevelt. He deliberately took the name "Rough Riders" for his unit because it was already internationally famous as the nickname for the "cowboys" and "Indians" of Buffalo Bill's Wild West show; the name gave his regiment instant celebrity status. Moreover, some battle scenes were staged for the cameras—the Spanish soldiers were given their guns back, but the bullets were removed from the cartridges. Finally, the Rough Riders were only one among several U.S. units fighting in the area that day.[1]

As president, Roosevelt hired the first full-time press secretary. He also instituted private interviews with correspondents and began to choreograph both his official and social activities for news photographers, including the early film crews. Roosevelt was particularly astute in symbolizing his philosophy of "rugged individualism" and his "speak softly and carry a big stick" foreign policy through having his hunting trips photographed. The cultural tradition of the heroic warrior-hunter who regenerates society through his victories was thus used to help persuade voters of the United States' rightful ascension to world empire.

Bush's manipulative political playing with symbolic virility followed this cultural tradition. One might have thought that after nearly ninety years, the U.S. press would have a more self-reflexive approach to choreographed role-playing by politicians. But the drama seems irresistible; the press acquiesces to its own manipulation and in turn shares responsibility for the reduction of democracy from discussion and action to the role of spectators watching a presidential *Wild Kingdom*.

Peter Pan-omics:
Happy-Talk on the Recession

May/June 1991

DOUG HENWOOD

No RECESSION'S DEMISE had ever been so widely predicted as that of the bust of 1990—which is probably appropriate, since no recession's arrival had ever been so widely anticipated. The 1980s "boom" was a product of smoke, mirrors, and borrowed money, so its longevity was in doubt from its birth. In 1991, Wall Street and the U.S. government relied on their loyal servants in the media to happy-talk the boom's corpse back to life.

A few headlines can summon the spirit of this cheerleading campaign: "Consumer Confidence Surges on Gulf War Success";[2] "Consumer Confidence Posts a Record Gain; Index Signals Better Days for Economy";[3] "Economists Say Reports Write Recession's Epitaph";[4] "Economy Index Up, Spurring Optimism on Recession's End."[5]

Of course, there were some dissenting views—a *Wall Street Journal* story by David Wessel reported that many blue-collar workers never recovered from the 1980–1982 recession,[6] while Michael deCourcy Hinds wrote in the *New York Times* that the "vast majority of Americans" have been "deeply stung" by the slump.[7] Both these exceptions are especially welcome, since they turn away from abstractions like gross national product (GNP) and money supply and toward the actual suffering experienced by folks outside the cushy precincts of corporate and editorial boardrooms.

But the media consensus generally took its cue from the latest *Economic Report of the President,* which explained: "The downturn in the U.S. economy in the latter part of 1990 does not signal any decline in its long-run underlying health or basic vitality. . . . Economic expansions end because of external shocks, imbalances in demand or policy mistakes."[8] In other words, there's nothing wrong with the economy that can't be explained by Saddam Hussein's hostile takeover of Kuwait, which forced up oil prices and forced down consumer and business confidence.

In the spring of 1991, Sylvia Nasar of the *New York Times* served as the media's most egregious optimist. On April 3, Nasar opined that the recession "may be the first in memory that can be attributed to a case of nerves. And now that confidence has come roaring back, signs are that an economic recovery is not far behind." Earlier recessions, she said, had been caused by external shocks like the 1973 oil embargo, "overexuberant" spending, or "blundering economic policy makers"—a list that reads as if it were cribbed from President Bush's chief economic adviser, Michael Boskin.

Dismal employment reports emanating from the Labor Department put a damper on such cheer, so on April 9, Nasar took on this troubling issue. "Layoffs Line the Road to Recovery," the headline said, and the first expert Nasar quoted to prove her case was . . . Michael Boskin. Nasar assured us that unemployment is the last indicator to show a recovery. True enough, but not even the mighty Boskin knew if the bottom was near, much less behind us.

John Liscio, a staff writer for *Barron's,* told *Extra!* that "Mosbacher, Brady, Boskin, Sununu and a gaggle of administration hacks couldn't have done any better" than Nasar at crafting such "complete and utter propaganda." No propagandist himself, Liscio wrote in the April 8, 1991, issue of *Barron's* that a "hot shot" Wall Street economist had called him earlier in the week to confess that "he really thought the economy was in terrible shape, but, being the face man for a big brokerage house, couldn't say as much publicly. 'It would be like the chief economist of A&P telling people not to buy food,' he quipped."

Was this "terrible shape" merely a difficult phase, to be cured by time and a sunny outlook? Recessions do come and, if history is any guide, go. Since World War II, the boom-bust cycle had repeated itself eight times, and this ninth recession would end as well.[9] So proper reporting of the recession wouldn't have projected the economy headed forever downward.

But by focusing on the twists and turns of the business cycle and cheerleading for an imminent economic recovery, media boosterism obscured the structural pathologies of the U.S. economy: the massive increases in federal, corporate, and household debt; an eighteen-year decline in real hourly wages, a deterioration unknown anywhere else in the industrial world; a savage fiscal crisis in thirty or more states and scores of major cities; a real poverty rate of 24 percent, as estimated by the Joint Economic Committee of Congress (in a study that was ignored by virtually every mainstream media outlet);[10] and a polarization along lines of race, sex, and class that worsened throughout what is universally described as "the longest peacetime economic expansion in U.S. history." Since these unpleasantries could not be ascribed to a crisis of confidence, they were mostly ignored.

Clarence the Credible: Media Delusions on the Thomas Story

November/December 1991

PRIOR TO Anita Hill's charges of sexual harassment against Clarence Thomas, most U.S. news media ignored extensive evidence of Thomas's ethically dubious behavior, both as a judge and a Reagan administration official. By downplaying the seamier side of Thomas's career, the press conveyed the impression that he was a person of integrity whose otherwise clean record was besmirched by Hill.

During the Thomas hearings, FAIR contacted numerous national media outlets, urging them not to overlook stories that raised serious questions about Thomas's credibility and character. When allegations of sexual harassment surfaced, FAIR distributed relevant material from the Equal Employment Opportunity Commission (EEOC) 1980 transition team, whose members included Clarence Thomas.

The transition team's final report criticized regulations on sexual harassment, saying, "The vagueness of the definition of discrimination has undoubtedly led to a barrage of trivial complaints against employers around the nation. The elimination of personal slights and sexual advances which contribute to 'an intimidating, hostile or offensive working environment' is a goal impossible to reach. Expenditure of the EEOC's limited resources in pursuit of this goal is unwise."[11]

Thomas endorsed this analysis as part of the full report. Moreover, as one of two members of the team's subcommittee on regulations and guidelines, he was directly responsible for inserting the passage. It was certainly a newsworthy insight into his views just before the alleged sexual harassment of Anita Hill began, particularly since the report dismisses exactly the kind of harassment that Thomas was charged with. FAIR provided this document to the press (along with another memo, signed by Thomas, that criticized sexual harassment rules as overly broad), but after a brief mention by a few national media,[12] it fell by the wayside during the hearings.

Likewise, the bulk of the media did little to pursue leads linking Thomas to lobbyists for the apartheid government of South Africa. One of these links was Jay Parker, Thomas's political mentor, of whom Thomas has said "I . . . hope I can have a fraction of [his] courage and strength." Parker is the founder of the *Lincoln Review,* a journal for right-wing blacks, which featured Clarence Thomas on its editorial advisory board. (Thomas remained on the board even after becoming an appeals court judge, in apparent violation of judicial ethics.)

In 1985, Parker and his associate William Keyes founded a firm called International Public Affairs Consultants (IPAC). Its sole client was the government of South Africa, which paid IPAC $360,000 a year to fight U.S. sanctions. One IPAC-sponsored event was a reception for the South African ambassador; the firm's report on the event listed Clarence Thomas as a participant.

FAIR gave news media a memo outlining these facts, but even when Thomas was questioned about the South Africa connection by Senator Paul Simon (D.–Ill.) in televised hearings, most media ignored it. (One exception was *New York Newsday,* which suggested that Thomas's answers to Simon were false.)[13]

Another facet of Thomas's career that was virtually ignored was the striking conflicts of interest he faced in his short tenure on the appeals court. He passed judgment on a case involving Ralston Purina, helping to overturn a $10.4 million civil award against the company, even though the firm was largely owned by the family of Thomas's close friend and patron, Senator John Danforth (R–Mo.).[14]

Although Thomas was a vocal supporter of Oliver North and his defiance of Congress, he did not excuse himself from ruling on the appeal of North's criminal convictions. (Thomas's fellow judge, Abner Mikva, did disqualify himself, because as a member of Congress he had voted to establish the Iran-contra special counsel.)

Thomas's participation in these cases appears to violate judicial ethics, which mandates that judges step down in cases where their "impartiality might reasonably be questioned."[15] Yet *New York Times* correspondent Neil Lewis concluded his postmortem on the Thomas hearings by citing Terry Eastland, a Reagan Justice Department official, who "said that if Judge Thomas believed he could not sit on a case because of any animosity resulting from the confirmation process, he would certainly excuse himself."[16]

Iran-Contra:
"Sweep It Away"

March 1993

Most of the major media reacted to George Bush's last-minute pardon of leading Iran-contra figures with something less than outrage. The conventional wisdom in media circles for years had been that the scandal was old news and that it should just go away. Robert MacNeil of the *MacNeil/Lehrer NewsHour* spoke for many in the media when he asked Tom Blanton of the National Security Archive, "Mr. Blanton, why does this issue remain important? Clearly, the public is bored with it. The polls all show that years ago they stopped being interested in it. Why not, as Mr. Bush describes in his pardon statement, why not bring in the healing power of the pardon and sweep it away and sweep the bitterness away?"[17]

Blanton pointed out that the polls actually showed that most voters did not believe that Bush was telling the truth about Iran-contra, and that this was a factor in Bush's electoral defeat. MacNeil then turned to his other guest, Richard Perle, a former assistant to pardon-recipient Caspar Weinberger, and demonstrated what he means when he says he asks tough questions of both sides: "Mr. Perle, I believe you would sympathize with the president and his desire to sweep the bitterness away with the pardon?"

Part of the reason the news media have been unable to "sweep away" the legacy of Iran-contra is that most news outlets have never fully dealt with the scandal, with the result that most people—including most journalists—don't understand what really happened or who was involved. The coverage of the pardons provided proof of this, as when the *Chicago Tribune*, trying to provide background on the arms-for-hostages deal, wrote, "There is no evidence that Bush had any knowledge about the other part of the affair: a covert weapons pipeline set up to aid the Nicaraguan contras after Congress prohibited direct government assistance in 1984."[18]

In fact, Bush's involvement with the contra operation was well documented. In 1986, then–Vice President Bush met with Felix Rodriguez, a former CIA operative who coordinated the illegal airlift of arms to the contras from El Salvador; according to a memo written by Bush's staff briefing him on the meeting, the two were to discuss "resupply of the contras."[19] Rodriguez was in frequent contact with Bush's office. Oliver North wrote in his diary that Rodriguez was "talking too much about VP connection."[20]

There was almost no hint of this record of Bush's involvement in coverage of either the pardons or Bush's reelection campaign. In fact, journalists themselves were quite critical of how they covered the Iran-contra issue during the 1992 election. Although journalists responding to a Times Mirror survey gave generally high ratings to their 1992 election campaign coverage, only 24 percent said coverage of the Iran-contra issue was good; 70 percent said it was fair or poor. In explanation of the low marks, the *Los Angeles Times* quoted a TV executive who said that only the *New York Times*, the *Los Angeles Times*, and the *Washington Post* had "done a good job of explaining this issue."[21]

That's not a particularly high standard to hold oneself to. In all of their '92 election campaign coverage, not one of those three papers printed a single story that quoted the "resupply of the contras" memo. (The *Los Angeles Times* did refer to it once in a story about former Bush aide Donald Gregg,[22] and the *Washington Post* mentioned it once—in a theater review.[23]) On the issue of illegal arms to the contras, the leading U.S. newspapers seemed to have given Bush a pardon of their own.

Notes

1. See James William Gibson, *Warrior Dreams: Paramilitary Culture in Post-Vietnam America* (New York: Hill and Wang, 1994).
2. *Los Angeles Times*, March 27, 1991.
3. *USA Today*, March 27, 1991.
4. *New York Newsday*, March 30, 1991.
5. *New York Times*, March 30, 1991.
6. *Wall Street Journal*, April 4, 1991.
7. *New York Times*, April 7, 1991.
8. Council of Economic Advisors, *Economic Report of the President* (Washington, D.C.: Government Printing Office, 1991).
9. According to the official (though private) National Bureau of Economic Research, the recession "ended" in March 1991. But unemployment didn't bottom out until February 1992, while year-to-year employment growth didn't turn positive until April 1992. By December 1992, job growth was still at only 1 percent; in a typical recovery, it's usually closer to 5 percent.
10. Joint Economic Committee of Congress, *Measuring Poverty* (Washington, D.C.: Government Printing Office, 1990).
11. *St. Louis Post-Dispatch*, October 10, 1991.
12. E.g., Associated Press, October 8, 1991; *Washington Post*, October 11, 1991.
13. *New York Newsday*, September 12, 1991.
14. Monroe Freedman, "Doubting Thomas' Ethics," *Texas Lawyer*, September 12, 1991, p. 15.
15. *United States Code Annotated*, Vol. 28, sec. 455 (Washington, D.C.: West Publishing, 1993).
16. *New York Times*, October 19, 1991.

17. *MacNeil/Lehrer NewsHour,* December 24, 1992.
18. *Chicago Tribune,* December 26, 1992.
19. Peter Kornbluh and Malcolm Byrne, eds., *The Iran-Contra Scandal: The Declassified History* (New York: New Press, 1993), p. 178.
20. Jeff Nason and Malcolm Byrne, "Will the Real George Bush Please Stand Up?" *In These Times,* February 10, 1988, p. 3.
21. *Los Angeles Times,* December 20, 1992.
22. *Los Angeles Times,* May 16, 1992.
23. *Washington Post,* June 20, 1992.

2 Rallying 'Round the Flag: The Panama Invasion

The Media Go to War: How Television Sold the Panama Invasion

January/February 1990

MARK COOK AND JEFF COHEN

Two weeks after the Panama invasion, CBS News sponsored a public opinion poll in Panama that found the residents in rapture over what had happened. Even 80 percent of those whose homes had been blown up or whose relatives had been killed by U.S. forces said it was worth it. Their enthusiasm did not stop with the ousting of General Manuel Noriega, however. A less heavily advertised result of the poll was that 82 percent of the sampled Panamanian patriots did not want Panamanian control of the canal, preferring either partial or exclusive control by the United States.[1]

A "public opinion poll" in a country under martial law, conducted by an agency obviously sanctioned by the invading forces, can be expected to come up with such results. Most reporters, traveling as they did with the U.S. military, found little to contradict this picture. Less than forty hours after the invasion began, Sam Donaldson and Judd Rose transported us to Panama via ABC's *PrimeTime Live*. "There were people who applauded us as we went by in a military convoy," said Rose. "The military have been very good to us [in escorting reporters beyond the Canal Zone]," added Donaldson.[2]

Obviously there was a mix of opinion inside Panama, but this was virtually unreported on television, the dominant medium shaping U.S. attitudes about the invasion. Panamanian opposition to the invasion was dismissed as nothing more than "DigBat [Dignity Battalion] thugs" who'd been given jobs by Noriega.

Few TV reporters seemed to notice that the jubilant Panamanians parading before their cameras day after day to endorse the invasion spoke near-perfect English and were overwhelmingly light-skinned and well dressed—this in a Spanish-speaking country with a largely mestizo and black population, where poverty is widespread. ABC's Beth Nissen was one of the few TV reporters to take a close look at the civilian deaths caused by U.S. bombs that pulverized El Chorillo, the poor neighborhood that ambulance drivers began referring to as "Little Hiroshima." The people of El Chorillo don't speak perfect English, and they were less than jubilant about the invasion.[3]

In the first days of the invasion, TV journalists had one overriding obsession: How many American soldiers have died? The question, repeated with drumbeat regularity, tended to drown out the other issues: Panamanian casualties, international law, and foreign reaction. On the morning of the invasion, CBS anchor Kathleen Sullivan's voice cracked with emotion for the U.S. soldiers: "Nine killed, more than fifty wounded. How long can this fighting go on?"[4] Unknown and unknowable to CBS viewers, hundreds of Panamanians had already been killed by then, many buried under rubble in their homes.

Judging from the calls and requests for interviews that poured into the FAIR office, European and Latin American journalists based in the United States were stunned by the implied racism and national chauvinism in the media display. The *Toronto Globe and Mail,* often referred to as the *New York Times* of Canada, ran a front-page article criticizing the United States and its media for "the peculiar jingoism... so evident to foreigners but almost invisible for most Americans."[5]

TV's continuous focus on the well-being of the invaders, and not the invaded, meant that the screen was dominated by red, white, and blue–draped coffins and ceremonies; honor rolls of the U.S. dead; drum rolls; remarks by Dan Rather about "our fallen heroes"[6] ... but no Panamanian funerals—despite the fact that the invasion claimed perhaps fifty Panamanian lives for every U.S. citizen killed.

When Pentagon pool correspondent Fred Francis was asked on ABC's *Nightline* on invasion day one about the extent of civilian casualties, he said he did not know because he and other journalists were traveling around with the U.S. Army.[7] Curiosity didn't increase in ensuing days. FAIR called the TV networks daily to demand that they address the issue of civilian deaths, but journalists said they had no way of verifying the numbers.

No such qualms existed with regard to Romania, where over the 1989 Christmas weekend CNN and other U.S. outlets were freely dishing out fantastic reports of 80,000 people killed in days of violence—greater than the immediate Hiroshima death toll—a figure that any editor should have greeted with extreme skepticism. Tom Brokaw's selective interest in civilians was evident when he devoted the first half of *NBC Nightly News* to Panama without mentioning noncombatant casualties, then turned to Romania and immediately referred to reports of thousands of civilian deaths.[8]

Not until the sixth day of the Panama invasion did the U.S. Army augment its estimated dead (23 American troops, 297 alleged enemy soldiers) to include a figure for civilians: 254. The few reporters who sought out independent sources—Panamanian human rights monitors, hospital workers, ambulance drivers, and funeral home directors—challenged this number as representing only a fraction of the true death toll. These sources also spoke of thousands of civilians injured and 10,000 left homeless. Many journalists, especially on television, were too busy cheerleading "the successful military action" to notice the Panamanians who didn't fare so successfully.

TV correspondents, so uncurious about civilian casualties, could not be expected to go beyond U.S. military assurances about who was being arrested and why. As the *Boston Globe* noted, U.S. forces were arresting anyone on a blacklist compiled by the newly installed government.[9] *Newsday*'s Peter Eisner reported, "Hundreds of intellectuals, university students, teachers and professional people say they have been harassed and detained by U.S. forces in the guise of searching for hidden weapons."[10]

In their coverage of the invasion of Panama, many TV journalists abandoned even the pretense of operating in a neutral, independent mode. Television anchors used pronouns like "we" and "us" in describing the mission into Panama, as if they themselves were members of the invasion force, or at least helpful advisers.

On the first day of the invasion NBC's Tom Brokaw exclaimed, "We haven't got [Manuel Noriega] yet."[11] CNN anchor Mary Anne Loughlin asked a former CIA official, "Noriega has stayed one step ahead of us. Do you think we'll be able to find him?"[12] After eagerly quizzing a panel of U.S. military experts on the *MacNeil/Lehrer NewsHour* about whether "we" had wiped out the Panamanian Defense Forces (PDF), Judy Woodruff concluded, "So not only have we done away with the PDF, we've also done away with the police force."[13] So much for the separation of press and state.

Nightline's Ted Koppel and other TV journalists had a field day mocking Noriega's Orwellianly titled "Dignity Battalions," but none were heard ridiculing the invasion's U.S. code name: "Operation Just Cause." The day after the invasion began, *NBC Nightly News* offered its own case study in Orwellian newspeak: While one correspondent referred to the U.S. military occupiers as engaged in "peacekeeping chores," another correspondent on the same show referred to Latin American diplomats condemning the United States at the Organization of American States (OAS) as a "lynch mob."[14] After the Soviet Union criticized the invasion as "gunboat diplomacy" (as had many other countries), Dan Rather dismissed the criticism as "old-line, hard-line talk from Moscow."[15]

Journalism gave way to state propaganda when a CNN correspondent dutifully reported on the first day of the invasion, "U.S. troops have taken detainees, but we are not calling them 'prisoners of war' because the U.S. has not declared war."[16] (That kind of obedient reporter probably still refers to the Vietnam "conflict.")

Similarly, on day one, many network correspondents couldn't bring themselves to call the invasion an invasion until they got the green light from Washington; instead, it was referred to variously as a military action, intervention, operation, expedition, affair, or insertion.

While they used euphemisms to describe the U.S. invasion, journalists went out of their way to use loaded language to demonize Noriega. Dan Rather placed him "at the top of the list of the world's drug thieves and scums."[17] Ted Koppel declared that "Noriega's reputation as a brutal drug-dealing bully who reveled in his public contempt for the United States all but begged for strong retribution."[18]

Many reporters uncritically promoted White House explanations for its breakup with Noriega. The *New York Times*'s Clifford Krauss reported that Noriega "began as a CIA asset but fell afoul of Washington over his involvement in drug and arms trafficking."[19] ABC's Peter Jennings told viewers on the day of the invasion, "Let's remember that the United States was very close to Mr. Noriega before the whole question of drugs came up."[20]

Actually, Noriega's drug links were asserted by U.S. intelligence as early as 1972. In 1976, after U.S. espionage officials proposed that Noriega be dumped as an asset because of drugs and double-dealing, the then-director of the Central Intelligence Agency (CIA), George Bush, made sure the relationship continued.[21] U.S. intelligence overlooked the drug issue year after year—as long as Noriega was an eager ally in U.S. espionage and covert operations, especially those targeted against Sandinista-led Nicaragua.

Peter Jennings's claim that the United States broke with Noriega after the "question of drugs came up" turns reality upside down. Noriega's involvement in drug trafficking was reportedly heaviest in the early 1980s, when his relationship with the United States was especially close. By 1986, when the Noriega–United States relationship began to fray, experts agree that Noriega had already drastically curtailed his drug links. The two drug-related indictments against Noriega in Florida covered activities from 1981 through March 1986.[22]

When, as vice president, Bush met with Noriega in Panama in December 1983, besides discussing Nicaragua, Bush allegedly raised questions about drug-money laundering. According to author Kevin Buckley, Noriega told top aide José Blandon that he'd picked up the following message from the Bush meeting: "The United States wanted help for the contras so badly that if he even promised it, the U.S. government would turn a blind eye to money-laundering and setbacks to democracy in Panama."[23] In 1985 and 1986, Noriega met several times with Oliver North to discuss the assistance Noriega was providing to the contras, including training contras at Panamanian Defense Force bases. Noriega didn't fall from grace until he stopped being a "team player" in the U.S. war against Nicaragua.[24]

The "war on drugs" rationale for the invasion would have been shredded if media outlets had reported the backgrounds of the new Panamanian leaders installed by the U.S. military. One journalist who did so was Jonathan Marshall, editorial page editor of the *Oakland Tribune*. In a series of editorials on "Panama's Drug, Inc.," Marshall reported that Panama's new president, Guillermo Endara, was a wealthy corporate attorney for several companies run by Carlos Eleta, a Panamanian business tycoon arrested in Georgia in April 1989 for conspiring to import tons of cocaine into the United States; that Vice President Guillermo "Billy" Ford was cofounder and part owner of Miami's Dadeland Bank, a repository for Medellín drug cartel money; and that Attorney General Rogelio Cruz served as a director of the First Interamericas Bank, which was owned by the leader of the Cali cocaine cartel and was shut down for drug-related "irregular operations" in 1985. "President Endara's appointments read like a who's who of Panama's oligarchy," Marshall concluded. "Many have personal or business associations with the drug-money laundering industry."[25]

Democracy had as little to do with Noriega's break with the United States as drugs. If Noriega believed Bush had given his strong-arm rule a green light in 1983, confirmation came the next year when Noriega's troops seized ballot boxes and blatantly rigged Panama's presidential election. Noriega's candidate, Nicolas Ardito Barletta, was also "our" candidate—an economist who had been a student and assistant to former University of Chicago professor George Shultz. Though loudly protested by Panamanians, the fraud that put Ardito Barletta in power was cheered by the U.S. embassy. Secretary of State Shultz attended his inauguration.[26]

On the December 20, 1989, *Nightline,* Ted Koppel summarized the often-cited incidents that were presented as justifications for the invasion: "When during the past few days [Noriega] declared war on the United States and some of his followers then killed a U.S. Marine, roughed up another American serviceman, also threatening that man's wife, strong public support for a reprisal was all but guaranteed." None of these supposed provocations could stand much scrutiny—particularly the claim that Noriega "declared war on the United States."[27]

The original Reuters dispatches, published on the inside pages of the *New York Times,* mentioned the supposed "declaration" in passing in articles dealing with other matters.[28] In the December 17 article, headlined "Opposition Leader in Panama Rejects a Peace Offer from Noriega," Reuters quoted the general as saying that he would judiciously use new powers granted him by the Panamanian Parliament and that "the North American scheme, through constant psychological and military harassment, has created a state of war in Panama." This statement of fact aroused little excitement at the White House, which called the Parliament's move "a hollow step."

The day after the invasion, *Los Angeles Times* Pentagon correspondent Melissa Healy told a call-in talk show audience on C-SPAN that Noriega had "declared war" on the United States. When a caller asked why that hadn't been front-page news, Healy explained that the declaration of war was one of a series of "incremental escalations." When another caller pointed out that Panama had only made a rhetorical statement that U.S. economic and other measures had created a state of war, Healy confessed ignorance of what had actually been said and suggested that it was certainly worth investigating.[29]

The incident symbolizes media performance on the invasion—dispense official information as gospel first and worry about the truth of that information later. It's just what the White House was counting on from the media. The Bush team set out to control television and front-page news in the first days, knowing that any exposés of official deception would not appear until weeks later, buried on inside pages of newspapers. Rulers do not require the total suppression of news; it's sufficient to delay the news until it no longer matters.

Besides uncritically dispensing huge quantities of official news and views, the TV networks had another passion during the first days of the Panama invasion: polling their public. It was an insular process, with predictable results. A *Toronto Globe and Mail* news story summarized it: "Hardly a voice of objection is being heard within the United States about the Panama invasion, at least from those deemed as official sources and thus likely to be seen on television or read in the papers. Not surprisingly, given the media coverage, a television poll taken yesterday by one network (CNN) indicated that nine of 10 viewers approved of the invasion."[30]

Journalists justified their role as distributors of government handouts in different ways. Asked on day one of the invasion why U.S. opponents of intervention were virtually invisible on the air, a CBS producer (who declined to give her name) told *Extra!*: "When American troops are involved and taking losses, this is not the time to be running critical commentary. The American people will be rallying around the flag."

Some TV reporters claim they were forced to rely on official U.S. versions because they had nothing else to do. "Peter Arnett, a Pulitzer Prize–winning combat journalist, was reduced to reporting on Noriega's alleged pornography collection," *Newsday* reported. "'They [the Pentagon] got away with it again,' Arnett said of the initial press blackout."[31] Arnett, who covered the invasion for CNN, was complaining that Pentagon officials failed to provide photo opportunities featuring wounded soldiers, suffering civilians, and general bang-bang.

Naturally, the Pentagon did everything possible to prevent such shots, in keeping with its belief that the Vietnam War was lost in American living rooms. "Two things that people should not watch are the making of sausage and the making of war," an Air Force doctor told *Newsday*. "All that front-page blood and gore hurts the military."[32]

Experienced combat journalists like Arnett should have known that the Pentagon's aim was to manipulate the pictures and stories that got out. "If you just looked at television, the most violent thing American troops did in Panama was play rock music," political media consultant Robert Squier told *Newsday*. "They feel if they can control the pictures at the outset, it doesn't make a damn [bit of difference] what is said now or later."[33]

Unhappiness with the Pentagon did not keep reporters from promoting the U.S. Army–approved image of Noriega as a comic book arch-villain. The Southern Command told reporters soon after the invasion that 110 pounds of cocaine had been found in Noriega's so-called "witch house," and this played big on TV news and the front pages. When, a month later, the "cocaine" turned out to be tamale flour, the government's deception was a footnote at best.[34] The initial headlines portraying Noriega as a drug-crazed lunatic had served their purpose: to convince the American people that he was a threat that needed to be removed.

You Be the Judge
January/February 1990

"[The Panama invasion was legal] according to all the experts I talked to."

—Rita Braver, CBS Evening News[35]

"As far as international law is concerned, even sources in the U.S. government admit they were operating very close to the line."

—John McWethy, ABC World News Tonight[36]

"The territory of a state is inviolable. It may not be the object, even temporarily, of military occupation or other measures of force taken by another state directly or indirectly on any grounds whatsoever."

—Article 20, Charter of the Organization of American States[37]

Notes

1. "Panamanians Strongly Back U.S. Move," *New York Times,* January 6, 1990.
2. *PrimeTime Live,* December 21, 1990.
3. *ABC World News Tonight,* December 27, 1989.
4. CBS, December 20, 1989.
5. *Toronto Globe and Mail,* December 22, 1989.
6. CBS, December 21, 1989.
7. *Nightline,* December 20, 1989.
8. *NBC Nightly News,* December 20, 1989.
9. *Boston Globe,* January 1, 1990.
10. *Newsday,* January 7, 1990.
11. NBC, December 20, 1989.
12. CNN, December 21, 1989.
13. *MacNeil/Lehrer NewsHour,* December 21, 1989.
14. *NBC Nightly News,* December 21, 1989.
15. *CBS Evening News,* December 20, 1989.
16. CNN, December 20, 1989.
17. CBS, December 20, 1989.
18. *Nightline,* December 20, 1989.
19. *New York Times,* January 21, 1990.
20. ABC, December 20, 1989.
21. *San Francisco Examiner,* January 5, 1990; "Talk of the Town," *New Yorker,* January 8, 1990, p. 25.
22. "Analysts Challenge View of Noriega as Drug Lord," *Washington Post,* January 7, 1990.
23. Kevin Buckley, "Noriega Could Give Some Interesting Answers," *St. Petersburg Times,* January 3, 1990.
24. Jim Naureckas and Peter Shinkle, "Senate Hearings Show U.S. Was Gen. Noriega's Partner in Crime," *In These Times,* February 24, 1988, p. 3.

25. *Oakland Tribune,* January 5, 1990; January 22, 1990.

26. See "Trouble in the Colonies: The Press Leads the Charge in Panama," *Extra!,* March/April 1988, p. 8; Richard Reeves, *San Francisco Chronicle,* December 25, 1989.

27. For a discussion of other "provocations," see Mark Cook and Jeff Cohen, "How Television Sold the Panama Invasion," *Extra!,* January/February 1990, p. 6.

28. *New York Times,* December 17–18, 1989.

29. C-SPAN, December 21, 1989.

30. *Toronto Globe and Mail,* December 22, 1989.

31. *New York Newsday,* January 14, 1990.

32. *New York Newsday,* January 14, 1990.

33. *New York Newsday,* January 14, 1990.

34. *Washington Post,* January 23, 1990.

35. *CBS Evening News,* December 20, 1989.

36. *ABC World News Tonight,* January 5, 1990.

37. General Secretary of the Organization of American States, *Organization of American States Charter* (Bogota, Colombia: Organization of American States, 1948).

3 Creating the New Hitler: The Gulf War

Media on the March: Journalism in the Gulf

November/December 1990

JIM NAURECKAS

FROM THE BEGINNING of the Persian Gulf crisis in August 1990, most of the mainstream U.S. media went into war mode: Their main mission was not journalism, but the creation of a national consensus in support of the U.S. military buildup.

The media acknowledged this mission as they begged to be allowed to report from Saudi Arabia: "A major military exercise cannot succeed without the sustained support and understanding of the American people, and it will not long be supported or understood without extensive and close-up news reporting," Max Frankel, executive editor of the *New York Times,* was quoted in his own paper.[1] Or as the *Times* editorialized more succinctly, "'Desert Shield' requires public support. Only credible information can assure that support."[2]

Given the one-sided information provided by the elite media, it was no wonder that consumers of news would endorse the Bush administration's policy in the Gulf. The adjectives "masterful" and "masterly"—not to mention "brilliant"—were repeatedly used to describe the president's military mobilization.

ABC's Sam Donaldson explained the softness of the coverage by saying, "It's difficult to play devil's advocate, especially against such a popular president as Bush."[3] But much of the analysis simply glowed with admiration: "In a single stroke Tuesday, George Bush ... brought the mantle of leadership back to

Washington," ran a front-page *Chicago Tribune* news analysis. "He has sent more troops, ships and planes into a trouble spot than any recent President. He has decided to act, setting himself eyeball to eyeball with a dictator—no puny leader of an obscure island but a tough militarist."[4]

"In forceful terms, Mr. Bush sought to prepare the whole American nation for the prospect of bloodshed," wrote R. W. "Johnny" Apple in an August 12, 1990, analysis of the president's speech on Iraq. Apple, one of the *New York Times*'s top domestic political analysts, wrote approvingly of Bush's message that "American soldiers and American hostages may have to die," referring to the president as "tough," "determined," and "statesmanlike." Saddam Hussein, on the other hand, was depicted by Apple in wormlike terms as "wiggling and squirming."[5]

With Saddam Hussein an unknown quantity to most U.S. citizens, the media made an all-out effort to turn him into a super-villain—not a mere human dictator, but a "beast,"[6] a "butcher,"[7] a "monster"[8] that "Bush may have to destroy."[9] Saddam Hussein's crimes had been well known—and underreported—for years, while Iraq was supported by the United States in its war against Iran. Journalists, suddenly outraged by Iraqi atrocities, expressed little self-criticism for letting Washington decide when Iraq's human rights record was worth reporting.

The *New York Post*'s front-page headline tagged Saddam Hussein "Child Abuser" for patting a young British hostage on the head.[10] Iraq's 1985 torture of hundreds of children to extract information about their relatives was documented by Amnesty International—but this was during the years when Baghdad's crimes were not big news.[11]

As if Saddam Hussein's actual record weren't brutal enough, the media turned to fictional atrocities: "I'll hang a hostage every day!" exulted a U.S. colonel, pretending to be the Iraqi leader for an *NBC Nightly News* "war game."[12] Reporters eagerly relayed every U.S. government speculation about Iraq's plan for terrorism: The only sources of one *Christian Science Monitor* article were terrorism "experts" from the Pentagon, the CIA, the National Security Council (NSC), the State Department, and the Federal Aviation Administration (FAA)—and, providing "balance," one of the most extremist leaders of the Palestine Liberation Organization (PLO).[13]

Portrayals of Saddam Hussein as the world's arch-villain frequently shaded into anti-Arab racism. "Disconcerting Arab customs" was the caption of a Pat Oliphant cartoon depicting Saddam Hussein with a gun pointed at a captive "guest."[14] "Not every Iraqi is an evil dreamer of death," was the most columnist A. M. Rosenthal was willing to concede.[15] (Rosenthal, who considers himself an expert on Mideast politics, mistakenly referred to both Iranians and Kurds as "Arabs" in an October 26, 1990, column.)

The most powerful method of demonizing Saddam Hussein, however, was the Hitler analogy: Again and again, Hussein was equated with Hitler, Iraq with Nazi Germany, and the '90s with the '30s—a metaphor that seemed intended to silence any debate or critical thought. *The New Republic* went so far as to put on its cover a subtly doctored photograph of Saddam Hussein with a Hitler-style mustache—a decision editor Hendrik Hertzberg defended as a "joke," but which came across more like subliminal propaganda.[16] ("I'll have to talk to my lawyer," the photographer's agent responded when informed by FAIR of the alteration. "It's something for us to consider if we want to work with people like this. . . . This is very unethical.")

The failure of the concessions made to Hitler at Munich was invoked as proof of Iraq's intention to take over Saudi Arabia, and Washington's prior relationship to Iraq was called "appeasement"— even though "alliance" would be a more realistic description for the way the United States supported Iraq during its decade-long war with Iran. "We can't stand to see Iraq defeated," Assistant Secretary of Defense Richard Armitage told Congress in 1987.[17]

SEPARATION OF PRESS AND STATE?

In the black-and-white world of the media, if Saddam Hussein is evil, then the U.S. government's goals and motives must be pure. A *New York Times* editorial dubbed Bush the "leader of all countries."[18] While U.S. diplomats "appeal to high moral values and the lessons of history," *New York Times* reporters wrote, "deep down the United States understands that many of its partners are in the coalition only because of a coincidence of interests, not because they share a common sense of moral purpose."[19] The hypothesis that the purpose of the United States—that it might, for example, want to continue its disproportionate control over the region's oil—might be more selfish than moral was not entertained by the *Times*.

It was not easy to portray the U.S. force as defending democracy—Saudi Arabia and Iraq have been given identical marks for repressiveness by Freedom House, a conservative foreign policy group. Democracy was therefore downplayed as an issue. A *Wall Street Journal* article took an approving look at Gulf monarchs and concluded that democracy might not only be bad for people in the region but also "could work against U.S. interests." The article quoted a State Department official: "You can't expect democracy to produce toadies to the U.S."[20]

Instead, the United States was praised in news reports for assuming the role of global policeman, "the only superpower . . . [able] to enforce international law against the will of a powerful aggressor."[21] In an assessment that could have appeared in a White House news release, *Newsweek* declared that "the president's grand plan for the post-cold-war world can be summed up simply: Stop International Bullies."[22]

The implication that the U.S. response to Iraq's invasion demonstrated a commitment to international law was a media myth. In fact, the administration frequently acted without legal authority throughout the buildup, as when it unilaterally imposed a naval blockade without U.N. sanction. (Once the blockade was in place, the United States got partial approval of its fait accompli.) Bush attempted to stop food from entering Iraq and Kuwait, although the Geneva Protocols state that "starvation of civilians as a method of warfare is prohibited."[23] Religious groups like the National Council of Churches and the American Friends Service Committee strongly protested the use of food as a weapon. But their objections were rarely noted in mainstream coverage.

Praising Bush as a guardian of international law was particularly jarring, given that only seven months earlier Bush had launched an equally illegal invasion of his own. But the word "Panama" was almost never mentioned in relation to the Gulf crisis, either in news reporting or in commentary. Indeed, a comparison between the coverage of Iraq's invasion of Kuwait and the U.S. invasion of Panama illustrates clearly how completely the media elite adopts the agenda and perspective of the White House. The *New York Times* editorial response to the invasion of Kuwait was called "Iraq's Naked Aggression";[24] its editorial on Panama was headlined "Why the Invasion Was Justified."[25] Iraq's invasion was instantly recognized as a violation of international law, but CBS's Rita Braver declared that the invasion of Panama was legal "according to all the experts I talked to."[26]

Graphically displaying the different approaches taken to the two invasions, *Time* magazine's logo on its Kuwait stories was a caricature of Saddam Hussein as an octopus;[27] for Panama, it was an American flag in the shape of a heroically flexed arm.[28] Though charts comparing Iraq's supposed "1 million-man army" with Kuwait's 20,000 troops were everywhere, no one had thought to contrast the United States' 2.3 million–member armed forces with the 4,000 combat troops in the Panamanian Defense Forces, or with the 700 Cuban construction workers in Grenada.

By one measure—the killing of civilians—the invasion of Kuwait appears to have been less devastating than the invasion of Panama. A *New York Times* article, entirely sourced to Kuwaiti refugees, gave an estimate of at least 300 deaths in the first days of the invasion, with another 225 to 300 executed later for resisting the occupation.[29] The death toll in Panama was many times higher, according to human rights and health experts. A *60 Minutes* segment—aired a full nine months after the Panama invasion—presented estimates ranging from 1,000 to 4,000 civilians killed by "Operation Just Cause."[30]

On the rare occasions when the Panama-Kuwait analogy was raised, it was instantly rejected. *Nightline*'s Ted Koppel, called a "TV statesman" in ABC News ads, dropped all pretense of objectivity as he and Barbara Walters lectured Iraq's ambassador to the United States on the differences between our good invasions, Panama and Grenada, and their bad one—Kuwait.[31] In Koppel's language during that exchange, the fuzzy line between U.S. press and U.S. government faded away completely: "We did not go in and seize Panama. We did not go in and seize Grenada," Koppel declared.

TV journalists spoke so often as though they were part of the government that even Jim Lehrer, not known for his distance from power, complained about the practice: "We never use 'we,'" he told the *Denver Post*. "That's just standard practice. . . . We don't need to cheerlead."[32]

WHO GOT TO SPEAK?

In the weeks after the invasion of Kuwait, the media played their traditional crisis role of defining and narrowing the range of viewpoints available to the U.S. public. To find out who was allowed to participate in the national debate on the Persian Gulf situation, FAIR analyzed the guest lists of programs dealing with the crisis on two of the most influential and in-depth TV news programs: *Nightline* and the *MacNeil/Lehrer NewsHour*. FAIR studied the first month of the Gulf crisis (August 1–31, 1990), when a wide-ranging debate—including both supporters and opponents of the military buildup—could have affected policy. But we did not find such a debate; not a single U.S. guest on *Nightline*, for example, argued against U.S. military intervention. Instead, we found the same narrow spectrum that FAIR had documented in its earlier studies of the two shows.[33]

In August 1990, nearly half the U.S. guests on both programs were current or former government officials (48 percent for *Nightline*, 47 percent for *MacNeil/Lehrer*); when international guests were included, the percentage of government officials was even higher.

/ The "experts" used by these shows generally came from conservative think tanks like the American Enterprise Institute and the Center for Strategic and International Studies, with analysts from the centrist Brookings Institution providing the "left" boundary of debate. Never tapped were progressive think tanks such as the Institute for Policy Studies or the World Policy Institute./

Only 3 percent of total guests on *Nightline* and 4 percent on *MacNeil/Lehrer* were from nongovernmental public interest or activist groups; this category included a hostage advocate, who appeared on both shows, and conservative activist Midge Decter, who appeared on *MacNeil/Lehrer* to attack U.S. policy as too pacifistic.

The guest lists were unrepresentative of the U.S. population: European-Americans made up a startling 98 percent of *Nightline*'s U.S. guests and 87 percent of the *NewsHour*'s. (The difference results mainly from *MacNeil/Lehrer*'s inclusion of Arab-Americans.) Only 9 percent of *MacNeil/Lehrer*'s and 14 percent of *Nightline*'s U.S. guests were female.

FAIR's earlier studies had been criticized by Ted Koppel, Robert MacNeil, and Jim Lehrer for focusing on discussion guests as opposed to people who provided sound bites in video segments. But when we examined the video clips dealing with the Gulf crisis, we found they represented an *even narrower* spectrum of views: Sound bites came from current or former government officials 62 percent of the time on *Nightline* and 63 percent of the time on *MacNeil/Lehrer* (72 percent on the latter, if troops and reservists are included). Less than 2 percent of

Nightline's and less than 1 percent of *MacNeil/Lehrer*'s taped-segment subjects represented public interest or activist groups.

No anti-interventionist U.S. guest appeared in the first month of the crisis on *Nightline,* but one *MacNeil/Lehrer* program included a panel of Arab-Americans (including FAIR advisory board member Casey Kasem) who had sharp criticisms of U.S. policy. After our study period, the *NewsHour* featured strong critics like Noam Chomsky, Edward Said, and *The Progressive*'s Erwin Knoll. But these exceptions did not change the overwhelming government-establishment bias of the vast majority of the show's coverage—especially in the crucial, early weeks after the invasion of Kuwait.

In some quarters, questioning the military mobilization was seen as dangerously unpatriotic: In a review of Bush's September 11 address on the Gulf crisis, the *New York Times*'s R. W. Apple approvingly noted that Bush "made it plain that he would not countenance . . . a buildup of doubts and caveats at home."[34]

Meg Greenfield, who as editorial page editor of the *Washington Post* has great influence over who will and will not participate in the national debate, complained in her *Newsweek* column that "the initial burst of national unity and collective confidence in the rightness of our purpose began to be assaulted" in the weeks following the Iraqi invasion. Referring to a radio talk show caller who argued that the homeless deserve money more than Saudi Arabia, Greenfield wrote, "The proper answer to the man was so complicated that it hardly stood a chance."[35] Perhaps this is why no column arguing against sending troops to Saudi Arabia had yet appeared on the pages Greenfield edited.

Other journalists marginalized dissenters by ignoring rather than attacking them: "Exceptional Consensus Backs U.S. Intervention," a *Washington Post* news analysis by E. J. Dionne was headlined. Although the article alluded to progressive critiques of the mobilization, its discussion of these views focused on the McCarthyite innuendo that "Soviet support for U.S. moves has quelled criticism on the left."[36]

The pro-intervention consensus alleged by Dionne did not include African Americans, who had been much more skeptical than whites of Bush's Persian Gulf policy from the beginning. Even though blacks were more at risk in the Gulf crisis, given their overrepresentation in the armed services, dissenting African-American leaders were rarely given an opportunity to have their views heard.

In many forums, right-wing hawks like Edward Luttwak or Jeane Kirkpatrick, who had tactical reservations about U.S. intervention in this particular context, provided the only questioning of U.S. policy. Patrick Buchanan, who has long protested the prosecution of Nazi war criminals, was often singled out by commentators as the leading "dove" on Iraq, in a manner that seemed calculated to tar opponents of military action as anti-Semitic.

Relegated to the margins of the debate were consistent critics of U.S. intervention. Unlike Ted Koppel, the *New York Times,* and most mainstream media, who had applauded the invasion of Panama, these analysts could condemn Iraq's invasion of Kuwait unhypocritically. The *Donahue* show featured three strong critics of White House policy: Ralph Nader, columnist Alexander Cockburn, and Richard Barnet of the Institute for Policy Studies.[37] But these appearances were exceptional; White House supporters were featured in almost every forum with drumbeat regularity.

BEATING THE WAR DRUMS

It would not be fair to say, however, that mainstream news outlets were totally supportive of Bush administration policy toward Iraq; much of the press was strongly critical of the U.S. government—for failing to immediately launch an attack against Baghdad. In fact, sometimes this was the only kind of "critic" the media recognized: "Critics of the Bush administration's goals in the Gulf say that unless Saddam Hussein is removed and his nation's military capacity is destroyed, he will continue to intimidate his neighbors, even if he withdraws from Kuwait," a *Christian Science Monitor* article read.[38]

While many columnists seemed to compete over who could produce the most bellicose rhetoric, advocacy of military violence was by no means limited to commentators. One of the most startling examples was Lesley Stahl's *60 Minutes* interview with Secretary of State James Baker, whom she badgered for a commitment to attack Iraq:

> This man, Saddam Hussein, has taken American citizens and put them at military installations and God knows what other kind of place. . . . Is that not provocation? . . . Several world leaders pressed the United States through you to go in to attack to take Saddam Hussein out. They want us to. There's a lot of pressure on us to do just that. . . . Is there any doubt in your mind that as this drags out and as we stay in this kind of stalemate situation right now, that Saddam Hussein is going to torture us with pictures of hostages and squeeze us by parading the Americans that he's holding prisoner in this country? . . . I mean, isn't it—well, how much do we want to go in and wipe him out? How can we leave him there with all those weapons at his disposal? How can we do that?[39]

FAIR's scrutiny of months of network news failed to reveal any example of equally hard-hitting interrogation—from a pro-peace perspective. Obvious questions went unasked: Why has the United States instantly rejected every proposal for a negotiated settlement? How is the Kuwait invasion illegal if the Panama invasion was legal? Why is the administration calling Saddam Hussein "Hitler" when it was lobbying to stop congressional sanctions against Iraq days before the invasion of Kuwait? Stahl's questioning showed that correspondents do know how to hold officials' feet to the fire—but only seem to do so from a hawkish perspective.

Some journalists pushed for the assassination of Saddam Hussein, which would violate both U.S. and international law: "The easiest way for the United

States to end the Persian Gulf crisis might be to have Iraq's Saddam Hussein removed—and don't think the idea hasn't occurred in Washington," wrote Mike Feinsilber of the Associated Press (AP). "Assassination is a much discussed topic in Washington because diplomacy seems to have such a scant chance of getting Iraq out of Kuwait and because the full-blown military alternative could result in the deaths of thousands of Americans and Iraqis."[40]

New York Times diplomatic correspondent Thomas Friedman, speaking on the *CBS Morning News,* called on the CIA to blow up Iraqi pipelines and then deny that it had done so—a rare case of a reporter actually *asking* to be disinformed.[41]

Whatever military solution to the crisis journalists envisioned, the actual human costs to both Iraq and the United States were seldom calculated. "A bombing campaign that shatters Saddam's military and secret-police apparatus can succeed without necessarily stirring resentment within the Iraqi nation," *Washington Post* columnist Jim Hoagland opined.[42] Given the Pentagon's estimate of 20,000 to 30,000 in U.S. casualties alone, Hoagland's speculation seemed like a particularly bloody form of wishful thinking.[43]

WRITING OFF NEGOTIATIONS

Although their colleagues in Washington may have called for war, journalists on the ground in Saudi Arabia bent over backwards to depict the U.S. military presence as a force for peace. Even when the United States sent F-16 and F-15 ground attack aircraft to Oman and Qatar, hundreds of miles from Iraq, *New York Times* military reporter Michael Gordon simply interpreted this as an extension of "the commitment to defend against an Iraqi attack."[44] Gordon's complaint about military censorship was that it prevented reporters from covering the real story— "how, or whether, the American military can fulfill its mission of defending Saudi Arabia."[45] Questions like, "Was there ever a real danger that Iraq would invade Saudi Arabia?" or "Is the U.S. force designed for defensive or offensive operations?" were apparently not on Gordon's or other reporters' agendas.

A few outlets provided coverage that was less one-sided. "The U.S. mobilization ... shows clearly that the aim all along has been to deploy offensive forces," according to an analysis in the London *Observer*.[46] In the United States, *New York Newsday* provided consistently independent reporting: "The Bush administration has decided against pursuing its own diplomatic efforts with Iraq to end the Persian Gulf crisis and is planning instead massive military attacks, mostly by air, if, as most officials expect, the economic embargo and U.N. initiatives fail," the paper reported on August 31, 1990.

Most of the media downplayed the Bush administration's rejection of negotiations as an option. When Iraq offered proposals, not only were there few calls from the press for Bush to test the proposals' sincerity but there was very little recognition that such offers had even been made. Saddam Hussein's claim that he would leave Kuwait with Syria's withdrawal from Lebanon and Israel's withdrawal from Lebanon and the Occupied Territories was generally ridiculed. "Unless you solve all the problems of the Middle East, we're going to stay in Kuwait," was how Barbara Walters characterized Iraq's position.[47]

When a front-page story by *New York Newsday*'s Knut Royce disclosed another offer by Baghdad, made August 23, 1990, to withdraw from Kuwait in exchange for control of the disputed Rumaila oil field and access to the Persian Gulf,[48] the *New York Times* reported the proposal on page 14, buried near the end of a story. The *Times* story featured a U.S. diplomat dismissing the proposal as "baloney" and noted that "a well-connected Middle Eastern diplomat told the *New York Times* a week ago of a similar offer, but it, too, was dismissed by the administration"[49]—and so was considered unworthy of reporting. During the week that the *New York Times* suppressed news of Iraq's overture, the mass media were repeatedly telling the public of Iraqi intransigence.

Given the way these proposals were buried, it is not surprising that the *New York Times* could claim—in an editorial warning against offering "face-saving formulas to Saddam Hussein"—that "he has proffered none himself, and he shows no signs of looking for a face-saving exit from Kuwait."[50]

Iraq's unwillingness to negotiate was only one of many myths that became "truth" through force of repetition. Another myth was the notion that Iraq's move against Kuwait was unexpected.

The *New York Times* editorialized on August 3, 1990, that Iraq invaded Kuwait "without warrant or warning." The editorialists would have had plenty of warning if they had read their own front page: On July 28, 1990, a *Times* article on the OPEC (Organization of Petroleum Exporting Companies) dispute over oil quotas reported that "Iraq has clearly threatened to use force against those who weaken the accord by overproducing—a threat mainly directed at the United Arab Emirates and Kuwait, which together have been exceeding their quotas by about a million barrels a day. And Saudi Arabia, by far the largest producer in OPEC, appears to be content to have Iraq play this role."

This myth was convenient for the Bush administration, which had signaled prior to the invasion that it might tolerate some sort of military action against Kuwait. A week before the invasion, the U.S. ambassador to Iraq, April Glaspie, emphasized to Saddam Hussein that the government had "no opinion on the Arab-Arab conflicts, like your border disagreements with Kuwait." Administration officials told the *Washington Post* only six days before the invasion that "an Iraqi attack on Kuwait would not draw a U.S. military response."[51]

PRO-IRAQ PRESS?

Despite the pro-administration puffery that characterized coverage of the Gulf crisis, some critics actually suggested that the media had been too "pro-Iraq." *Newsweek* "balanced" Bush's call for "objective reporting" instead of "Iraqi cheerleading" with a CBS executive's claim that "the reporting has been very fair and very accurate."[52] A true opposing viewpoint, that the cheerleading was all in Bush's favor, was not represented.

When *Nightline* ran a program on whether the TV networks were being used for "propaganda," the guests were conservative columnist Fred Barnes, conservative Senator Trent Lott (R.–Miss.), and ABC News President Roone Arledge.[53] Since progressive media critics were excluded by *Nightline,* it was no wonder that Baghdad was the only source of propaganda seriously considered. Following his debate with the Iraqi ambassador to the United States on *Nightline,* Ted Koppel referred to the exchange as "a propaganda war that is being waged on American television, where the Iraqi government is trying to go over the heads of the American government, directly to the American people, and hoping that it's going to sow some seeds of dissension."[54]

The footage Iraq produced of Saddam Hussein mingling with hostages obviously was propaganda and was labeled as such when rebroadcast on U.S. television. But the media constantly disseminated material carrying the U.S. government agenda, based on government sources and often reported under conditions of U.S. military censorship. It was this propaganda, much more skillful than Saddam Hussein's, that made up the bulk of reporting on the Gulf crisis. Unfortunately, it carried no labels.

Gulf War Coverage: The Worst Censorship Was at Home

May 1991

JIM NAURECKAS

THE MORNING AFTER the United States began the bombing of Iraq, NBC's Robert Bazell reported the Pentagon's assessment via the *Today* show: "It was spectacular news," Bazell summarized. "We've lost only one casualty."[55]

Other networks were similarly ecstatic. CBS's Charles Osgood described the early bombing of Iraq as "a marvel," while the same network's Jim Stewart spoke of "two days of almost picture-perfect assaults."[56]

The war ended on the same note of enthusiastic cheerleading from the media, with CBS's Dan Rather pumping a general's hand after an interview and gushing, "Congratulations on a job wonderfully done!"[57]

The euphoria at the beginning and the end of the Persian Gulf War bracketed one of the most disturbing episodes in U.S. journalistic history—a period in which many reporters for national media abandoned any pretense of neutrality or reportorial distance in favor of boosterism for the war effort. As Hodding Carter, who once served as a State Department spokesperson, put it: "If I were the government, I'd be paying the press for the kind of coverage it is getting right now."[58] Or in the words of a U.S. colonel who handed out little flags to pool reporters: "You are warriors, too."[59]

A few journalists chafed at sacrificing professional standards: "We have sort of become adjuncts of the government," one correspondent in Saudi Arabia told *New York Newsday*. "The line between me and a government contractor is pretty thin."[60]

But many TV journalists did not need to be coerced into abandoning the appearance of independence, instead accepting the task of guiding public opinion in favor of the war as their natural role. In discussing the prospect of increased casualties, Jim Lehrer presented the government and the media as an information team: "Have officials and the press prepared the American people for what may happen next?"[61] NBC's Tom Brokaw was skeptical of the idea that reporters have a right (let alone a duty) to cover the return of dead U.S. servicepeople: "Do you think that's in the best interest of the U.S.?" he asked.[62]

Reporters treated officials, particularly military officials, with kid gloves. When they did engage in tough questioning, it was usually to stake out a more hawkish position than that of the Pentagon. When ABC's Cokie Roberts, for example, interviewed General H. Norman Schwarzkopf, she pressed him, "Why not go after [Saddam Hussein] and end this? . . . Wouldn't it be smarter to institute a draft and get 18-year-olds?"[63] Or as Tom Brokaw asked on day one of the Gulf War, "Can the United States allow Saddam Hussein to live?"[64]

The use by journalists of "we" to mean U.S. military forces was constant, so that one seemed to hear of CBS taking out half the Iraqi Air Force, Saddam Hussein targeting NBC's command and control center, and even Walter Cronkite manning Patriots: "We knocked one of their Scuds out of the sky."[65] As Christopher Hitchens of *The Nation* put it, describing the limited range of debate on U.S. network television, "If you can't, in discussing something like this war, use the word 'we' for everything that's done, as if we are one and we're all agreed . . . you really aren't in the discussion at all."[66]

"We" weren't fighting "them," but "him." Journalists constantly asked, "How long will it take to defeat Saddam Hussein?" or "How badly are we hurting him?"—as if wars are fought against single individuals, rather than nations. For all the media talk about "punishing Saddam Hussein," he was clearly one of the few Iraqis who had three meals a day and a warm place to sleep. Even after the country of Iraq lay in ruins, ABC's Ann Compton continued the fiction that the war targeted a single person: "If there is any use of chemical weapons [against rebels], it will bring down more air attacks on Saddam Hussein's head."[67] Not only was Saddam the only target in Iraq, but the only fighter as well: Journalists said "Saddam Hussein launched another Scud tonight"; they didn't say "George Bush dropped another round of bombs on Baghdad."

SPIN CONTROL THROUGH CENSORSHIP

The extent to which war reporting was controlled by the Bush administration was seldom detailed by the press and hence was widely misunderstood by the public, which largely bought the argument that restrictions were necessary for some vaguely defined "security" reasons. Such arguments were belied by the Pentagon's arbitrary ban on coverage of coffins returning to Dover Air Force Base and by the "48-hour news blackout" at the beginning of the ground war, which was abandoned as soon as the news turned out to be good for the Pentagon.

Nor were the press pools formed because there would otherwise be too many reporters for the military to safely manage: The Pentagon actually flew in, at taxpayer expense, 450 local U.S. reporters to cover their "hometown troops." Meanwhile, reporters from the foreign and alternative press, who would not produce such predictably favorable coverage, were almost entirely excluded from the pools.

The restrictions were aimed not at protecting lives but at protecting the Bush administration's popularity by keeping unpalatable images away from the U.S. public.

"I've never seen anything that can compare to it, in the degree of surveillance and control the military has over the correspondents," stated *New York Times* war correspondent Malcolm Browne. "When the entire environment is controlled, a journalist ceases to be a reporter in the American or Anglo-Saxon tradition. He works a lot like the PK"[68]—referring to the Nazi's Propaganda Kompanie.

The policy had its roots not only in the Pentagon's successful efforts to control the flow of information during the invasions of Panama and Grenada but also in the sophisticated techniques of spin control developed by the Reagan and Bush administrations, techniques whose finest flowering was in the 1988 election campaign. The key principle used by both Reagan and Bush was that if you could control where and when journalists (particularly TV journalists) can report, you could control the imagery and its emotional impact on the public. Michael Deaver, Ronald Reagan's minister of photo opportunities, marveled at the Pentagon's media mastery during the war: "If you were going to hire a public relations firm to do the media relations for an international event, it couldn't be done any better than this is being done."[69]

The prime function of the pool reporting concept was to limit the imagery available to TV cameras. Thus we saw much heroic imagery of missiles rocketing off into the wild blue yonder; images of soldiers killed or wounded by "friendly fire" or "noncombat related accidents" were not considered suitable photo opportunities. As Howard Stringer, president of the CBS Broadcast Group, noted approvingly: "There are more people routinely killed across the spectrum of American television in a given night than you saw in any of the coverage of this war."[70]

Since so much of U.S. action was in the air, where reporters are naturally excluded, the Pentagon provided its own visuals—the video-game footage from laser-guided "smart bombs" hitting seemingly uninhabited buildings, always dead on target. That the military selected the best examples of its handiwork for its show-and-tells was obvious, but that didn't stop TV from rerunning the footage endlessly, or pundits from citing it as evidence of how well the expensive high-tech weaponry worked.

Though some journalists abandoned the pools and set off on their own in search of more independent reporting, others seemed to prefer the comforts and privileges of being a kept press. When Robert Fisk of the London *Independent* tried to report without official permission on the battle of Khafji, NBC correspondent Brad Willis reported him to the Marines. "You asshole," the reporter told Fisk. "You'll prevent us from working. You're not allowed here. Get out. Go back to Dhahran."[71]

Reporters who tried to cover the war outside the Pentagon's press pools were sometimes detained and threatened by U.S. soldiers. Marines held a wire service photographer for six hours, threatening to shoot him if he left his car—"We have orders from above to make this pool system work," they told him. A French TV crew was forced at gunpoint to turn over to Marines footage of soldiers wounded at the battle of Khafji.[72]

The power to control where pool reporters go—and to remove uncooperative reporters from the pool, as was done to Douglas Jehl of the *Los Angeles Times*—was not enough to satisfy Pentagon information managers. Journalists were also accompanied by military escorts who intervened in reporting, blocking interviews on sensitive subjects such as the practice of religion by U.S. soldiers in theocratic Saudi Arabia.[73]

Military officials had right of approval over the final copy and footage (although the benign verb "cleared" was usually used in place of the more ominous "censored"). The censors were known to delete details that struck them as embarrassing—the fact that Stealth pilots were watching X-rated movies before bombing missions, for example, or a *Detroit Free Press* reporter's description of a returning bomber pilot as "giddy." (The censor changed that to "proud," but finally compromised with "pumped up."[74])

The response of the mainstream media to being censored by their government was strikingly muted, considering that in the case of Nicaragua the U.S. media often treated wartime censorship as a plausible justification for overthrowing the Sandinista government. Mainstream news outlets could have legally challenged the Pentagon restrictions; the Center for Constitutional Rights, on behalf of a number of journalists and liberal and progressive publications, filed a lawsuit seeking the abolition of the restrictions on the grounds that there is no wartime exception to the First Amendment. But not only did mainstream media not join the lawsuit, or file friend-of-the-court briefs (as FAIR did), they hardly even reported on the suit.

Before the war, NBC News President Michael Gartner made a strong statement about the dangers of censorship to the *Washington Post:* "I don't think you can hide the horror of war.... War is not like primetime television, where people are dying peacefully or whatever. It's horrible. And you have a duty in news to tell people what's going on. And if something is horrible, you tell them it's horrible, you show them it's horrible.... Any time [someone] tries to somehow crimp that, it's very, very bad for the viewer. It's very bad for the country, it's very bad for democracy."[75]

During the war, Gartner ordered NBC not to air exclusive footage of how U.S. bombing had devastated the city of Basra in Iraq.[76] He saw nothing wrong with journalists censoring themselves: "I have no problem with [*Today* show executive producer] Tom Capra making that decision. I just don't want [Defense Secretary] Dick Cheney to make that decision."

PENTAGON "EXPERTS"

The Pentagon usually either provided the networks' information about the war or managed the news from the front through censorship and press restrictions. The networks' "analysis" of this information, which filled up hours of airtime between real news, was not itself censored by the Pentagon, but it might as well have been. Network TV featured a one-sided procession of retired military brass, ex-government hawks, right-wing pundits and politicians, scholars from think tanks with generally conservative bents, and—for supposed balance—Democratic politicians rallying 'round the president.

"You know who I feel sorry for?" quipped *Saturday Night Live*'s Dennis Miller. "It's the one retired army colonel who didn't get a job as a TV analyst."[77] NBC's satirical news anchor is paid to tell jokes; real anchor Tom Brokaw is not. But after introducing a retired U.S. Army colonel, Brokaw announced that "the Fairness Doctrine is in play here tonight," and introduced, for balance, a retired U.S. Navy admiral. Army versus Navy was often what passed for balance on U.S. TV.

ABC's Anthony Cordesman, a former Pentagon and National Security Council official and, until the day the war began, an aide to Senator John McCain (R.–Ariz.), was the analyst who showed up most often in a FAIR survey of network news sources—eleven times in fourteen days. His message could be summed up in one sentence: "I think the Pentagon is giving it to you straight."[78] Cordesman could be counted on to defend the Defense Department position—whether by referring to dead civilians as "collateral damage" or by explaining that if reporters on the roof of the bombed neighborhood shelter in Baghdad couldn't find the camouflage paint the Pentagon said was there, it must have flaked off when the bombs hit.[79]

Not all military consultants were as slavish as Cordesman in parroting the official line. But all shared a common history and set of assumptions with the current Pentagon leaders and tended to reinforce rather than question the messages coming out of official briefings. Some of the military analysts had another kind of conflict of interest, like CNN's General James Blackwell, who has also served as a consultant to Lockheed, the manufacturer of many of the weapons that Blackwell was called upon to praise.

Perhaps the most questionable choice as a network TV military consultant was General Michael Dugan, the U.S. Air Force chief of staff until September 1990. Dugan was fired by the Air Force for asserting, among other things, that the U.S. should target Saddam Hussein's family and level Iraq's most important cultural sites—both violations of the Geneva Protocols.[80] Yet he was hired as a consultant by CBS, where he argued that the United States would never deliberately harm civilians in wartime.[81]

With the discussion dominated by retired military men, media analysis demonstrated a near-worship of military technology. Journalists revered U.S. weaponry—a CNN reporter described the "sweet, beautiful sight" of bombers taking off from Saudi Arabia[82]—and attributed moral failings to Iraqi munitions, as when NBC's Arthur Kent called the Scud "an evil weapon, but not an accurate weapon."[83] While ABC's Cordesman talked about the "brilliance of laser-guided bombs,"[84] Peter Jennings described the Scud as "a horrifying killer"[85]—even though the effects of the U.S. bombs were demonstrably more deadly.

The contest between good U.S. weapons and evil Iraqi ones seemed to be summed up in the comparison between the Patriot and the Scud. (The media universally chose to use the nickname given to the Iraqi missile by the Pentagon—which often gives silly or sinister-sounding names to the enemy's products—rather than using the Soviet designation, SS–1.) Richard Blystone of CNN described the Scud as "a quarter-ton of concentrated hatred,"[86] while the Patriot was described by *USA Today* as "three inches longer than a Cadillac Sedan de Ville."[87]

Pundits like George Will and most of the *McLaughlin Group* took advantage of the Patriot's celebrity status to call for more "Star Wars" antimissile research—although the Patriot has nothing to do with Star Wars technology[88]—and to celebrate the 1980s military buildup in general. As Lee Cullum, editorial writer for the *Dallas Times Herald*, said on the *MacNeil/Lehrer NewsHour*, "It's gratifying to know all this money was well spent."[89]

Justifying further military spending, of course, was a major goal of Pentagon management of the news. Sometimes the spin control was so effective that reporters ignored the evidence in front of their own eyes. On January 20, 1991, NBC's Tom Aspell in Baghdad marveled over the accuracy of Tomahawk cruise missiles—"accurate to within a few feet." He had just finished saying that one such accurate missile had hit "the [al-Rashid] hotel employees' housing compound."

The ultimate in weapons fetishism came in discussion of the ultimate weapon—the nuclear bomb. During the Gulf crisis, journalists gave serious, sometimes sympathetic, consideration to the use of atomic weapons against Iraq. "Should a Nuclear Bomb Be Used Against Iraq?" was one of the "ethical dilemmas" that *Time* magazine examined in its February 4, 1991, issue.

In a lengthy segment that considered whether to use nuclear bombs against Iraq "to save U.S. lives," CBS's Robert Krulwich marveled over the advances made in tactical, low-yield nuclear weapons: "You can drop one over the Empire State Building and control the blast to within five blocks and there'd be almost no significant damage in the rest of Manhattan. Even fallout is less of a problem."[90]

Most of the corporate-owned media have close relationships to the military and oil industry: The chair of Capital Cities/ABC, for example, was on the board of Texaco, and CBS's board included directors from Honeywell and the Rand Corporation.[91] But no news outlet was as potentially compromised as NBC, wholly owned by General Electric (GE).

The Boston-based corporate watchdog group, INFACT, reported that in 1989 alone GE received nearly $2 billion in U.S. military contracts for systems employed in the Gulf War effort. Conflicts of interest at NBC were an ongoing problem, as when the network aired a laudatory segment on the Patriot missile, for which GE produces parts. Brokaw called the Patriot "the missile that put the Iraqi Scud in its place."[92]

NBC's conflicts of interest went beyond weaponry. The government of Kuwait was believed to be a significant GE stockholder, having owned 2.1 percent of all GE stock in 1982, the last year for which figures are available.[93]

Having profited from weapons systems used in the Gulf, and anticipating lucrative deals for restocking U.S. arsenals, GE was also poised to profit from the rebuilding of Kuwait. GE told the *Wall Street Journal* that it expected to win contracts worth "hundreds of millions of dollars."[94]

HEARD AND UNHEARD

The nonmilitary consultants used by the networks hardly provided more balance than the parade of generals and colonels. For political commentary and expertise, CBS relied on Fouad Ajami, a Lebanese-born academic whose hawkish views made him the media's favorite Arab-American pundit. He served to "explain" Arab culture for the United States with such comments as "We get lost in the twisted alleyways of the Middle Eastern bazaar."[95] He dismissed Arab opposition to the U.S. war, referring to "the Palestinian mob"[96] and "some few gullible souls ... demonstrating in Algeria."[97] William Safire called Ajami the best commentator of the war, "for the amazing way he reads the Arab mind."[98]

Ajami was unwaveringly pro-war, declaring, "We went over there to do what had to be done, we went over there to thwart a despot."[99] For an "objective" analyst, he had a strikingly skewed view of the political spectrum. When a caller to CBS's *America Tonight* asked if people who "opposed this war" were adequately covered by the media—a question translated by Lesley Stahl as "Do you believe that pro-Arab views are not getting enough of a hearing on television?"—Ajami replied, "I think everyone is being heard; the people who favor this war, the people who think it's a just war are being heard; the people who think it is just barely a just war are being heard; the people who believe Saddam is a hero are getting their airtime from Amman and from the West Bank and so on."[100]

ABC's Middle East consultant was the Brookings Institution's Judith Kipper, who was "impressed" by the bombing of Iraq[101] but who found Iraqi missile attacks on Israel "an incredible escalation."[102] For analysis of the region, NBC went to Edward Peck, a former U.S. ambassador to Iraq. An example of Peck's analysis was this explanation of the difference between U.S. and Iraqi culture:

> Where we in the West tend to think of our New Testament heritage, where you turn the other cheek and you let bygones be bygones and forgive and forget, the people of the Middle East are the people of the Old Testament, if you will, if the Muslims will let me say that, where there's much more of an eye for an eye and a tooth for a tooth and you don't forget and you don't forgive and you carry on the vendetta and the struggle long after people in the West would be prepared to say all right, it's over, let's not worry about it any longer.[103]

Offered as the bombs were beginning to fall on Baghdad, these observations on the vengeful nature of non-Christian societies came across as somewhat surreal.

Usually missing from the news was analysis from a perspective critical of U.S. policy. The media's rule of thumb seemed to be that to support the war was to be objective, while to be antiwar was to carry a bias. *Washington Post* editorial page editor Meg Greenfield made clear in her *Newsweek* column who she felt should be left out of the debate: "If the capacity of the American political system to function effectively is not itself soon to become a victim of the crisis . . . a few premises [will have] to be accepted. The first of these premises is that just about everybody engaged in the argument hoped to prevent war."[104] Those who believe that George Bush pushed for war all along, then, had little chance of making that point in the *Post*.

A survey conducted by FAIR of the sources on the ABC, CBS and NBC nightly news in the first two weeks of the war found that of 878 on-air sources, only one was a representative of a national peace organization—Bill Monning, of International Physicians for the Prevention of Nuclear War. By contrast, seven players from the Super Bowl were brought on to comment on the war.[105]

From the outset of the Gulf crisis, national television news marginalized critics. Mainstream media so ignored the months of mobilizing by antiwar activists that ABC's Cokie Roberts could announce on January 17, 1991, "The peace movement has instantly sprung up." Hours before the war started, a CNN correspondent concluded his report on Atlanta's Martin Luther King commemoration, which turned into an impassioned protest against Bush's Gulf policy: "Antiwar sentiment in Atlanta is more fervent than anyone knew."[106] CNN is based in Atlanta. Why didn't it know?

Media also tended to downplay the size of antiwar demonstrations. The *New York Times* coverage of the first national rally against the war (the January 19, 1991, march in Washington, D.C.) consisted of a single photo and caption, which put the size of the crowd at a mere 15,000[107]—less than the official police count of 25,000 and far less than the 75,000 estimated by the organizers. The photo's caption read: "Across America, Demonstrators Take Sides in Persian Gulf War"—placing the thousands of peace activists on par with the handful of pro-war demonstrators on the scene.

No matter how vast the number of antiwar demonstrators or how puny the number of war supporters, some media insisted on giving the pro-war side equal or greater coverage. When a handful of Young Republicans marched into a rally of at least 600 war opponents at the University of California (UC) at Berkeley, the *San Francisco Chronicle* covered the event by dedicating the headline ("War Backers March on UC Protest"), the photo, and the only quote of a student offering an opinion to the Young Republican minority.[108] When George Bush's visit to New York on a rainy night in February brought out 3,500 antiwar protesters and a half-dozen pro-war demonstrators, the *New York Times* devoted a sentence on page D5 to the 3,500; the accompanying photo was of the pro-warriors, including a woman carrying a placard: "If You Don't Support Our President and Our Country, Get Out."[109]

At times, the media displayed open hostility toward the peace movement: *Newsweek* was offended that the peace movement upset the "noble spirit of common purpose and national unity."[110] CBS seemed to mock protesters when its morning program reported that "the voices of protest are being heard loud and clear," as it showed a clip of protesters being dragged off a basketball court by police in Montana. The segment ended with the crowd chanting "USA, USA."[111] In another CBS segment, correspondent Jerry Bowen described as one of the "signs of patriotism" a bumper sticker that read: "Save a Flag/Burn a Protester."[112]

In Los Angeles, ABC affiliate KABC-TV actually banned coverage of peace demonstrations soon after the war began, according to station employees quoted by *Los Angeles Times* TV critic Howard Rosenberg. "Nothing is on paper, but it's understood and it's been reaffirmed repeatedly," a staffer, who asked for anonymity, told Rosenberg. "We may occasionally drop in a line [about antiwar demonstrations] at the end of coverage of pro-war demonstrations, but we do not put those protest stories on the air."[113]

On the rare occasions when mainstream journalists defended protesters, it became one more opportunity to boost the war policy. Tom Brokaw challenged a pro-war guest to acknowledge the right to dissent, saying, "After all, that's what those people in the Gulf are defending, the right, among others, to have freedom of expression."[114] It's hard to see the reinstallation of the emir of Kuwait, whose government has long forbidden criticism, as a blow for freedom of expression.

When antiwar voices were heard, it was very rarely as in-studio guests partaking in substantive discussions. Instead, typical coverage of the peace movement resembled nature footage—outdoors, in the demonstrators' "natural habitat."

Many TV viewers must have wondered if peace advocates were capable of expressing themselves in more than slogans, chants, or sound bites. But even sound bites were rare: Only about 1.5 percent of nightly network news sources were protesters, about the same number as people who were asked about how the war had affected their travel plans.[115]

Relying on random protesters to present a movement's views, as network TV did, denied that movement its most articulate and knowledgeable spokespeople. The situation is comparable to depending on interviews with the crowd at a Republican rally to convey the views of the Bush administration.

In a broadcast debate, a local TV news director bristled at the suggestion by FAIR's Martin Lee that television news had systematically slighted U.S. opponents of the war. "How can you do any better than having Saddam Hussein piped into our homes live?" the news director asked. "How can you do any better than that?"[116]

CIVILIAN DEATHS AS "PROPAGANDA"

With policy critics basically excluded from the discussion, few had any interest in bringing up one of the most important issues of the war: civilian casualties. No one was on hand to contradict claims like Ted Koppel's that "great effort is taken, sometimes at great personal cost to American pilots, that civilian targets are not hit"[117] or Brokaw's statement that "the U.S. has fought this war at arm's length with long-range missiles, high-tech weapons . . . to keep casualties down."[118] The unstated but obvious truth was that by carrying out an air war that was unprecedented in its ferocity, U.S. strategy sought to reduce U.S. military losses at the expense of thousands of Iraqi civilian casualties.

Again and again, the mantra of "surgical strikes against military targets" was repeated by journalists, even though Pentagon briefers acknowledged that they were aiming at civilian roads, bridges, and public utilities vital to the survival of the civilian population. One was reminded of Harry Truman's announcement of the dropping of the atomic bomb: "Sixteen hours ago, an American airplane dropped one bomb on Hiroshima, an important Japanese Army base."[119]

Journalists and pundits were rightfully outraged when Baghdad advertised its violations of the Geneva Protocols by parading prisoners of war on TV. They failed to object, however, when the United States proved its own violations by showing footage of laser-guided bombs destroying hydroelectric dams (forbidden as targets under Protocol I, Article 56).

While civilian targets deliberately hit by U.S. bombs were transformed by the media into military targets, the civilians accidentally killed by U.S. bombs became Saddam Hussein's fault. "We must point out again and again that it is Saddam Hussein who put these innocents in harm's way," Brokaw announced.[120] Reporting on Iraqi civilians killed by U.S. bombs, Mark Phillips of CBS intoned, "Saddam Hussein promised a bloody war, and here was the blood."[121]

Some of the media apologies were ill-timed. The same week that high-tech, armor-piercing bombs destroyed a Baghdad bomb shelter and its civilian inhabitants and a British laser-guided bomb killed 150 Iraqis in a market, the *Newsweek* cover on newsstands read: "The New Science of War; High-Tech Hardware: How Many Lives Can It Save?"[122] The next week's *Newsweek* was able to turn even the shelter bombing into a moral victory for the United States: "The mere fact that the bombing was such a big event suggested how few civilian casualties this war has produced in the first place."[123]

When they were not apologists for U.S. killing, journalists often assumed a dubious evenhandedness: "The Iraqis say the main targets are civilians. The U.S. insists their targets continue to be military. In war, there are no independent judges."[124] Unless, of course, an independent press commits itself to cutting through the propaganda on both sides.

British journalist Patrick Cockburn took exactly such an approach in his reporting from Baghdad for the London *Independent*. "From the beginning, the allies' bombs and missiles were never as accurate as might have appeared," he concluded.

> There were craters where missiles had hit houses or waste ground, or were far from any obvious targets.... Often the bomb that had hit a civilian house was one of a stick of bombs, most of which had fallen on open ground. Sometimes an obvious target was visible in the distance.... The allied air forces have become victims of their own propaganda. They have pretended they can carry out surgical strikes; but mass bombing remains a blunt instrument.[125]

Other reporters in Baghdad, such as ABC's Bill Blakemore, also did creditable jobs of reporting the facts as they saw them, sometimes under considerable pressure from their anchors to conform to the official Washington version.

The U.S. media's most effective—and offensive—tool for dismissing civilian casualties was to treat the whole issue as a propaganda ploy on the part of Saddam Hussein. As CBS's Bruce Morton commented, "If Saddam Hussein can turn the world against the effort, convince the world that women and children are the targets of the air campaign, then he will have won a battle, his only one so far."[126] Viewers—and CBS employees—could only draw the conclusion that aggressive pursuit of the issue of civilian deaths would give aid and comfort to the enemy. The media were warned away from the subject by writers like *Newsweek*'s Jonathan Alter: "The voracious American media will use human-interest stories to prey on the sensibilities of the American people, who are extremely sensitive to casualties."[127]

NBC's Dennis Murphy, concluding a segment on video evidence of victims provided by the Iraqi government, took a tone that was widespread throughout the media: "Until we get some Western reporters and photographers in there to vouch for it, I think we'll have to call it propaganda." Anchor Garrick Utley agreed: "That's a pretty good name for it."[128] It's a name that the media gave to dead Iraqis again and again.

There is no doubt that U.S. journalists are able to convey sympathy for civilian victims of war; the coverage of the aftermath of the Scud attacks in Israel was proof of that. The networks took great pains not to underplay the seriousness of the missile attacks; when a CBS reporter noted that the situation after an air raid was "as would be expected, quite normal," Dan Rather stepped in: "That is not to say, when we say normal and expected, that we are insensitive to the people who were affected by the attack."[129] But when, as a FAIR survey showed, more than three times as much attention is given to victims in Israel—where four people had been killed by missiles—than to civilians in Iraq and Kuwait—where thousands died—such coverage ceases to be sympathy and becomes exploitation.

Sometimes the deaths occurring in Iraq were literally forgotten, as when Ted Koppel, on a day when clearing weather allowed 2,000 bombing runs over Baghdad, said, "Aside from the Scud missile that landed in Tel Aviv earlier, it's been a quiet night in the Middle East."[130]

The compassion that might have been extended to the innocents under U.S. bombing seemed reserved instead for another "victim"—the U.S. citizen. Experts on economics and psychology were brought on TV to explain how Saddam Hussein was hurting the American public, which helped to dissolve any residual guilt they might feel over the destruction of Baghdad. But the main way the media established the living-room participant as a sort of vicarious casualty was by the incessant repetition of the terrorism theme.

Report after report about terrorism was based on nothing more than the speculation of self-styled terrorism "experts," as in "Anti-terrorism experts say an attack in the U.S. can be expected. . . . [The question is] not if an attack, but when."[131] The experts usually turned out to be either Bush administration officials putting out the line of the day or corporate security consultants for whom fear means business, or sometimes both. Billie Vincent, a member of Bush's anti-terrorism task force and president of a company that designs security systems for airports, wrote a *New York Times* op-ed piece with the unsurprising rallying cry, "Improve Airline Bomb Detection."[132]

The truth is that while there is little history of foreigners committing organized political violence in the United States, there is a long tradition of governments using the specter of such violence for political ends, as in the "Libyan hit squads" supposedly stalking Reagan in 1981—an apparent creation of then-CIA director William Casey.

One could argue that the upsurge in hate crimes against Arab-Americans that accompanied the war frenzy, as documented by an Arab-American Anti-Discrimination Committee report, constituted a form of terrorism. The committee found more than 100 instances of hate crimes against Arab-Americans from August 1990 through March 1991, including a bomb found in a San Diego mosque and an Arab restaurant burned down in Detroit.[133] But these crimes were not treated by the media as terrorism; the terror, after all, could not be blamed on Iraq.

Coverage of the "terrorist threat" sometimes hit the higher frequencies of hysteria, as when Dan Rather interviewed Federal Bureau of Investigation (FBI) chief William Sessions: "If you're an American mother who happens to be of Jewish heritage ... do you send your child to school?" Rather asked earnestly. "What should our attitude toward Americans of Arab heritage be?" he queried. Sessions was reassuring: The children were safe, and Arab-Americans "all support the president's policy."[134]

The Rand Corporation's Brian Jenkins argued on *Nightline:* "If we think of terrorism as not only the sum of terrorist actions but also comprising the atmosphere of fear and alarm created by terrorist actions or by the threat of terrorist actions, then the war here has already begun.... People are alarmed."[135] If TV news is running unsubstantiated stories designed to increase ratings by frightening viewers, wouldn't that make the networks terrorists as well?

THE THREAT OF PEACE

If mere demonstrations for peace had annoyed the media, the prospect of actual peace breaking out sent many journalists into convulsions. The *Wall Street Journal*'s Karen Elliot House called the prospect of a negotiated settlement a "tragedy," while for Tom Brokaw it was "a nightmare ... the worst possible scenario."[136] Dan Rather seized upon the perfect metaphor to depict Soviet peace proposals as threatening and dangerous: "If you consider this a kind of Iraqi-Soviet Scud—diplomatically ... Marlin Fitzwater at the White House has fired what amounts to a diplomatic Patriot at it."[137]

David Brinkley promoted his February 17, 1991, program thus: "Sunday on *This Week:* What next in the war after Saddam Hussein's phony peace offer? Secretary of Defense Richard Cheney will be our guest." The *New York Times* offered this smug editorial comment in response to the Soviet peace effort: "The same question can be asked about peace that is reasonable to ask about ground war: What's the rush?"[138]

Saddam Hussein was consistently presented as a madman with whom it was impossible to negotiate. "His one success was deeply atavistic: toppling all standards of reasonable discourse, rejecting every rational approach, he managed to throw everyone back into antique ways of settling their disputes," *Newsweek* reported.[139]

When breaking news made it clear that Iraq was willing to negotiate its withdrawal from Kuwait, the idea of negotiating itself had to be discredited. Commentary dwelt on racial stereotypes about "haggling in the bazaar"; one NBC newscast actually illustrated a report about negotiations with footage of rug merchants.

Commentators seemed oblivious to the racism inherent in talk about the "Arab mind": "We go in a straight line; they zig-zag," Judith Kipper remarked. "They can say one thing in the morning, another thing at night, and really mean a third thing."[140] The Bush administration's flip-flops on the war's aims and justifications did not evoke similar speculations about WASP psychology.

By the end of the war, U.S. troops were actually maneuvering to prevent Iraqi troops from leaving Kuwait before they could be killed—a fact the *Washington Post* referred to two weeks later as a "grim irony."[141] The media shied away from describing the massive cost in human lives of such a policy, euphemizing instead that the United States was seeking the "humiliation" of Saddam Hussein. The *New York Times*'s Leslie Gelb gave an original explanation of why such a "humiliation" of Saddam was necessary: "If he were to survive the war as a hero, he would be like a giant starship emitting undeflectable death rays."[142]

Why were the American people surprised at the weakness of the Iraqi ground resistance? Because they trusted the media, and the media trusted the U.S. military. *New York Newsday*'s Susan Sachs reported how the Pentagon had intentionally placed false estimates of Iraqi defenses in the U.S. press: "There was a great disinformation campaign surrounding this war," one senior commander boasted. "We've known for weeks that the lines weren't that formidable," General Walter Boomer told Sachs. "But we wanted to let Iraqis think we still thought they were big."[143]

One might question whether it's legitimate to corrupt the U.S. political debate in order to fool Saddam Hussein. But given the fact that the U.S. military knew that it would face little or no resistance from the Iraqis, it seems more likely that this "great disinformation campaign" was aimed directly at the American people—first justifying a massive military buildup, then making the Pentagon into a hero for knocking down a straw man.[144] George Bush's unprecedented rating in the polls was the fruit of this deception.

THE "EVENHANDED" PRESS

The media's performance in the Gulf War prompted extensive self-analysis by journalists—much of it focused, in self-congratulatory fashion, on whether the press is *too* independent, *too* aggressive, *too* willing to present both sides. Typically, TV discussions on the subject pitted right-wing press-bashers on the attack against mainstream journalists defending the media, with progressive critics largely excluded. One of the most extreme examples of this imbalance was a panel on the *MacNeil/Lehrer NewsHour*, which included, on the right, *Wall Street Journal* press critic Dorothy Rabinowitz and not one but two representatives of the far-right organization Accuracy In Media (AIM)—Reed Irvine and Admiral Thomas Moorer, an AIM board member. These panelists were "balanced" with three journalists—including Bernard Kalb, formerly a spokesperson for the Reagan State Department, and Harrison Salisbury, who stated, "It is fair to have a prejudice in favor of our side and I always have had that."[145]

MacNeil and Lehrer could hardly claim to be unaware that there were critics who would call this view unprofessional; just that morning, FAIR activists were outside their New York office, protesting their one-sided coverage of the Baghdad shelter bombing the night before.

The extensive airtime handed to right-wing critics was the media's reaction to an alleged upswelling of public anger over the disloyal press. Not all of this "outrage" was spontaneous: The Republican National Committee, for example, sent out a half-million copies of form letters to be passed on to the media, complaining about "the attention given to war protesters."[146]

But attacks from the hysterical right are useful to the media in burying serious press criticism. *Time* devoted a three-page article to the charge that the media served as conduits for Iraqi propaganda, with only one paragraph allotted for those arguing that U.S. dissidents were being slighted. This was followed by, "Is this anything more than the usual partisan carping at the press? The attacks from both sides probably mean that the press is situated just about where it usually is: in the evenhanded middle ground."[147]

Just where this "evenhanded middle ground" is situated was illustrated by an article on the war's effect on network profits. In an effort to increase ad sales, CBS executives "offered advertisers assurances that the war specials could be tailored to provide better lead-ins to commercials. One way would be to insert the commercials after segments that were specially produced with upbeat images or messages about the war, like patriotic views from the home front."[148]

The Polling Game

May 1991

THERE'S NO DOUBT that U.S. public support for the Bush policy greatly increased after fighting began, but the polls cited to demonstrate this phenomenon did as much to shape public opinion as to measure it.

Before the war, a *Los Angeles Times* poll offered this slanted choice: "If Hussein pulls his troops out of all of Kuwait, should the U.S. keep a military presence in the Persian Gulf to maintain stability in the region, or not?" Unsurprisingly, only 26 percent chose to vote against "stability."[149] People would have responded far differently to, for example, "Should the U.S. keep a potentially destabilizing military force in the Persian Gulf, or not?"—which many Mideast experts would have seen as a more realistic question.

The question Gallup asked in mid-February 1991, which echoed those asked by other pollsters, was "Do you think U.S. and allied forces should begin a ground attack soon to drive the Iraqis out of Kuwait—or should we hold off for now and continue to rely on air power to do the job?"¹⁵⁰ Since a cease-fire for negotiations was not given as an option—and certainly not presented as an appealing choice that would "drive the Iraqis out" or "do the job"—a respondent who had doubts about both the air and the ground war had no option but to appear uninformed or apathetic: "No opinion."

After the ground offensive began, the *New York Times*/CBS poll let people choose between agreeing that "the U.S. did the right thing in starting the ground war," or maintaining that it should have "waited longer to see if the bombing from the air worked."¹⁵¹ Even though the Soviets had already gotten the Iraqis to agree to their plan for withdrawal from Kuwait, those who favored a diplomatic solution could only respond "no opinion."

Establishment journalists use polls to claim that they're reflecting public opinion, not shaping it. But the spectrum of opinion and debate was far wider outside the official Washington circles the media tended to cover.

On the eve of war, for example, a *New York Times*/CBS poll indicated that a 56 percent to 33 percent majority favored a Mideast peace conference rather than war as a means of dislodging Iraq from Kuwait. By 47 percent to 37 percent, respondents favored a negotiated Iraq-Kuwait border settlement as a means of averting war.¹⁵² But since these views were not advocated inside the Beltway, they were almost never included in the mainstream media debate.

Even after the war began, when one-sided media coverage added to public support for the war, a *Washington Post* poll still found 42 percent approving of peace talks to bring the war to a quicker end.¹⁵³ On TV, the percentage advocating peace talks did not exceed a fraction of 1 percent.

"Slaughter" Is Something Other Countries Do

May/June 1991

"**M**ARK THOMPSON, defense correspondent for Knight-Ridder Newspapers, says his days feel shapeless without the comforting rhythm of the morning briefing from Riyadh and the afternoon session at the Pentagon," the *Washington Post*'s Howard Kurtz reported after the war.¹⁵⁴ "There's nothing better for a journalist than to know what the story of the day is," Thompson told Kurtz. "The worst thing for reporters is to mope around sifting through ashes looking for a story, and that's what everyone is doing now."

In the aftermath of the Gulf War, reporters were generally able to avoid ash-sifting in favor of dutifully reporting the story of the day. The main theme was the violence being inflicted on the Iraqi people by the Iraqi government—somehow a more interesting subject than the violence inflicted on the Iraqi people by the U.S. government.

"Americans are appalled by the spectacle of Iraqi forces slaughtering Kurds and Shiites," wrote New York Times columnist Leslie Gelb.[155] Why were they appalled by those killings and not by the several-times-greater death toll inflicted by U.S. bombing? Was it because mass media outlets played down reports by refugees fleeing U.S. bombs, and played up those featuring Iraqi guns? Or was it because commentators like Gelb scrupulously avoided using words like "slaughter" to describe damage caused by their own government?

NBC's John Chancellor similarly lamented that Saddam Hussein was "slaughtering his own people"[156]—an act presumably much worse than slaughtering someone else's people, since Chancellor managed not to use the word "slaughter" during the six weeks that U.S.-led forces were killing as many as 30,000 Iraqis per week.

A news analysis in the New York Times carried the headline, "'Clean Win' in the War With Iraq Drifts into a Bloody Aftermath." "Clean win," a quote from Colin Powell, was not used ironically: The story's lead used the phrase "clean win" as an accurate description of a victory that "was being soiled by the bloodbath it had unleashed inside Iraq."[157]

Reporting on atrocities by Iraq was specific and graphic, whereas accounts of damage caused by the United States were vague and abounded in euphemisms. Maintaining the economic embargo with the aim of causing famine and epidemic in Iraq was described by the New York Times as a policy of "making life uncomfortable for the Iraqi people," in order to "encourage them to remove" Saddam from power.[158] A map in U.S. News & World Report identified the area of Iraq occupied by the U.S. as "American Protection."[159]

A New York Times chart titled "Re-examining the Toll" included detailed breakdowns on Iraqi losses of tanks, artillery, and armored personnel carriers—but no mention of human life.[160] The Iraqi people also disappeared in a Washington Post chart listing U.S. casualties (Americans killed, wounded, missing, or taken prisoner) along with "Iraqi losses" (2,085 tanks, 962 armored vehicles, 1,005 artillery pieces, and 103 aircraft destroyed).[161]

To find the human toll caused by U.S. weapons, one often had to look in the nooks and crannies—such as U.S. News & World Report's "Washington Whispers" page, which featured this one-paragraph item, captioned "The Grim Math": "Although top U.S. commanders last week estimated that Iraq suffered at least 100,000 military deaths during the war, other sources in the Gulf say the final total—including civilian fatalities—will be at least twice that. These sources say the allied aerial attacks inflicted far more casualties than previously thought."[162]

The report of a possible 200,000 dead took up little more than an inch of space. At that rate, the Nazi Holocaust against the Jews would take up about 30 inches—and could almost be contained on a single page in *U.S. News & World Report*.

Back to Iraq: News Reporting Echoes Bias of Desert Storm

March 1993

SAM HUSSEINI

As U.S. PLANES resumed the bombing of Iraq in the beginning of 1993, ABC's Jim Laurie cautioned viewers, "Bear in mind that most Iraqis, because of the incredibly tightly controlled media here, never understood why it was this attack was carried out. There is nothing really in the media to help them explain all this."[163]

But were Americans much better off? The U.S. press was full of explanations for the attack, many of them misleading or wrong. Leading news outlets frequently claimed that the United States was acting on behalf of the U.N. in establishing "no-fly zones" over Iraq. In fact, the restriction of Iraqi flights was decided unilaterally by the United States and a small group of European allies. As the Center for Constitutional Rights pointed out, "None of the U.N. Security Council resolutions call for the establishment of the current 'no-fly zone.'"[164]

That didn't stop *New York Newsday* from using the headline "U.N. Foot's Down" over an article about a U.S. ultimatum regarding the "no-fly zone";[165] or the *New York Times* from referring to an "Iraqi jet flying over southern Iraq in violation of the United Nations ban";[166] or CBS's Dan Rather from announcing that the U.S. attack was "on behalf of the United Nations."[167]

There were some U.N. resolutions that Iraq may have been violating, but as the Bush administration acknowledged, they were not the primary reason for the bombing. When Ted Koppel asked if the United States would have called off the raids if Iraq had promised to abide by U.N. resolutions, the National Security Council's Richard Haass replied, "Probably not," explaining that "the most important issue on the proximate cause of today's action" was "the placement of missiles and so forth in the no-fly zone."[168] But most media reports blurred the difference between U.S. and U.N. restrictions, in effect giving an international cover to what was essentially a unilateral action.

As the U.S. government replayed the Gulf War, the press seemed to have learned precious little from Desert Storm. The same government and military experts dominated the coverage, and voices that would lend an independent perspective were once again marginalized.

The same propagandistic use of language was evident: While Baghdad's attempts to fly aircraft over its own territory were "threatening," "provocative," and "defiant," the U.S. attacks were "restrained."

Journalists again spoke as if they were part of the U.S. government, using the words "we" and "us" when talking about military action. "Are we going to retaliate?" ABC's David Brinkley asked military analyst Anthony Cordesman. "I think we have to retaliate," Cordesman replied.[169]

Just as in the Gulf War, journalists trivialized the human impact of military action, treating war as a kind of game. In an interview with Defense Secretary Dick Cheney, Jim Lehrer remarked of Saddam Hussein, "It must give you some sense of satisfaction to pop him one before you go."[170]

For Jim Stewart of CBS, "The problem with bombing is you don't always know if you destroyed everything you aimed at."[171] A similar neglect of human costs was evident in Tom Aspell's NBC report from Baghdad that "the sanctions are only now taking effect."[172] In fact, the *New England Journal of Medicine* estimated that more than 46,000 Iraqi children had died from the combined effects of war and trade sanctions in the first part of 1991 alone.[173]

Despite overwhelming evidence released after the Gulf War that much of the U.S. weaponry had been highly inaccurate, news outlets still relied on analysts who uncritically accepted Pentagon claims. When a hotel full of civilians—including foreign journalists—was bombed, CBS's Randall Pinkston insisted from his base in Washington, "Whatever hit the al-Rashid Hotel, it wasn't a U.S. missile."[174] If journalists (including Bob Simon of CBS) had not been on hand to contradict the official story, the Pentagon might never have acknowledged that a U.S. cruise missile had in fact hit the hotel.

And again, when journalists did raise questions about the bombing of Iraq, it was usually from a position more hawkish than the administration's. ABC's John McWethy reported, "There are questions about why the raid was not bigger, to send an even stronger message to Baghdad."[175] Dan Rather began one broadcast by asking, "Was President Bush's parting shot at Saddam a sock on the jaw or a slap on the wrist?"[176]

On the *McLaughlin Group,* Morton Kondracke, a long-time foreign policy analyst on PBS, took this convoluted position in favor of Bush's raid: "It's good that Bush hit Saddam as lightly as he did, because if that sort of encourages Saddam to make another big blunder and test the United States, this will give Clinton the opportunity to hit him hard and to show at the outset of his administration that he's a tough guy."[177]

Notes

1. *New York Times,* August 10, 1990.
2. *New York Times,* August 11, 1990.
3. *Wall Street Journal,* August 28, 1990.
4. *Chicago Tribune,* August 8, 1990.
5. *New York Times,* August 12, 1990. Apple wrote in a strikingly similar vein on the Panama invasion, declaring that Bush had completed "a presidential initiation rite," joining "American leaders who since World War II have felt a need to demonstrate their willingness to shed blood to protect or advance what they construe as the national interest. . . . Panama has shown him as a man capable of bold action." *New York Times,* December 21, 1989.
6. Mary McGrory, *Washington Post,* August 7, 1990.
7. Mortimer B. Zuckerman, "Showdown in the Sand," *U.S. News & World Report,* August 20, 1990, p. 72.
8. Charles Lane, "The Making of a Monster," *Newsweek,* August 20, 1990, p. 29.
9. Evan Thomas, "Staring Down the Bully," *Newsweek,* September 3, 1990, p. 17.
10. *New York Post,* August 30, 1990.
11. Alexander Cockburn, *Wall Street Journal,* August 16, 1990.
12. *NBC Nightly News,* August 8, 1990.
13. *Christian Science Monitor,* September 21, 1990.
14. Pat Oliphant, cartoon in "Press and Prejudice: Anti-Arab Racism on Display," *Extra!,* May 1991, p. 20.
15. *New York Times,* August 9, 1990.
16. "Furor in the Gulf," cover story, *The New Republic,* September 3, 1990.
17. Joe Stork, "Reagan Re-Flags the Gulf," *Middle East Report,* September/October 1987, p. 2. The Reagan administration allegedly used third-country cutouts to send sophisticated weaponry to Iraq, in violation of U.S. arms export laws. See *Village Voice,* December 18, 1990.
18. *New York Times,* August 12, 1990.
19. *New York Times,* September 23, 1990.
20. *Wall Street Journal,* October 8, 1990.
21. *Boston Globe,* August 20, 1990.
22. Evan Thomas, "Staring Down the Bully," *Newsweek,* September 3, 1990, p. 17.
23. See Center for Constitutional Rights, "U.S. Intervention in the Middle East Violates U.S. and International Law," press release, September 17, 1990.
24. *New York Times,* August 3, 1990.
25. *New York Times,* December 21, 1990.
26. CBS, December 20, 1989.
27. Lisa Beyer, "Iraq's Power Grab," *Time,* August 13, 1990, p. 16.
28. George J. Church, "Showing Muscle," *Time,* January 1, 1990, p. 20.
29. *New York Times,* October 17, 1990.
30. *60 Minutes,* September 30, 1990.
31. *Nightline,* August 17, 1990.
32. *Denver Post,* September 12, 1990. This "standard practice" was not in effect during the Panama invasion, when *MacNeil/Lehrer*'s Judy Woodruff (December 21, 1989) went on about how "not only have we done away with the PDF, we've done away with the police force."

33. William Hoynes and David Croteau, "Are You on the Nightline Guest List?" *Extra!*, January/February 1989, p. 1; William Hoynes and David Croteau, "All the Usual Suspects: MacNeil/Lehrer and Nightline," *Extra!*, Winter 1990, p. 1; David Croteau and William Hoynes, *By Invitation Only: How the Media Limit Political Debate* (Monroe, Maine: Common Courage, 1994).

34. *New York Times*, September 12, 1990.

35. Meg Greenfield, "Another Kind of 'Hostage,'" *Newsweek*, August 20, 1990, p. 72.

36. *Washington Post*, August 8, 1990.

37. *Donahue*, October 2, 1990.

38. *Christian Science Monitor*, September 10, 1990.

39. *60 Minutes*, September 9, 1990.

40. Associated Press, September 4, 1990.

41. *CBS Morning News*, August 4, 1990.

42. *Washington Post*, September 26, 1990.

43. *Chicago Sun-Times*, November 4, 1990. The estimates leaked by the Pentagon, of course, turned out to be wild overestimates.

44. *New York Times*, September 4, 1990.

45. *New York Times*, August 28, 1990.

46. London *Observer*, September 9, 1990.

47. *Nightline*, August 17, 1990.

48. *New York Newsday*, August 29, 1990.

49. *New York Times*, August 30, 1990.

50. *New York Times*, October 1, 1990.

51. *Washington Post*, July 26, 1990. See also Alexander Cockburn, "Did the U.S. Want Iraq to Attack?" *The Nation*, October 8, 1990, p. 370. While Glaspie later claimed that her statement was taken out of context, an article in the January 22, 1991, *Village Voice* by Murray Waas showed that Glaspie's statement was part of a concerted effort by the Bush administration to signal that the U.S. would wink at an Iraqi military action.

52. Ned Zeman, "An Angry President," *Newsweek*, September 3, 1990, p. 4.

53. *Nightline*, August 28, 1990.

54. *Nightline*, August 17, 1990.

55. *Today*, January 17, 1991.

56. CBS, January 17, 1991.

57. CBS, February 27, 1991.

58. C-SPAN, February 23, 1991.

59. London *Independent*, February 6, 1991.

60. *New York Newsday*, January 23, 1991.

61. *MacNeil/Lehrer NewsHour*, January 23, 1991.

62. *NBC Nightly News*, January 22, 1991.

63. *This Week with David Brinkley*, January 20, 1991.

64. NBC, January 16, 1991.

65. CBS, January 17, 1991.

66. C-SPAN, February 4, 1991.

67. *Nightline*, March 11, 1991.

68. *New York Newsday*, January 23, 1991.

69. *New York Times*, February 15, 1991.

70. *New York Times*, March 4, 1991.

71. London *Independent,* February 6, 1991; *Washington Post,* February 11, 1991.
72. Fund for Free Expression, "Managed News, Stifled Views; U.S. Freedom of Expression and the War: An Update," research memo, February 27, 1991.
73. Fund for Free Expression, "Managed News, Stifled Views; U.S. Freedom of Expression and the War: An Update," research memo, February 27, 1991.
74. *Village Voice,* February 5, 1991.
75. *Washington Post,* January 7, 1991.
76. "Casualties at Home: Muzzled Journalists," *Extra!,* May 1991, p. 15.
77. *Saturday Night Live,* January 19, 1991.
78. ABC, January 21, 1991.
79. *ABC World News Tonight,* February 13, 1991.
80. *Washington Post,* September 16, 1990.
81. CBS, February 13, 1991.
82. CNN, January 16, 1991.
83. NBC, January 17, 1991.
84. ABC, January 21, 1991.
85. ABC, January 22, 1991.
86. CNN, January 22, 1991.
87. *USA Today,* January 22, 1991.
88. *New York Times,* January 27, 1991.
89. *MacNeil/Lehrer NewsHour,* January 18, 1991.
90. CBS, February 22, 1991.
91. Doug Henwood, "Capital Cities/ABC: No. 2, and Trying Harder," *Extra!,* October/November 1989, p. 8; Doug Henwood, "CBS: Tiffany Goes to K-Mart," *Extra!,* March/April 1990, p. 8.
92. *NBC, Nightly News,* March 6, 1991.
93. Richard P. Mattione, *OPEC's Investment and the International Financial System* (Washington, D.C.: Brookings Institution, 1985).
94. *Wall Street Journal,* March 21, 1991.
95. CBS, March 5, 1991.
96. CBS, February 8, 1991.
97. CBS, January 18, 1991.
98. *New York Times,* February 28, 1991.
99. CBS, March 5, 1991.
100. *America Tonight,* February 14, 1991.
101. ABC, January 16, 1991.
102. ABC, January 17, 1991.
103. NBC, January 16, 1991.
104. Meg Greenfield, "The Hardest Judgment Call," *Newsweek,* January 21, 1991, p. 64.
105. FAIR, "Gulf War Sources Survey: January 17–January 30, 1991," research memo, February 22, 1991.
106. CNN, January 16, 1991.
107. *New York Times,* January 20, 1991.
108. *San Francisco Chronicle,* January 31, 1991.
109. *New York Times,* February 7, 1991.
110. Jerry Adler, "The War Within," *Newsweek,* February 4, 1991, p. 58.
111. *CBS Morning News,* January 18, 1991.

112. CBS, February 16, 1991.

113. *Los Angeles Times,* February 26, 1991.

114. NBC, January 28, 1991.

115. FAIR, "Gulf War Sources Survey: January 17–January 30, 1991," research memo, February 22, 1991.

116. WPIX–TV, February 5, 1991.

117. *Nightline,* January 17, 1991.

118. NBC, January 29, 1991.

119. Quoted in Paul Boyer, "The Cloud over the Culture," *The New Republic,* August 12, 1985, p. 27.

120. NBC, January 16, 1991.

121. CBS, February 14, 1991.

122. "The New Science of War; High-Tech Hardware: How Many Lives Can It Save?" cover story, *Newsweek,* February 18, 1991, p. 38.

123. Jonathan Alter, "The Propaganda War," *Newsweek,* February 25, 1991, p. 38.

124. NBC, February 5, 1991.

125. London *Independent,* February 14, 1991.

126. CBS, February 9, 1991.

127. Jonathan Alter, "Does Bloody Footage Lose Wars?" *Newsweek,* February 11, 1991, p. 38.

128. NBC, January 27, 1991.

129. CBS, January 18, 1991.

130. *Nightline,* January 23, 1991.

131. NBC, January 22, 1991.

132. *New York Times,* February 26, 1991.

133. Arab-American Anti-Discrimination Committee, *Report on Anti-Arab Hate Crimes* (Washington, D.C.: Arab Anti-Discrimination Committee, 1991).

134. CBS, January 16, 1991.

135. *Nightline,* January 15, 1991.

136. Quoted in *New York Newsday,* January 24, 1991.

137. CBS, February 12, 1991.

138. *New York Times,* February 20, 1991.

139. Tom Mathews, "Saddam's Last Stand," *Newsweek,* March 4, 1991, p. 18.

140. Steven V. Roberts, "Bush in the Bazaar," *U.S. News & World Report,* December 24, 1990, p. 24.

141. *Washington Post,* March 11, 1991.

142. *New York Times,* February 17, 1991.

143. *New York Newsday,* March 1, 1991.

144. When the *St. Petersburg Times* (January 6, 1991) had former government image analysts examine commercially available satellite photos of Kuwait taken in September 1990, they failed to find any sign of the massive Iraqi force the Bush administration claimed was poised to invade Saudi Arabia, raising doubts about the veracity of the administration's intelligence claims. While the alternative weekly *In These Times* (February 27, 1991) picked up on the story, the Associated Press and other mainstream media outlets ignored it.

145. *MacNeil/Lehrer NewsHour,* February 14, 1991.

146. *New York Times,* February 21, 1991.

147. Richard Zoglin, "Just Whose Side Are They On?" *Time,* February 25, 1991, p. 52.

148. *New York Times,* February 7, 1991.

149. *Los Angeles Times,* December 14, 1990.
150. *New York Newsday,* February 17, 1991.
151. *New York Times,* February 26, 1991.
152. *New York Times,* January 14, 1991.
153. *Washington Post,* January 22, 1991.
154. *Washington Post,* March 25, 1991.
155. *New York Times,* March 31, 1991.
156. NBC, March 20, 1991.
157. *New York Times,* March 31, 1991.
158. *New York Times,* March 22, 1991.
159. Steven Budiansky et al., "Saddam's Revenge," *U.S. News & World Report,* April 15, 1991, p. 26.
160. *New York Times,* March 25, 1991.
161. *Washington Post,* March 1, 1991.
162. Warren Cohen, "Washington Whispers," *U.S. News & World Report,* April 1, 1991, p. 16.
163. ABC, January 13, 1993.
164. Center for Constitutional Rights, "International Human Rights Groups Condemn Bombing of Iraq," press release, January 14, 1993.
165. *New York Newsday,* January 7, 1993.
166. *New York Times,* January 14, 1993.
167. CBS, January 17, 1993.
168. *Nightline,* January 13, 1993.
169. *This Week with David Brinkley,* January 17, 1993.
170. *MacNeil/Lehrer NewsHour,* January 13, 1993.
171. CBS, January 18, 1993.
172. NBC, January 20, 1993.
173. A. Ascherio, "Effect of the Gulf War on Infant and Child Mortality in Iraq," *New England Journal of Medicine,* September 24, 1992, p. 931.
174. CBS, January 17, 1993.
175. ABC, January 17, 1993.
176. CBS, January 14, 1993.
177. *McLaughlin Group,* January 17, 1993. Clinton did end up "hitting Saddam hard" in June 1993, in response to a supposed Iraqi assassination attempt on President Bush. A November 1, 1993, *New Yorker* article by Seymour Hersh argued persuasively that the evidence for the supposed assassination attempt was dubious—and that the Clinton administration was largely motivated by fear that the media would portray it as weak if it did not "retaliate" against Iraq.

PART TWO

The '92 Election

4 The Primaries: Limiting Choice

On the Campaign Trail: Public Logic Versus Press Logic

April/May 1992

JOSHUA MEYROWITZ

Joshua Meyrowitz, a professor of communications at the University of New Hampshire, wrote an article for the March/April 1992 Columbia Journalism Review *on the media blackout of Larry Agran, the former mayor of Irvine, California, who ran for the 1992 Democratic presidential nomination on a "peace dividend now" platform. Meyrowitz reported that national media in effect "airbrushed" Agran out of the campaign: He was often excised from reports of forums in which he participated with the "major candidates." Some photographers asked him to stand off to the side so that they could crop him out of published photos. When Agran at one point passed Jerry Brown in New Hampshire opinion polls, with 4 percent naming him as their choice versus 3 percent for Brown,* ABC News *ignored Agran and reported Brown's standing.*[1]

When Meyrowitz interviewed members of the press corps about Agran's candidacy, he found a discrepancy between the way national journalists and ordinary people think about political campaigns. He described those differences in a memo to FAIR, *which is excerpted below.*

THE RELATIVELY LOW national stature of the "major" Democratic candidates might logically have led people to pay attention to alternative candidates. But when I spoke to journalists, many immediately adopted the perspective of their sources in the Democratic Party leadership, which they told me was more concerned than ever about not giving the impression of putting forward a "field of unknowns." Thus, the journalists seemed even more concerned about giving "undue" coverage to "fringe" candidates. (Journalists seemed very sensitive to the possibility that giving Larry Agran coverage might unduly boost his campaign, but they were hesitant to admit that not covering him might unduly hurt his campaign.)

When even the *New York Times* wrote that George Bush had no "blueprints for the future" of our country, and that he had little competition among the major presidential contenders or in Congress, many people I know saw this as evidence that the mainstream media should look beyond the typical political spotlight.[2] But the national journalists I spoke with seemed to see this state of affairs as a reason to protect the "insiders" even more. One journalist told me: "One of the problems that people in D.C. see in the presidential primary season is that anyone can run. There's a body of thought among insiders that this is not necessarily a good thing." He noted that there is a "divisiveness" that comes from candidates attacking and running against "the institutions that run the country."

When Governor Douglas Wilder dropped out of the race, many people I spoke with felt that there was now an "empty chair" for another candidate. But journalists had the opposite reaction: "We can't wait to winnow the race down even further," said one. Another journalist complained that "every extra candidate means another reporter and another $150-a-day hotel room."

Asked about the lack of media coverage of Democrats not supported by the party hierarchy, and of third-party candidates, a journalist told me, "That battle was lost 200 years ago, when we didn't set up a parliamentary system. We have two parties and that's it."

Most of the voters I know are hungry for a candidate with new ideas, and they see a presidential primary campaign as fostering a national dialogue on key issues. But the national journalists I spoke with mostly saw the campaign as a horse race: "If we don't think that you have at least some chance of being elected, you don't get any coverage," said a senior editor at *Newsweek*.

"An election is not a matter of who is the smartest, the most articulate, or who has the best ideas," a reporter at the *Los Angeles Times* told me. "It's much more complicated than that. What it really comes down to is who can win the most votes."

Sex, Polls, and Campaign Strategy: How the Press Missed the Issues of the '92 Election

June 1992

JANINE JACKSON

"THIS SORT of thing was not supposed to happen in 1992," the *New York Times*'s John Tierney wrote.[3] After the 1988 presidential campaign, the press had been accused, not least by itself, of "obsessive coverage of supposed character issues, [and] endless analysis of strategies and polls instead of who stood for what." Voters wanted substance, it was said, and reporters pledged to do better. But, Tierney said of his fellow journalists in the 1992 election season, "It didn't take them long to be distracted by questions of sex, polls and campaign strategy."

Self-conscious articles like Tierney's were a prominent feature of 1992's election coverage, often running alongside stories that exhibited the very characteristics they decried. To see how papers were following through on their promise of more substantive reporting, FAIR surveyed news articles on the presidential election in three nationally prominent papers—the *New York Times*, *Washington Post*, and *Los Angeles Times*—from January 14, 1992, when the *New York Times* began its special campaign section, through February 19, 1992, the day after the New Hampshire primary (Table 4.1).

Articles were put in one of several general categories according to their main content: "Campaign Analysis," "Polls/Voter Mood," "Personal Biography," "Issues," "'Hard' News," "Human Interest/Local Color," and "Media Self-Analysis." Headlines and leads helped determine a few ambiguous cases; stories that clearly belonged in two categories were credited as one-half in each. The results produced a picture of how the "papers of record" divided their attention—and that of their readers.

Coverage in the early, pre–New Hampshire primary phase of a presidential campaign is critical. Candidates need to receive attention in order to recruit supporters and raise money. Voters need a full and balanced presentation of each candidate's proposals and record in this early stage of the process; after the field has been "winnowed," it may be too late.

CAMPAIGN ANALYSIS

The largest category of campaign stories (38 percent) focused on "campaign analysis"—articles that told us which candidate was "breaking from the pack,"[4] which was "feeling the heat,"[5] and which might "fade in the stretch."[6]

Such "horse race" articles are characterized by an emphasis on the packaging and selling of a candidate's "message" or image, rather than on a critical examination of the content of that message. They reduce candidates' positions to snappy phrases (e.g., Tom Harkin is an "old-fashioned Democrat") and tend to rely heavily on the opinions and speculations of assorted "experts," "strategists," and "political professionals," who often go unnamed.

Typical of this approach was Robin Toner's January 14, 1992, *New York Times* piece, which reported that, according to "the buzz inside the Capital Beltway," Bill Clinton was "the hot candidate of the post-Cuomo period," who might "wrap up the nomination early." This was because polls showed Clinton "at the head of the pack in New Hampshire, neck and neck" with Paul Tsongas. Bob Kerrey, meanwhile, was "clearly—perhaps desperately—looking for an opening" and could "ill afford another week of underachieving," while Jerry Brown was "running more of a crusade than a campaign."

Although a later *New York Times* story by R. W. Apple cautioned that "there can't really be a frontrunner until a vote is cast,"[7] Toner had already laid odds, decisively labeling the candidates and "framing" the race itself as practically a done deal—three weeks before the Iowa caucuses and a month before the New Hampshire primary. This article, and many others like it, contained no information at all about any of the candidates' proposals, their history of policymaking, or their ideas—so readers learned nothing more than who the pundits thought was ahead. The closest the piece came to discussing an issue was its mention that Kerrey's latest TV ad had a "trade-oriented message."

The flimsiness of most horse race stories was highlighted by their empty language. Tsongas "ran against politics-as-usual."[8] Which candidate ran in favor of it? And Clinton's position papers, according to the *Los Angeles Times,* gave his candidacy "an image of substance."[9] There were also "insights" of dubious acuity, such as Apple's assessment in the *New York Times* that "for Mr. Kerrey, the challenge is to make himself seem the logical alternative to Mr. Clinton for those who find the Arkansan unsatisfactory for one reason or another."[10] For the same paper's Elizabeth Kolbert, on the other hand, "probably the most important thing for Mr. Kerrey to do . . . is to persuade voters that he could convincingly play the lead." This because "analysts say Mr. Kerrey must show that he has the elusive but seemingly all-important quality: electability."[11] It is hard to see what readers were meant to gain by such surface-skimming "analysis."

When strategy pieces did touch on issues, it was often to portray them as merely political brokering "chits," as when the *Washington Post*'s David Broder reported Democratic criticism of President Bush's health care plan as "evidence of the opposition party's determination to keep the health care issue for itself."[12]

Likewise, a January 26 Toner piece in the *New York Times* on candidates' stands on abortion rights turned out to be not about principles but "electoral consequences": "Many analysts say that the Republican Party's anti-abortion stance can hurt among moderate suburban voters." The piece concluded that Bush must maintain his hard antichoice line because "changing again could turn into a 'character' issue."

Kolbert's January 25 *New York Times* story on the publication by some candidates of position papers focused on these pamphlets as marketing tools or props. It was not the content of their economic plans but simply which candidates were printing them and which were not that was, in Kolbert's view, one of the "hot new issues of the primary campaign." Kolbert even quoted a Kerrey aide who explained that their campaign had no plans to publish a pamphlet but that "if it did," it would be "40 to 45 pages."

Of course, stories that focus on campaign strategies, rather than on the issues, need not be shallow and lingo-ridden. "Insider" political pieces that go beyond the latest tracking poll and campaign stop can give readers something to think about. A February 13 *Washington Post* article by Frank Swoboda and Charles Babcock on President Bush's campaign tactics questioned whether Bush's use of sub-Cabinet members to promote his reelection violated the Hatch Act. And Ann Devroy used a story about Bush's campaign strategy to contrast words and actions, pointing out Bush's "pattern of substantive shifts on issues" over the years.[13]

At the *New York Times,* Andrew Rosenthal wrote critical pieces on the financing of Bush's campaign trips and the "White House power struggle,"[14] and Maureen Dowd skewered Bush's and Patrick Buchanan's tactical self-portrayals as "outsiders," warning readers that "these two old Washington hands believe that they can give the impression of being fiery populists with their rhetoric."[15]

The president appeared to be the most popular subject for critical analyses. But a Ronald Brownstein article in the *Los Angeles Times* thoughtfully analyzed the changing tactics of Brown's campaign, indicating both possible weaknesses and signs of success for Brown's "'guerrilla' approach" and noting that most "pundits have refused to take his White House bid seriously."[16] And Thomas B. Edsall had an interesting discussion in the *Washington Post* of Clinton's Southern support network that featured interviews with party leaders, officials, and voters with a number of different perspectives.[17]

A few informative articles dealt not with the strategies of individual candidates but with the campaign process itself: In the *New York Times,* reporter Peter Applebome used the case of David Duke to explain some of the intricacies of state ballot laws and to point out "unresolved legal issues about the roles that parties play in elections."[18] Another *New York Times* piece gave readers a peek at the process of gathering endorsements, "an elaborate courtship ritual" between candidates and backers.[19]

A quarter of the campaign analysis stories were about candidates' media strategies, with the *New York Times* and *Los Angeles Times* running special series devoted to candidates' TV ads ("The Ad Campaign" and "Ad Watch"). The *Los Angeles Times*'s Thomas Rosenstiel occasionally used the feature to examine the claims made in commercials; he pointed out, for example, that although a Bush ad "implies that all Democrats opposed him on the Persian Gulf War, in fact many sided with him."[20] The *Washington Post*'s Howard Kurtz pointed out that the "economic emergency" Tsongas's ads said he would declare would have no legal force and showed how a Harkin ad attacking other candidates' tax plans was misleading.[21]

But those articles that inserted a little information into the rhetoric were exceptional; the majority of the "eye on media" stories didn't get past the stylistic level, confining themselves to describing candidates' ads and often simply parroting their transcripts verbatim. The underlying assumption seemed to be that there was nothing more to know: The presidential race really is little more than a show, and recognizing spin was just the same as penetrating it.

POLLS

If there was one thing we were not supposed to see a lot of in the 1992 election, it was small-scale tracking polls, those "most volatile indicators of public moods,"[22] whose margins of error often exceed the trumpeted daily "surges" and "slippages" they purportedly register. The *New York Times*'s Michael Kagay, quoted in the *Washington Post*, called them "the riskiest and least substantial use of the polling technique that exists."[23] The 9 percent of coverage categorized in FAIR's survey as "Polls" represents only those articles that focused entirely on poll results and does not begin to represent the number of stories that cited polls.

Opinion poll stories almost never provided readers with a complete picture of the questions as asked. For example, the day after the New Hampshire primary, the *New York Times*'s Robin Toner reported that polls indicated that much of Tsongas's support was "from people who wanted a candidate with specific ideas, as well as one who has shown strength and courage."[24] Was this as opposed to those who would have preferred a weak, cowardly nincompoop?

In an attempt to deflate Harkin's claims that polls showed him rallying, the *Los Angeles Times*'s David Lauter explained, "Tracking polls taken in the final days of New Hampshire campaigns are notoriously unreliable."[25] Why, then, did 17 percent of all *Los Angeles Times* campaign stories in the final days of the New Hampshire race—February 14–18, 1992—cite these "notoriously unreliable" polls? (For the *Washington Post* in the same period, the figure was 23 percent; for the *New York Times*, 29 percent.)

Despite protestations, then, the 1992 election season started off just as poll-laden as any other. In the period FAIR looked at, for example, *Los Angeles Times* readers were favored with up-to-the-minute "data" ranging from the merely confusing—"Clinton and Tsongas lead as the fall-back choice for voters who may reconsider their votes"[26]—to downright brain-teasers: "Moreover, nine in 10 of those polled believe that the nation remains stuck in recession, and most do not

TABLE 4.1 Types of Articles in Campaign Coverage, January 14, 1992–February 19, 1992

Number of Articles in Category; Percentage of Total Campaign Coverage

	New York Times (No.)	(%)	Washington Post (No.)	(%)	Los Angeles Times (No.)	(%)	Total Campaign Coverage (No.)	(%)
Campaign Analysis	**83.5**	**43**	**51.5**	**32**	**56.0**	**37**	**191**	**38**
Strategy and tactics	36.5		22.5		20.5		79.5	
Speculation and horse race analysis	27.5		16.0		24.5		68.0	
Campaign media strategy	19.5		13.0		11.0		43.5	
Polls/Voter Mood	**16.0**	**8**	**13.5**	**8**	**14.0**	**9**	**43.5**	**9**
Polls	5.0		1.5		9.5		16.0	
Personal Biography ("Character issues")	26.5	14	21.5	13	16.5	11	64.5	13
Issues (Policies, public record)	20.5	11	23.0	14	16.5	11	60.0	12
"Hard" News (Includes campaign stops)	25.5	13	21.5	13	16.5	11	64.5	13
Human Interest / Local Color	17.0	9	15.0	9	7.0	4	39.0	8
Media Self-Analysis	4.0	2	1.5	1	3.0	2	8.5	2

see any immediate prospects for improvement. About one-fifth of those surveyed believe that the economy will improve in the next three months, but about one-fourth expect continued decline and half forecast little change."[27]

"CHARACTER" AND PERSONAL BIOGRAPHY

The Star tabloid's release of Gennifer Flowers's allegations of an extramarital affair with Bill Clinton occasioned a great deal of soul-searching in the mainstream press. All three papers ran stories with headlines like "Reports on Clinton Pose Quandary for Journalists."[28] But the papers' real quandary appeared to be deciding how many stories they could print about the charges while still claiming to be unsure whether to cover them.

The popular solution appeared to be to claim to write not about the allegations themselves (which were acknowledged to be "unsubstantiated") but about the possible, or expected, or imagined effect of the reporting of the allegations on Clinton's candidacy. Papers divided against themselves, printing stories headlined "Clinton Lied in Denying Affair, Woman Insists,"[29] alongside breast-beating columns denouncing such coverage, while "voter mood" pieces illustrated how unhappy the public was about the turn the coverage had taken.

The story, and all the stories about the story, added up to an at times dizzying display of journalistic self-reflexiveness. "Is it all right to report a supermarket tabloid's allegation of adultery? And if not, why did we just do it, and why can't we stop talking about it?" agonized Tierney in the *New York Times*.[30] (*The Star* was so ubiquitously derided as a "supermarket tabloid" that the phrase began to sound like a disclaimer—as if, having shared the gossip, the dignified dailies winked to the reader, "but you didn't hear it from us.")

If John Tierney was the *New York Times*'s appointed conscience, the *Washington Post*'s Howard Kurtz adopted a similarly "distanced" and strangely passive tone, wondering abstractly "whether the mainstream press will pursue the allegations, regardless of whether they ultimately prove to be true or relevant to voters."[31] At that point, Kurtz's paper had already run five articles devoted to *The Star*'s story in as many days.

A January 29, 1992, *Los Angeles Times* article by Rosenstiel explained that editors, while expressing "distaste" for the Flowers story, felt they "had little choice but to follow" it. The "key reason" the allegations were newsworthy, the article says, was the fact that Clinton answered reporters' questions about them. Editors conceded that there was "a certain circularity" to this reasoning: "Reporters raise the issue by asking questions, and then say it is news because the candidate answered." The *Washington Post*'s managing editor, Robert Kaiser, admitted that this was "sort of a cop-out answer" to the question of why the story no one wanted to run wound up as the story of the week.

Rosenstiel's piece described the *New York Times* as the "most circumspect" of the major dailies and quoted executive editor Max Frankel as saying, "In the only language we have, where we play a story, how big we play it, we are telling the reader what we think of this stuff and whether we can vouch for it or not." With this in mind, FAIR noted that the *New York Times* mentioned the "unsubstantiated allegations" in their campaign coverage at least once a day, every day, from January 24 through February 7.

For a story it disdained, the *New York Times* certainly drummed an awareness of the allegations into its readers' heads. For instance, a February 7 article on TV ads commented that, in a commercial, Clinton was surrounded by flags and family, "symbols of American virtue," while "in news reports, Mr. Clinton has been forced to battle charges that he had a 12-year extramarital affair."

A striking expression of the *New York Times*'s contradictory stance came on January 28, when it ran an 850-word story on the accusations ("Clinton Attempts to Ignore Rumors") alongside results of a national poll indicating that 80 percent of the public thought the matter had no place in election news. (The story next to that, a "horse race" piece, also devoted six of fourteen paragraphs to the accusations of the "former nightclub singer.")

From January 14 through February 19, 1992, the *New York Times* produced ten stories wholly concerned with Flowers's allegations, Clinton's denials, and assessments of the political fallout. The *Washington Post* ran six stories and the *Los Angeles Times* eleven. A similar pattern was followed with the subsequent charges of draft-dodging. Allegations that Clinton had used deception to avoid the draft received ten stories in the *New York Times,* including a 21-column-inch box detailing Clinton's draft status from 1964 to 1969.[32] The *Washington Post* ran eleven draft stories; the *Los Angeles Times* ran three. The total of fifty-one stories exclusively about either Flowers or the draft in all three papers represented 10 percent of total campaign coverage in the period studied.

Journalists did acknowledge that the coverage was out of sync with voters' interests. As Robin Toner reported in the *New York Times* on a Clinton campaign stop: "Throughout the day, the voters asked Mr. Clinton about Medicare, AIDS, the deficit and the future of the Haitian refugees; but the reporters who swarmed around him at every stop asked about the draft."[33] And there were plenty of interviews demonstrating the public's (not to mention the candidates') dissatisfaction. "I know the press is in the business of selling newspapers and getting ratings, but I don't think it's right," the *New York Times* quoted a young woman complaining. "I want to hear about the issues."[34]

MISSING ISSUES

The papers of record may defend their decision to print all those stories about and references to alleged affairs, about Tsongas's "sad-eyed expression," and Kerrey's Vietnam experience. But can they defend as easily their decision not to ask other questions—not to balance the fluff with serious discussions of social problems and the candidates' specific policies? In the end, the biggest problem with election coverage was not what was in it but what was missing.

From the papers of record we learned that Hillary Clinton likes "medium-hot" chili;[35] that, as a boy, Jerry Brown "once refused to wear a funny hat" to a parade;[36] and that, according to an old Tsongas friend, "no one sat around the pool when Paul was on duty" as a lifeguard, whatever that means.[37] But did we learn enough about the candidates' proposals and their public records to make an informed choice on election day?

Only 12 percent of the campaign stories could be deemed substantive, in that they provided information on candidates' ideas more concrete than Harkin's pledge to be a "true Democrat" or Buchanan's call to "send a message" to the president. Many of the articles that were counted as issue stories only recited a few facts out of context or buried them near the end of the piece.

Among the notably informative stories, some were single-candidate "spotlight" features, like David Maraniss's February 3 *Washington Post* article, which detailed Clinton's policy record as governor of Arkansas, or the Paul Richter and Ronald J. Ostrow piece in the February 14 *Los Angeles Times*, examining Tsongas's lobbying history. The *Post*'s Dan Balz reported on the specific points made in a January 23, 1992, speech by Harkin on military spending cuts without once mentioning Harkin's "craggy face" or his poll standings.[38] The *Los Angeles Times* ran a version of the *Post*'s story, also sticking to Harkin's ideas.[39] (The *New York Times* didn't cover the speech at all; perhaps its space was taken up that day by "Clinton Denounces New Report of Affair.")

There were only a handful of campaign stories that addressed a particular social or economic issue and compared two or more candidates' ideas about it. A February 15 article in the *Washington Post* by Mary Jordan outlined Democratic candidates' proposals for education reform and contrasted them with those of the Republicans. And a February 1 *Post* story by Michael Weisskopf discussed candidates' environmental records, but it also pointed out that environmental concerns appeared to be "far down on the agenda." The thrust of both stories, in fact, was the virtual absence of these and other issues from the campaign.

The focus of coverage would seem to indicate that, as some of Weisskopf's sources suggested, voters "are so preoccupied with the economy that other issues seem irrelevant." But perhaps reporters just weren't asking the right questions.

If such issues as education, reproductive rights, and the environment were pushed to the background, didn't we at least see some serious attention given to questions of economic policy in the 1992 election? Not exactly. Although it's true that economic issues were often mentioned, the press' explanations usually didn't get beyond the "short form." FAIR's survey found a total of twelve stories containing sustained critical examination of candidates' economic proposals; five of these were about President Bush.

Anyone who picked up a paper knew that Kerrey had a "health care plan." But how exactly was it supposed to work, how would it be funded, and what services would it include? A Kenneth J. Cooper article in the February 6 *Washington Post* was the only one in the period studied that answered these questions with more than a couple of sentences and that substantively compared Kerrey's approach with that of other candidates. Most stories on health care were content to repeat candidates' stump speeches on the matter.

And certainly, readers would have heard that Tsongas was "pro-business," or that he was "no Santa Claus." But did they know that he agreed with Bush on the line-item veto, that he opposed legislation barring employers from permanently replacing striking workers, and that he called for loosening antitrust legislation? If they didn't read David Broder's February 16 article in the *Washington Post*, chances are they didn't know these facts before the New Hampshire primary.

Perhaps no phrase was bandied about more in discussions of candidates' economic proposals than the call for (or against) a "middle-class tax cut." But only an article by James Risen in the February 2 *Los Angeles Times* cleared away the smoke around the phrase, noting that the "nation's median household income . . . stands at $35,353. But that kind of income no longer represents the middle class as it is defined by political Washington." Risen also illustrated how parts of Bush's tax package that "appear to provide broad-based relief to the entire middle class . . . actually target their benefits at a much narrower group: the suburban professional class."

A January 19 *New York Times* story by Gwen Ifill echoed Risen's themes. Its subject was the "invisibility" of the poor and their concerns in the 1992 race, as candidates from both parties fell over themselves to "woo the middle class." Ifill questioned whether Democrats were "abandon[ing] their traditional role as champions of the disenfranchised" and cited spokespeople from the Institute for Policy Studies and "antipoverty" advocacy groups.

Ronald Brownstein's February 15 *Los Angeles Times* article was a careful comparison of Clinton's and Tsongas's "intellectual lineage," their differences and agreements on economic renewal, tax reform, labor-management relations, and some social issues and foreign policy. The article was a model in its reliance on real data instead of stock phrases and in its contrasting what the candidates said with what they had done. It's unfortunate, though, that Clinton and Tsongas were the only candidates deemed worthy of such thoughtful attention. FAIR could find no such stories comparing the other Democratic candidates.

Reports of debates would seem like natural opportunities for the press to compare (Democratic) candidates' ideas. But while they did repeat snippets of dialogue, these "day after" articles were more interested in fights—who had raised his voice, who had insulted whom—than in what was said or not said. The February 16, 1992, Democratic candidates' debate was "bland" according to the *New York Times*'s R. W. Apple because only when "his rivals ganged up on . . . Senator Tsongas" were there any "fireworks." Apparently, the candidates merely discussing their ideas made for "less-than-gripping television viewing."[40]

The other preferred angle on debates concerned who looked best on television: Kerrey was "mostly distinguished for energy of expression," while Tsongas's "hangdog look conforms to his sober message," Walter Goodman wrote in the *New York Times*.[41]

The *New York Times* facetiously endorsed telegenicness as a criterion for electing a president: After all, "with candidates so well-trained to avoid the specific or the unpopular, voters can't be sure what Presidential policies they will have to suffer through, but they know they'll have to endure the President's talking head every night on television."[42] But we might ask more seriously: Whose fault is it that candidates, who speak to reporters every day, can so easily avoid the specific and the unpopular? And don't readers, and voters, deserve more than ironic commentary on such a state of affairs?

LOST OPPORTUNITY

The media's tendency to neglect the discussion of issues in favor of more "colorful" but less important campaign fare is distressing, and not only because readers don't get to learn enough, early enough, about the candidates. Presidential elections should be about more than who wins the White House—they should put issues on the national agenda, begin dialogues and create coalitions among different constituencies, define national priorities, and focus public attention on the democratic process. The primary and caucus season is a chance to generate awareness and discussion of questions that matter. The reduction of this process to a winner-take-all horse race represents a lost opportunity for public education and for the discourse and debate vital to democracy.

The press is not solely responsible for voter apathy or cynicism. Still, journalists might do something to combat that apathy by providing election coverage that critically investigates candidates' proposals and records and links their ideas to the issues that affect readers' lives. A look at the coverage of the first few weeks of the 1992 campaign indicates that while the papers of record acknowledged that challenge, they did not live up to it.

Media Campaign to Limit Voters' Choices

April/May 1992

MEDIA COVERAGE of the Democratic primaries went far out of its way to narrow the choices available to the voters. From the outset, national pundits and political journalists tried to hand the election to Governor Bill Clinton, presenting him as "Mr. Electable"—even though, as the *New York Times*'s R. W. Apple acknowledged, "everyone in politics" knew about the sex and draft evasion stories in Clinton's history.[43] Discussions of more serious aspects of Clinton's record were difficult to find—you could read about Clinton's dismal labor and environmental records in the sensationalistic *New York Post*,[44] but not in the *New York Times*.

Meanwhile, the pundits overcame their major complaints about Paul Tsongas—he's boring and untelegenic—and warmed up to his corporate-friendly message. An obvious question went unasked: After eleven years of Republican administrations coddling big business nearly bankrupted the nation, why should more coddling by a Democrat be expected to turn things around?

The candidates not anointed by the media were marginalized—either by denying them media exposure, or by ridicule and attack. One common tack was to accuse them of representing the traditional Democratic constituencies—women, minorities, labor, the elderly, and so forth—who were dubbed "special interests."

During CNN's Democratic debate two days before the New Hampshire primary, correspondent Ken Bode lectured Senator Tom Harkin (D.-Ia.) on the way that "PACs [political action committees] and special interests get a lever and a hold on politicians and public policy" and then challenged the candidate: "Can you tell me where specifically you disagree with the legislative programs and goals of organized labor in America today?" Bode went on to ask Jerry Brown about one of "the most active and powerful of all of our special interest groups in this country"—senior citizens—pressing him to "take them on" over Social Security.[45]

When did we see the 2 percent of the country that would benefit most from Bush's (and Tsongas's) proposed capital-gains tax cut described as a special interest? And when did we see Bush or Tsongas challenged by reporters to "take on" these moneyed interests?

The media's contortions in support of favorite candidates could be breathtaking. On February 11, 1992, the national media gave more prominence to the "news" that Paul Tsongas was ahead in a New Hampshire public opinion poll than to the results of the first real voting of the campaign, Senator Tom Harkin's 78 percent victory in the Iowa caucuses. Harkin's acquisition of forty-eight delegates, more than twice the number at stake in New Hampshire, was relegated to the back pages and the ends of newscasts, with CBS giving the story all of eight seconds.[46]

Most news "analysis" showed a striking lack of historical perspective. One reporter in the *New York Times* tried to play down Jerry Brown's near tie with Paul Tsongas for first place in Maine, saying, "The Maine caucuses are not necessarily a gauge of nationwide sentiment—Jesse Jackson finished a strong second here in 1988."[47] Maine was quite a good "gauge of nationwide sentiment" in 1988: Jackson finished a strong second across the country that year, winning 7.5 million votes and 29 percent of the total, compared to Michael Dukakis's 10 million and 42 percent.

What the media did use as their gauge of nationwide sentiment was the primary in New Hampshire—a tiny, Republican, virtually all-white state—determining that from then on, only two candidates, Tsongas and Clinton, warranted serious coverage.

The Philandering Front-Runner and the Mad Monk

June 1992

WHILE THE NATIONAL media seemed to have almost a love-hate relationship with Bill Clinton during the 1992 primary, their view of Jerry Brown was less complex: They hated him.

New York Times reporter Maureen Dowd was on the mark when she described the press corps' attitude toward Clinton before the New Hampshire primary as "smitten and worshipful."[48] Though Clinton's performance with actual voters was lackluster until Super Tuesday, he'd already won the "invisible primary" among pundits and fund-raisers by a landslide.

The New Republic's Hendrik Hertzberg asked "several dozen" national political journalists covering the 1992 New Hampshire primary whom they would vote for if they were New Hampshire Democrats. He got the same answer from everyone: Clinton. Hertzberg, who has conducted similar surveys since 1968, wrote that "such unanimity is unprecedented" among the press corps.[49]

The media's obsession with tabloid-style "character" stories—marital problems, draft history, decades-old drug use—certainly hurt Clinton; journalists elevated evasive answers about his private life to a major "integrity" problem. George Bush's deceptions about his role in public policy matters—Iran-contra, for example—never caused the same drumbeat of media questions about honesty.

But as Clinton sewed up the 1992 Democratic nomination, he had the press to thank for helping to drive key rivals out of the race. A decisive moment was "Junior Tuesday," March 3, a day with six Democratic electoral contests that produced four winners: Paul Tsongas in Maryland and Utah, Tom Harkin in Minnesota and Idaho, Brown in Colorado, and Clinton in Georgia—Clinton's first win anywhere. *USA Today* accurately assessed these results as "a muddle."[50] But the prevailing media spin was that of the *New York Times,* whose lead story stated that as a result of Tsongas's and Clinton's victories, the "Democratic presidential campaign moved decisively toward a two-man struggle."[51]

With political reporters and pundits asserting repeatedly that only Clinton or Tsongas had a chance of winning the nomination, funding for the others dried up, forcing them out of the race. Even as every candidate who dropped out—including Tsongas, eventually—attributed his decision to an inability to raise funds,

Jerry Brown continued to be treated like a crank or a hypocrite for saying that money had too much influence in campaigns.

No presidential candidate in recent memory was more tarred and feathered with media put-downs and epithets than Jerry Brown. Some descriptions implied imminent violence. NBC's Lisa Myers led off a segment on Brown: "He's been called the Pied Piper of Protest and the political equivalent of a drive-by shooting. He's both."[52] On the *MacNeil/Lehrer NewsHour*, commentator David Gergen called Brown a "political assassin."[53] A *New York Times* article depicted him as "a dangerous opponent because he seems to revel in throwing bombs."[54]

Most journalists just dismissed Brown as a nuisance. The day of the Connecticut primary, the *New York Times*'s R. W. Apple described Brown as "flailing about, spewing out charges like sparks from a Fourth of July pinwheel, in a last-ditch effort to establish himself ... as a credible alternative" to Clinton.[55] (Brown beat Clinton in that primary.) In *Newsweek*, Brown was described as "the mad monk of presidential politics" and a "masterful annoyance."[56] The same week's *Time* referred to him as "a walking Experiment in Living" with "terminal flightiness."[57]

Many politicians have courted the support of both labor and environmentalists. When Brown did it, *Time* dubbed him "Samuel Gompers in Earth shoes"[58] and "a noisy sideshow for dyspeptic interest groups."[59] Selling oneself to voters is what all candidates do. When Brown did it, he was "as brash as a late-night television pitchman"[60] or "an odd, fringe actor shouting an 800 telephone number."[61]

On the eve of the New York primary, in a piece purporting to point out the positive aspects of Brown's campaign, *Newsweek*'s Jonathan Alter called him "a chameleon, a character assassin and a first-class cynic." Alter labeled Brown's platform "demagogic," "silly," and "sketchy"; he accused the candidate of "engaging in his typical hype" and his supporters of "turning a blind eye to their candidate's unfitness."[62]

Like those of any politician, Brown's record and proposals should have been held up to tough scrutiny. But can anyone imagine a *Newsweek* senior editor talking about George Bush's "typical hype" or his "unfitness"—and getting away with it?

Buchanan and Duke: Playing the Same Hand

March 1992

PATRICK BUCHANAN and David Duke found themselves in the same place in the 1992 Republican primaries—using nearly identical issues and rhetoric to challenge George Bush from the right. But they took different paths to get to that point: Duke rose to prominence through the use of Ku Klux Klan robes, while Buchanan rode a more conventional vehicle—television.

Although Duke often received soft treatment on national TV,[63] he was still considered outside the mainstream by the political press corps. By contrast, Buchanan was one of the boys. Among TV pundits, he had been the leader of the pack—the only one to appear on national TV seven days a week, as cohost of CNN's *Crossfire*, host of CNN's *Capital Gang*, and a regular member of public TV's *McLaughlin Group*. Besides these recurring gigs, he had been a frequent guest on ABC's *Nightline* and *Good Morning America*.

Buchanan had served up his far-right positions so incessantly, they'd become almost commonplace. His fellow TV pundits appeared incapable of noticing the striking similarities in the ideologies of Buchanan and Duke.

On TV, Buchanan's sparring partners "from the left" were folks like Jack Germond (*McLaughlin Group*), Michael Kinsley (*Crossfire*), and Mark Shields (*Capital Gang*). They reacted to "Pat's candidacy" largely with good-natured jesting, not the hostility reserved for Duke. After CNN telecast Buchanan's speech launching his campaign, network analyst Jack Germond said, "I've known Pat for 25 years or more and I know him well and I'm very fond of him."[64] Kinsley and Shields (the latter was referred to in a *Newsweek* profile of Buchanan as "another friend from the left")[65] wrote nearly identical columns, saying, in essence: I rarely agree with Buchanan's principles but at least he's got principles.[66]

In fact, Buchanan, like Duke, has long displayed authoritarian inclinations and sympathy for fascism. In his autobiography, *Right from the Beginning*, Buchanan waxed nostalgic about his dad's hero, General Francisco Franco.[67] Buchanan has referred to the Spanish dictator as a "Catholic savior" and, like Chile's General Augusto Pinochet, a "soldier-patriot who saved his country from Communism."[68] Buchanan also admired apartheid-era South Africa—which he called the "Boer Republic"—and asked, "Why are Americans collaborating in a U.N. conspiracy to ruin her with sanctions?"[69]

For years, Buchanan has championed accused Nazi war criminals and campaigned for the U.S. Justice Department to stop "running down 70-year-old camp guards."[70] His columns questioning the historical record about the gassing of Jews at Treblinka have appeared in pro-Nazi publications that claim the death camps are a Jewish hoax.[71] Buchanan has been credited with crafting Reagan's line that called the Nazi troops buried at Bitburg "victims just as surely as the victims in the concentration camps."[72]

In a bizarre 1977 column, Buchanan said that despite Hitler's anti-Semitic and genocidal tendencies, "he was also an individual of great courage. . . . Hitler's success was not based on his extraordinary gifts alone. His genius was an intuitive sense of the mushiness, the character flaws, the weakness masquerading as morality that was in the hearts of the statesmen who stood in his path."[73]

Buchanan is contemptuous of what he calls "the democratist temptation, the worship of democracy as a form of governance." The would-be president once wrote: "Like all idolatries, democratism substitutes a false god for the real, a love of process for a love of country."[74] He has written disparagingly of "the one man, one vote Earl Warren system."[75] In one column, he suggested that "quasi-dictatorial rule" might be the solution to the problems of big municipalities and the federal fiscal crisis: "If the people are corrupt, the more democracy, the worse the government."[76]

Like Duke, Buchanan has a demonstrated attraction to white-supremacist views. In the Nixon White House, he referred to an *Atlantic* magazine article on intelligence and heredity as "a seminal piece of major significance for U.S. society." The piece, he wrote to Nixon, indicates that "integration of blacks and whites—but even more so, poor and well-to-do—is less likely to result in accommodation than it is in perpetual friction—as the incapable are placed consciously by government side by side with the capable."[77]

Buchanan was one of the first to advocate that the Republican Party exploit racial issues. In another memo to Nixon, he wrote:

> There is a legitimate grievance in my view of white working-class people that every time, on every issue, that the black militants loud-mouth it, we come up with more money. . . . The time has come to say—we have done enough for the poor blacks; right now we want to give some relief for working-class ethnics and Catholics—and make an unabashed appeal to these patient working people, who always get the short end of the stick. If we can give 50 Phantoms to the Jews, and a multibillion dollar welfare program for the blacks . . . why not help the Catholics save their collapsing school system.[78]

Buchanan couched many of his 1992 campaign themes, from trade policy to the "underclass," in racial terms. In a discussion of immigration, for example, he asked whether "Zulus" or "Englishmen" would be easier to assimilate.[79]

Given their similarities, it was ironic to see Buchanan trying to distance himself from Duke in 1992. (He complained that Republican officials "are beginning to treat me like David Duke.")[80] Three years earlier, when Duke ran for the Louisiana state legislature and shared a phone with the Klan, Buchanan wrote a column ridiculing national Republican leaders for overreacting to Duke and his Nazi "costume": "Take a hard look at Duke's portfolio of winning issues," Buchanan advised, "and expropriate those not in conflict with GOP principles."[81]

Buchanan said Duke was right on target attacking "reverse discrimination against white folks" and crime committed by the "urban underclass"—Buchanan's code phrase for blacks. He saluted Duke for walking "into the vacuum left when conservative Republicans in the Reagan years were intimidated into shucking off winning social issues." His column concluded: "The GOP is throwing away a winning hand, and David Duke is only the first fellow to pick up the discards." But Buchanan's friends in the media seemed unwilling to look too closely at the cards Buchanan was holding.

Some went out of their way to blur perceptions of Buchanan's far-right views: William Safire described Buchanan's supporters as a "network of the nativist right and isolationist left,"[82] while Stephen Rosenfeld in the *Washington Post* wrote that although Buchanan's America First platform raises "fair questions," the "come-home movement" might be "captured or severely tainted by extremists, including David Duke."[83]

Get Me Rewrite
June 1992

In an early edition of the March 12, 1992, *New York Times,* an R. W. Apple article speculated about Pat Buchanan's chances in Michigan: "He might also find support in Macomb County, north of Detroit, to which many white workers fled when their neighborhoods were taken over by blacks." By the late edition, the race-baiting terminology had been removed: Macomb was now the place where "many white workers moved when blacks began to settle in their neighborhoods."

Notes

1. *ABC World News Tonight,* January 26, 1992.
2. *New York Times,* February 2, 1992.
3. *New York Times,* January 31, 1992.
4. *New York Times,* January 14, 1992.
5. *Los Angeles Times,* February 14, 1992.
6. *New York Times,* January 28, 1992.
7. *New York Times,* February 18, 1992.
8. *New York Times,* February 19, 1992.
9. *Los Angeles Times,* January 31, 1992.
10. *New York Times,* January 21, 1992.
11. *New York Times,* February 8, 1992.

12. *Washington Post,* February 7, 1992.
13. *Washington Post,* January 15, 1992.
14. *New York Times,* January 18, 1992; January 21, 1992.
15. *New York Times,* January 17, 1992.
16. *Los Angeles Times,* February 8, 1992.
17. *Washington Post,* February 11, 1992.
18. *New York Times,* February 6, 1992.
19. *New York Times,* January 21, 1992.
20. *Los Angeles Times,* February 8, 1992.
21. *Washington Post,* February 14, 1992.
22. *Los Angeles Times,* February 12, 1992.
23. *Washington Post,* February 15, 1992.
24. *New York Times,* February 19, 1992.
25. *Los Angeles Times,* February 16, 1992.
26. *Los Angeles Times,* February 9, 1992.
27. *Los Angeles Times,* February 5, 1992.
28. *Washington Post,* January 30, 1992.
29. *Los Angeles Times,* January 28, 1992.
30. *New York Times,* January 31, 1992.
31. *Washington Post,* January 30, 1992.
32. *New York Times,* February 14, 1992.
33. *New York Times,* February 14, 1992.
34. *New York Times,* January 31, 1992.
35. *Los Angeles Times,* January 29, 1992.
36. *Washington Post,* February 6, 1992.
37. *Washington Post,* February 4, 1992.
38. *Washington Post,* January 24, 1992.
39. *Los Angeles Times,* January 24, 1992.
40. *New York Times,* February 17, 1992.
41. *New York Times,* January 20, 1992.
42. *New York Times,* January 19, 1992.
43. *New York Times,* February 16, 1992.
44. *New York Post,* January 10, 1992; January 23, 1992. The coverage seemed to have been prompted by the Republican-oriented paper's distaste for the likely Democratic nominee, and by reporter Deborah Orin's personal hostility toward Clinton.
45. CNN, February 16, 1992.
46. Even though the Iowa caucuses have been covered intensively in presidential elections from 1976 through 1988, in 1992 they were all but ignored, with the excuse that a victory by Harkin, one of Iowa's senators, was a foregone conclusion. Other victories by Harkin in Minnesota and even Idaho were similarly discounted because he was a "regional candidate." On the other hand, a win by Southerner Bill Clinton in Georgia was trumpeted as proof that he was in fact the front-runner—as the media had said all along. See FAIR's campaign newsletter *CounterSpin,* March 6, 1992; March 13, 1992.
47. *New York Times,* January 24, 1992.
48. *New York Times,* February 16, 1992.
49. Hendrick Hertzberg, "Press Pass," *The New Republic,* March 9, 1992, p. 46.
50. *USA Today,* March 4, 1992.

51. *New York Times,* March 4, 1992.
52. *NBC Nightly News,* March 25, 1992.
53. *MacNeil/Lehrer NewsHour,* March 27, 1992.
54. *New York Times,* March 22, 1992.
55. *New York Times,* March 24, 1992.
56. Howard Fineman, "The Method in His Madness," *Newsweek,* March 23, 1992, p. 36.
57. Margaret Carlson, "Why Jerry Keeps Running," *Time,* March 23, 1992, p. 27.
58. Margaret Carlson, "Why Jerry Keeps Running," *Time,* March 23, 1992, p. 27.
59. Jon D. Hull, "Sweet Smell of Success," *Time,* March 30, 1992, p. 20.
60. *New York Times,* March 28, 1992.
61. *New York Post,* March 28, 1992. Brown's use of a toll-free number to raise funds—because he refused the large donations that other candidates relied on—was widely mocked. "Isn't Jerry Brown making a complete joke of himself, carrying on like this?" Michael Kinsley asked on *Crossfire,* after Brown was barred from the show for insisting on giving out his number. Three years later, as Kinsley's chief debating partner, Patrick Buchanan, announced on *Crossfire* that he would run for president (February 16, 1995), Kinsley helped Buchanan hold up a sign announcing his 800 number.
62. Jonathan Alter, "Jerry's Date with History," *Newsweek,* April 13, 1992, p. 31.
63. Martin A. Lee, "Friendly Fascism: National Media Give Duke a Face-Lift," *Extra!,* January/February 1992, p. 6.
64. CNN, December 10, 1991.
65. Tom Mathews, "Why Is Buchanan So Angry?" *Newsweek,* January 27, 1992, p. 22.
66. Michael Kinsley, "Can We Stand Pat?" *The New Republic,* January 27, 1992, p. 6; Mark Shields, *Washington Post,* January 21, 1992.
67. Patrick Buchanan, *Right from the Beginning* (Boston: Little, Brown and Company, 1988).
68. *New York Post,* September 17, 1989.
69. *New York Post,* September 17, 1989.
70. Cited by Anthony Lewis, *New York Times,* May 16, 1985.
71. "Patrick Buchanan, Equal Opportunity Maligner," *Extra!,* November/December 1990, p. 14.
72. Anthony Lewis, *New York Times,* May 16, 1985.
73. Quoted in Jacob Weisburg, "The Heresies of Pat Buchanan," *The New Republic,* October 22, 1990, p. 22.
74. Patrick J. Buchanan, *Patrick J. Buchanan: From the Right,* newsletter, Spring 1990, p. 7.
75. Quoted in Jacob Weisburg, "The Heresies of Pat Buchanan," *The New Republic,* October 22, 1990, p. 22.
76. *Washington Times,* January 9, 1991.
77. *Boston Globe,* January 4, 1992. The argument in the September 1971 *Atlantic* article, by Richard J. Herrnstein, later became the basis for a widely publicized defense of racial superiority: Richard Herrnstein and Charles Murray, *The Bell Curve: Intelligence and Class Structure in American Life* (New York: Free Press, 1994). See Jim Naureckas, "Racism Resurgent: How Media Let *The Bell Curve*'s Pseudo-Science Define the Agenda on Race," *Extra!,* January/February 1995, p. 12.
78. *Boston Globe,* January 4, 1992.

79. *This Week with David Brinkley,* December 8, 1991.
80. Associated Press, December 17, 1991.
81. Patrick Buchanan, syndicated column, *New York Post,* February 25, 1989.
82. *New York Times,* December 16, 1991.
83. *Washington Post,* December 13, 1991.

5 The Presidential Campaign: Unfair to Voters

Democracy Versus Punditocracy: The Handful of Insiders Who Shaped Campaign News

October/November 1992

LAWRENCE SOLEY

In 1990, NBC News senior vice president Tim Russert penned a widely read op-ed article criticizing broadcast coverage of the 1988 presidential campaign. According to Russert, "The public felt cheated by the emphasis on flag-waving and furloughs rather than on deficits and defense." Russert insisted that in the future, the networks needed to avoid photo opportunities, while providing coverage of the issues and candidates' records.[1]

Despite Russert's lofty suggestions, network television coverage of the 1992 presidential campaign looked eerily like that of 1988, complete with liberal-baiting, stories of marital infidelity, an overemphasis on strategy and "horse race" coverage, and sound bites from the same small group of political pundits—nearly all white and male—who monopolized discourse during the 1988 campaign.

Horse race stories, which focus on predicting who will win, have always been broadcast media's main fare, and 1992 was no exception. Campaign strategy, polls, and discussion of advertising tactics predominate; if issues are discussed at all in horse race stories, they are merely fodder for color commentary down the backstretch.

A CBS evening newscast that used abortion as the backdrop for a story on campaign strategy illustrated this kind of coverage. Paula Zahn's lead-in stated: "It's just what the Bush-Quayle campaign didn't need. Another election year controversy involving the vice-president. It began with a statement that Dan Quayle made about abortion that appeared to put him at odds with the president."[2] The impact of the vice president's comment on the campaign was discussed; the implications of the president's proposed abortion ban were not probed.

Two of the most important sources in horse race stories are spin doctors and political analysts. Spin doctors are the hired guns of electoral campaigns who typically insulate their candidates from probing questions. Political analysts are usually retired spin doctors or spin doctors whose candidates have already dropped out of the race.

According to Burrelle's Broadcast Database, which contains transcripts of news broadcasts from ABC, CBS, NBC, and National Public Radio (NPR), the three leading spin doctors of President Bush's reelection campaign—Robert Teeter, Fred Malek, and Charles Black—made more than 129 broadcast news appearances between August 1991, the month that Bill Clinton decided to establish a presidential campaign committee, and July 15, 1992 (Table 5.1).

The three leading advisers to Bill Clinton—James Carville, Frank Greer, and Mickey Kantor—made eighty-two appearances. Ross Perot's troika of spin doctors—James Squires, Thomas Luce, and Morton Meyerson—made the news on eighty occasions.

Many other political analysts from both parties appeared during the primary season. Between August 1, 1991, and June 3, 1992, when he was named comanager of the Perot campaign, Republican Ed Rollins made seventy appearances. On the Democratic side, Bob Beckel, Robert Squier, and Ann Lewis were the most-featured strategists. Other Republican consultants who appeared included Eddie Mahe and Douglas Bailey.

Typically, such sources contribute a partisan spin to a horse race or strategy story, as when William McInturff, identified as a Republican strategist, told CBS: "Sooner or later, you've got to remind people of what it is that you're proud you have done as president and what you're going to do in the future. And I just don't know that that's coming across right now."[3] McInturff's suggestion that Bush had a record to be proud of went unexamined in the report.

Pollsters also play an important role in horse race stories, pontificating about the meaning of the previous day's survey. Frequently appearing pollsters in 1991–1992 included Democrats Stan Greenberg, Harrison Hickman, and Peter Hart and Republicans Neil Newhouse and Linda DiVall.

Rounding out the horse race and strategy stories are Washington pundits, who claim to know what voters in the rest of the country are thinking. As pundit Thomas Mann noted on the CBS evening newscast of April 18, 1992, "The public is unhappy. It's anxious, believes the country's on the wrong track. It's hard to get excited about a race when the constant refrain is the inadequacy of the people

TABLE 5.1 Leading Campaign News Shapers. Newscast Appearances, August 1, 1991–July 15, 1992

Profession	Affiliation	Number of Appearances
Spin Doctors		
For George Bush		
Robert Teeter	campaign chair	63
Frederick Malek	campaign manager	36
Charles Black	campaign adviser	30
For Bill Clinton		
James Carville	senior adviser	46
Frank Greer	media adviser	21
Mickey Kantor	campaign chair	15
For Ross Perot		
Thomas Luce	petition manager	53
James Squires	campaign director	15
Morton Meyerson	senior adviser	12
Political Analysts		
Ed Rollins (before 6/3/92)	Sawyer-Miller Group	70
Bob Beckel	Bob Beckel and Associates	55
Robert Squier	The Communications Company	53
Ann Lewis	former Democratic National Committee	17
Eddie Mahe	Eddie Mahe, Jr., & Associates	15
Douglas Bailey	Bailey-Deardourff	14
Pollsters		
Harrison Hickman	Hickman-Maslin Research	30
Linda DiVall	American Viewpoint	28
Peter Hart	Garin-Hart Strategic Research	21
Neil Newhouse	Decisionmaking Information	12
Stan Greenberg	Clinton campaign	9
Washington Pundits		
Kevin Phillips	columnist/publisher	97
Joe Klein	*Newsweek*	42
David Gergen	*U.S. News & World Report*	32
Thomas Mann	Brookings Institution	32
Norman Ornstein	American Enterprise Institute	30
Merle Black	Emory University	17
Advertising and Media Analysts		
Kathleen Hall Jamieson	University of Pennsylvania	17
Larry Sabato	University of Virginia	8

SOURCE: Burrelle's Broadcast Database (Livingston, N.J.: Burrelle's Information Services).

seeking office."[4] (Mann didn't mention whether voters were tired of hearing from Beltway-based savants.)

Unlike the horse race analysts, who rarely say anything not related to winning elections, the Washington pundits frequently speak about policy issues. In the 1987–1988 election cycle, a small group of former Republican officials and representatives of Beltway think tanks had a virtual lock on these discussions on network television. In the two years preceding George Bush's election, Washington punditry was dominated by former Republican officials like Kevin Phillips, Stephen Hess, and David Gergen, and by William Schneider and Norman Ornstein of the American Enterprise Institute (AEI), a conservative think tank.

According to Burrelle's Broadcast Database, the Washington pundits who monopolized discourse during the 1988 campaign did so again in 1992. Between August 1, 1991, and July 15, 1992, Kevin Phillips was quoted ninety-seven times by the three television networks and NPR—about two times a week. David Gergen appeared thirty-two times, not counting his weekly appearances on the *MacNeil/Lehrer NewsHour*. Norman Ornstein appeared thirty times, not counting appearances on CNN, where his AEI colleague William Schneider was employed as a news analyst. Other AEI representatives who shaped the news during the 1991–1992 campaign period included Suzanne Garment and Ben Wattenberg.

Aside from Schneider, who was under contract with CNN, the only top political pundit to make fewer appearances in 1992 than in 1988 was Stephen Hess of the Brookings Institution.[5] He appeared only eight times between August 1, 1991, and July 15, 1992. During his limited appearances, Hess managed to explain why Bush's popularity had plummeted ("I think what's happened was the president was up so high that he almost forgot what it's like to be down")[6] and why marital fidelity has remained a campaign issue. ("Jefferson was accused of having a black woman as a mistress. Andrew Jackson was accused of being an adulterer. Grover Cleveland was accused of siring an illegitimate child.")[7]

Although Hess's appearances declined, appearances by his Brookings colleague, Thomas Mann, were up. Mann appeared only three times in 1987 and 1988, but popped up thirty-two times during the 1992 campaign period. Because Mann was considered a "congressional expert" by the media, he was used to comment on Capitol Hill in addition to news about the presidential race.

The pundits who dominated discourse in broadcast news also provided analysis for much of what appeared in print. CBS "news consultant" Joe Klein wrote for *Newsweek*, David Gergen was with *U.S. News & World Report*, and Kevin Phillips was a columnist for the *Los Angeles Times*. William Schneider was a columnist for the *National Journal* and a contributing editor of *Atlantic* magazine and the *Los Angeles Times* opinion section.

The oft-quoted TV pundits not only wrote for print media but also were a constant source of quotes for reporters at leading newspapers such as the *New York Times, Los Angeles Times,* and *Washington Post*. Even regional newspapers were filled with their analyses: Between January 1991 and March 31, 1992, the

Minneapolis *Star Tribune* quoted sages from the Brookings Institution ninety-four times. Kevin Phillips was quoted ten times, and the newspaper carried three of his op-ed pieces.

When *Chicago Tribune* media critic James Warren asked about the repeated use of the same pundits on network newscasts, NBC's Tim Russert said, "People doing a TV piece say, 'All I need is somebody saying X.' And you know the familiar people who'll say that and can speak in 8- to 10-second soundbites." Although Russert described this as "incestuous," he insisted that "there is nothing conspiratorial." Nevertheless, NBC was making a "deliberate effort" to expand contacts with lower-profile academics and others, he said.[8]

The Anti-Democratic Convention: Corporations, the Real "Special Interests," Got Little Play

September 1992

JIM NAURECKAS

IT WAS FASHIONABLE to bemoan the networks' lack of gavel-to-gavel coverage of the 1992 conventions. ABC's Peter Jennings told the *Washington Post* that it was "a little sad" that the networks were passing up "a chance to present the democratic process in the purest sense."[9]

Of course, modern stage-managed conventions are anything but a democratic process—and the media bear a lot of the blame for that. Anything at a convention that resembles democracy—a debate over a contested issue, a resolution that isn't preapproved—is denounced by media pundits as "mischief" from "special interests."

There was to be none of that in 1992: "Certainly the portents are brighter than they were at the conventions of 1980, 1984 and 1988, when turmoil marred the nomination spectacle," wrote the *Washington Post*'s David Broder.[10] Juan Williams, in the same paper, praised Clinton for having "a strong enough hand to control Jesse Jackson and Jerry Brown, thereby staging a peaceful, unified convention."[11]

During the convention, reporters pushed for more exclusion, not inclusion. "Are you annoyed that you have to deal with people like Jerry Brown and Jesse Jackson?" PBS's Jim Lehrer asked Clinton.[12] "Should Brown be allowed to speak if he hasn't endorsed the ticket?" NBC's John Cochran asked a Brown delegate.[13] Reporters seemed to endorse the evolution of these events from a political party's convention to a nominee's coronation by repeatedly calling it "Clinton's convention," which intrusive delegates were trying to disrupt.

The national media were constantly on the alert against grassroots activists, usually referred to as some kind of "interests": One Thomas Edsall piece in the *Washington Post* featured "liberal interests," "various minority interests," and (in a quote from a Clinton delegate) "every weird special interest that could exist on the face of the Earth."[14] The conflict at the convention was supposed to be between these "interests"—defined by Edsall as "blacks, gays, unions, feminists"—and the "middle class" (as if most blacks, gays, union members, and feminists weren't middle class), whose representatives were said to have taken back control of the party.

Journalists' acceptance of the view that the party was moving toward the middle class showed their failure to "follow the money." It's not that journalists don't understand that there's a connection between money and politics—as a David Broder column on Jackson illustrated: "Clinton played hardball politics with Jackson, especially after Ross Perot's comments about homosexuality made it clear that the gay community, whose financial support is critical to Jackson's operations, would find no alternative to Clinton in November."[15]

Broder can analyze this kind of political triple-bank shot—when he's writing about relatively powerless sectors of the party. But the national media made little effort to interpret the role of the Clinton campaign's corporate backing in changing the direction of the party.

There was little talk, for example, about Clinton's campaign manager, Mickey Kantor, whose law firm represented such tribunes of the middle class as General Electric, Martin Marietta, United Air Lines, ARCO, and Chemical Bank.[16] Two important fund-raisers for Clinton were Robert Barry, a longtime lobbyist for GE, and Thomas Boggs,[17] a $1.5 million-a-year lawyer whose firm has represented various corporate interests, including the notorious Bank of Credit and Commerce International (BCCI). Democratic National Committee (DNC) chair Ron Brown was a partner in Boggs's firm, where Brown personally represented the Haitian dictatorship of Jean Claude ("Baby Doc") Duvalier, as well as the association of foreign auto dealers.[18]

The money Clinton used to achieve early "front-runner" status didn't come from the middle class. As William Greider noted in *Rolling Stone*, "Half or more of Clinton's funding came from conservative corporate interests"—including Wall Street investors and Washington lobbyists.[19]

The Democratic Leadership Council, the group fronted by center-to-right Democratic politicians (including Clinton and Al Gore) that assumed control of the Democratic Party, was not a middle-class organization. It was bankrolled by—and spoke for—corporate America: ARCO, Dow Chemical, Georgia Pacific, Martin Marietta, the Tobacco Institute, the American Petroleum Institute, and so forth.

There was little attempt to make any connection between these corporate ties and the program Clinton espoused, except in the alternative press: Thomas Ferguson in *The Nation,* for instance, related Clinton's vague, timid position on health care reform to his support from the medical industry;[20] John Judis in *In These Times* connected Clinton's trade policies to donations from investment bankers who deal in overseas capital.[21]

Perhaps there would have been more discussion of these connections if the spectrum of commentary on the convention hadn't been so narrow. On the issue of the Democratic platform, you could turn to CNN's *Capital Gang* to hear it criticized as "anti-capitalist" by Robert Novak and "mildly socialist" by Mona Charen.[22] For an opposing view, you could read "Column Left" on the *Los Angeles Times* op-ed page, where Elaine Ciulla Kamarck praised the Democratic platform for avoiding Republican attacks by adopting Republican rhetoric and positions on everything from crime to welfare to corporations.[23] A progressive perspective that holds that it's a bad idea for a Democratic platform to adopt Republican positions apparently would have been too far out to be considered.

Conventional Wisdom: How the Press Rewrites Democratic Party History Every Four Years

September 1992

JIM NAURECKAS

COVERAGE OF THE 1992 Democratic convention often drew sharp contrasts with earlier Democratic conventions—particularly 1984 and 1988. A look back at the coverage of those conventions, however, shows that they had been covered in almost exactly the same terms.

Like 1992, both 1984 and 1988 were treated as landmarks, a new start for a party whose old ways had led to defeat. The *New York Times* reported in 1984 that it was "with justification" that Mondale aides called the 1984 convention "the most successful since 1964."[24] According to a 1988 *Chicago Tribune* editorial, "The Democratic Party of 1988 is more unified, more single-minded, more obsessed with winning and less with ideology, more in control of its own destiny than it has been in decades."[25] But within four years, each convention became a symbol of what had to be changed about the Democratic Party to give it "winnability."

In the conventional wisdom of 1992, the main problem with the '84 and '88 conventions was the meddlesome power of Jesse Jackson. "There have been Democratic conventions, back in 1984 and 1988, that Mr. Jackson all but held in the palm of his hand," wrote the *New York Times*'s B. Drummond Ayres.[26] In various 1992 news reports, Walter Mondale and Michael Dukakis had been "humbled" by Jackson,[27] "acquiesced to Jackson's terms,"[28] or were "anxious to appease Jesse Jackson."[29]

The contemporary coverage of the '84 and '88 conventions presented a very different picture: A Jackson supporter quoted in the *Washington Post* "complained just before Mondale's crushing platform victory over Jesse L. Jackson that when Jackson's negotiators sought to compromise, the Mondale camp stayed firm."[30]

In 1988, according to William Schneider in the *Los Angeles Times,* "The Jackson forces were persuaded to give up or compromise most of their proposed amendments, all of which would have committed the party to a liberal position. Only two amendments were subjected to a convention vote—both lost by better than 2 to 1."[31]

If any "humbling" went on, it was in the other direction: "Without getting much of what he wanted," *Chicago Tribune* columnist Jon Margolis wrote of Jackson, "he went to Dukakis' hotel suite to eat breakfast and surrender with honor."[32]

Mondale's and Dukakis's "appeasement" of Jackson was always presented in 1992 as politically costly. "Walter F. Mondale and Michael S. Dukakis both exhausted valuable resources trying to satisfy Jackson," according to the *Boston Globe*.[33] "Mondale and Dukakis aides said they believed the efforts to satisfy Jackson had weakened the image of the nominees as they started the general election campaign," wrote Thomas Edsall and David Broder of the *Washington Post*.[34]

But at the time, reporters and pundits had talked of the "firmness" demonstrated by Mondale and Dukakis. "Walter F. Mondale tonight took firm control of the Democratic National Convention," Broder wrote in 1984, reporting on Mondale's defeat of Jackson's platform amendments.[35]

George Will in 1988 saw Dukakis's putting down of Jackson as a political coup for the Democratic nominee. "Jackson's overreaching gave Dukakis an opportunity to act presidential and he seized it, giving Jackson nothing but rhetoric as he cut Jackson, the would-be co-quarterback, down to the subservient role of blocking back."[36] According to a post-convention Gallup poll, only 17 percent of respondents said that Dukakis went too far in addressing Jackson's concerns.[37]

In the mass media's distorted history, Democratic conventions before 1992 were controlled by so-called "special interest groups"—meaning minorities, feminists, labor, environmentalists, and other progressive constituencies. But in contemporary coverage, every convention since 1984 has been hailed by journalists as the one in which the "special interests" lost their influence. "With the nomination of Walter S. Mondale for president," reported the *Christian Science Monitor,* "the Democratic party has moved full circle," with control shifting from "amateur activists" back to "experienced political hands."[38] Four years later, the rewrite was on: Mondale was seen by William Schneider as "the leader of the Old Party, the advocacy politician who spoke for 'special interests.'"[39]

Writing in 1988 about that year's convention, columnist Elaine Ciulla Kamarck asserted, "Interest groups and their demands were barely visible."[40] A *Chicago Tribune* editorial was effusive: "Unlike too many of his defeated predecessors, Mike Dukakis devoted neither his campaign nor his convention to buying the love of a jungle of special-interest groups with promises that could mortgage the heart and soul and pocketbook of a prospective administration."[41]

Chris Wallace on NBC's *Meet the Press* framed the key question of the 1988 Democratic convention as: "How far can Dukakis go to meet Jackson without appearing, like 1984, to be caving in to every special interest?"[42] When FAIR asked Wallace at the convention why he never applied the "special interest" label to the corporate interests behind such candidates as Democrat Lloyd Bentsen or Republican George Bush, he challenged FAIR to watch his network's coverage of the upcoming Republican convention. FAIR watched. "Special interests" were nowhere to be found; Republicans apparently just represented the national interest.[43]

According to mass media, Clinton ran for president as a moderate who appealed to the "middle class"—a plan that was seen as a contrast to previous Democratic campaigns. "The platform is not Mondale-Dukakis liberal, but Clinton moderate," reported the *Christian Science Monitor.*[44]

Actually, both Mondale and Dukakis tried to win by moving the party to the right. "Look at our platform," said Mondale in his acceptance speech. "There are no defense cuts that weaken our security, no business taxes that weaken our economy, no laundry lists that raid our treasury."[45] At the time, journalists agreed: "Democrats' Platform Shows a Shift From Liberal Positions of 1976 and 1980," ran the headline of the *New York Times*'s analysis of Mondale's platform.[46] "The minority planks that could have crippled his campaign were blocked," the *Christian Science Monitor* wrote of Mondale in 1984.[47]

It was the same story with the 1988 platform. Wrote the *Washington Post:* "The expansive promises of Democratic Party platforms of earlier years—the crowded bazaar of special interests and special pleadings—have been streamlined into the version that will go before the convention here Tuesday."[48]

Nor was Clinton the first to think that talking about the middle class is the way to get votes. Mondale portrayed himself as "embodying all the traditional, middle-class values of the rural Midwest," according to Broder.[49] In 1988, Anthony

Lewis described Dukakis's strategy as "go for the middle ground and the middle class."[50] The buzzwords that the *Chicago Tribune* praised Dukakis for using would have been familiar to any viewer of the 1992 convention: "family, community, honesty, patriotism, accountability, responsibility, opportunity."[51]

The nomination of conservative Lloyd Bentsen as the 1988 vice-presidential candidate was a powerful signal of the party's priorities that by 1992 had been largely forgotten: "When Michael Dukakis chose Sen. Lloyd Bentsen as his running mate, he turned his back not just on Jesse Jackson, but on two decades of Democratic Party thinking," wrote David Broder at the time. "He sent an unmistakable message to the activist constituencies of the Democratic Party that the days of litmus-test liberalism are over."[52]

How is it that Democratic Party history gets revised every four years? It's largely because the "left" perspective in mainstream debate is represented by centrists who identify with the establishment politicians who dominate the Democratic Party and feel estranged from the party's progressive constituencies. These pundits and political journalists seem reluctant to acknowledge that it was insiders, not activists, who led the party to crushing defeat in 1984 and 1988.

After describing the 1988 convention as a transition between the "Old Party" dominated by liberal "special interests" and the "New Party" characterized by post-ideological "problem-solvers" like Dukakis, William Schneider made a prediction in the *Los Angeles Times*: "If the problem-solvers can't win ... there is every likelihood that Democrats will go back to what they really believe in."[53] What actually happened, of course, was the same move that was made in 1984: When the "pragmatists" lost badly with their centrist approach, they were repainted after the fact as radicals, so the strategy of tilting to the right could be tried again and again.

Working the Refs
October/November 1992

"There is some strategy to it. I'm the coach of kids' basketball and Little League teams. If you watch any great coach, what they try to do is work the refs. Maybe the ref will cut you a little slack next time."

—Republican National Committee chair Rich Bond, on Republican complaints about media bias[54]

Issues, Images, and Impact: A FAIR Survey of Voters' Knowledge in the 1992 Campaign

December 1992

JUSTIN LEWIS AND MICHAEL MORGAN

ALTHOUGH THERE WAS no shortage of polls published during the 1992 presidential election campaign, most opinion surveys offered little more than a snapshot of attitudes or voting intentions. FAIR's survey of the U.S. electorate during the 1992 presidential election campaign, by contrast, was concerned not only with what people thought but also with the knowledge that lay behind those attitudes, and the sources of that knowledge.[55]

Democracy in the United States depends increasingly upon the news media. Surveys show that for most citizens the media are the principal source of information about political candidates and politics in general. Of the many news outlets available, the most important is network television, which is the place—to paraphrase ABC News—where most Americans get their news. Our study focused on the role played by the news media (and TV news in particular), asking the following questions:

- Did the news media successfully communicate enough information for voters to understand the political issues?
- How did the public's knowledge of substantive issues compare with more trivial knowledge, and how did this relate to media exposure?
- Did the information people received suggest any bias toward certain political positions? Did, for example, the media effectively communicate more "pro-Bush facts" or "pro-Clinton facts?" Did the information communicated by the news media make voters more inclined toward the left, the right, or the center?

The study was based on a nationwide telephone survey, conducted September 30 to October 3, 1992, of 601 randomly selected Americans who said they would "probably" or "definitely" vote. These likely voters tended to have more years of education than the average American.

Why do people vote for one candidate rather than another? This question is never as simple as it looks, and the many possible answers to it are enough to stimulate the thriving industry of political punditry. What we can say with some degree of certainty is that people make their voting decisions based on what they know about the candidates. This led us, in this survey, to ask people not so much what they thought of the candidates, but what they knew about them. The answers often exhibited a disheartening ignorance.

Similar to most other surveys taken at the beginning of October, FAIR's poll showed Clinton leading with 41 percent, Bush with 32 percent, Perot with 10 percent, and 17 percent undecided.

Despite voters' proclaimed desire to base their votes on the issues rather than on more trivial information about the candidates, most people, we discovered, knew very little about the former and a great deal about the latter. Asked about the candidates' policies and backgrounds, the only questions that a majority answered correctly were "Which candidate's family has a dog called Millie?" and "Do you recall which TV character Dan Quayle criticized for setting a poor example of family values?" Eighty-six percent knew that Millie belonged to the Bush family, and 89 percent correctly identified Murphy Brown, compared with 19 percent who could name the Reagan-Bush Cabinet member recently indicted for his role in the Iran-contra scandal, Caspar Weinberger. (Perhaps the only surprise, in this respect, was that only 23 percent could correctly recall the name of the woman alleged during the early primaries to have had an affair with Clinton—Gennifer Flowers.)

Even an issue that was topical in the week the survey took place had a majority confused. At the beginning of the week, President Bush vetoed an attempt by Congress to impose sanctions on China for human rights abuses, in keeping with his long-held position on China. Despite this, when asked what position Bush had taken on China since the massacre at Tiananmen Square, only 44 percent knew that Bush was against sanctions, while roughly the same amount (43 percent) stated that Bush had actually imposed trade sanctions. In other words, people were as likely to link Bush with a policy he steadfastly opposed as they were to link him with the one he actually pursued.

When it came to Clinton's record in Arkansas, perceptions of the candidate on various issues bore even less resemblance to reality. According to independent calculations, Arkansas state taxes were among the lowest in the nation. Despite this, when asked, "To your knowledge, how high were Arkansas state taxes while Clinton has been governor?" only 21 percent responded correctly that they were "among the lowest in the nation," while more—32 percent—reported that they were "among the highest in the nation."

Similarly, the Green Index, compiled by an independent monitoring group, has put Arkansas near the bottom of all states in most areas of environmental policy.[56] But when asked, "How has Governor Clinton's record on the environment been rated by an independent monitoring group?" only 19 percent correctly stated "among the worst in the nation." (Fifty-two percent said "about average" and 7 percent "among the best.")

Of the twenty-one factual questions about the candidates and the issues, the average percentage of correct responses was 32 percent, a figure that dropped to 27 percent if the more trivial, less "issue-oriented" questions were excluded.

Not surprisingly, those with a college education tended to score higher than those without. But although Clinton supporters were more likely to be drawn from less educated groups (his lead among those with no college education stretched to 25 percentage points), they were, overall, the *best* informed group of voters in this survey, followed by Perot supporters, with Bush supporters scoring the lowest.

These differences become even more striking when we look at the most knowledgeable 20 percent and the least knowledgeable 20 percent. Among the most knowledgeable group, Clinton led by almost 30 percentage points (55 percent to 26 percent) over Bush (with Perot at 9 percent). Among the least knowledgeable, on the other hand, Bush had a commanding 44-to-26 percent lead (with Perot at 8 percent). Predictably, FAIR found more undecided voters—22 percent—among the least knowledgeable, while only 10 percent of the most knowledgeable were undecided.

It was also notable that exposure to the main information source in our culture, television, did not increase knowledge. Heavy TV viewers knew slightly less than light TV viewers. Similarly, those who relied on TV as their main source of news scored slightly lower than those who relied on other sources, such as newspapers.

Many in the Bush campaign lamented (in public, at least) Bush's failure to get his message across—often blaming the "liberal media" for this failure. FAIR's survey suggested that on a number of issues, Bush's message got through, while the Clinton campaign's did not. This related not simply to Clinton's record on taxes but to other areas in which Republican attacks appeared to have hit home.

Take, for example, a question about the candidates and the draft: "Of the four candidates for president and vice president [Bush, Clinton, Quayle, and Gore], have any been accused of using family influence to avoid being sent to Vietnam?" This statement applied to both Bill Clinton and Dan Quayle, yet only 23 percent named both, while almost three times as many picked only Clinton (41 percent) as picked only Quayle (15 percent). To put it another way, we could say that in a competition among a Republican campaign answer, a Democratic campaign answer, and the correct answer, the Republican answer won.

An issue that potentially undermined Vice President Quayle was the fact that, despite his criticisms of the "cultural" or "media elite," he himself comes from a family that owns a newspaper chain. The good news for Quayle was that few people were aware of this—only 24 percent in our survey.

Several Democratic attacks on the Bush record, on the other hand, didn't hit home. Democrats complained, for example, that despite Bush's account of the "tax and spend" Congress, he proposed a bigger budget in 1991 than the one Congress finally approved.[57] Although this charge was true, most people believed the opposite to be the case. When asked, "Last year, [1991] which do you think was greater: the amount of money President Bush proposed spending on the Federal Budget, or the amount Congress actually passed?" Sixty-six percent said Congress spent more, and only 22 percent answered correctly. Even Clinton supporters chose the wrong answer by a margin of more than two to one.

Other surveys suggested that on what voters considered to be the most important "family" issues (such as family leave), most preferred Clinton's proposals over Bush's.[58] Yet Bush was still seen as more supportive of "family values" than his opponent. When asked which candidate was more supportive of "family values," 45 percent chose Bush and only 28 percent said Clinton.

One tactic that Democratic strategists seemed to have more success with than the Republicans was tying their opponent to a symbol of elite privilege, the Ivy League. Fifty-seven percent named Bush as a "candidate who had attended an Ivy League university," while 44 percent named Clinton. In fact, both attended the same Ivy League school (Yale), although only 14 percent chose the "both" answer.

Despite the apparent success of the GOP in getting much of its message across, the fact remains that people who stated a preference tended to choose Clinton over Bush. This suggests that the general level of antipathy toward Bush was so deep-rooted that voters could absorb Republican criticisms of Clinton as a "draft-dodging, tax-and-spend liberal"—and *still* vote for him.

The Republican claim that the news media promoted "pro-Clinton facts" more aggressively than "pro-Bush facts" was not supported by this survey. Far from evidence of "liberal bias," the data on the media's impact on public attitudes suggest that the reverse is more plausible.

A more profound problem was also highlighted by these results. The news media's emphasis on reporting campaign rhetoric over facts, their reluctance to focus on the record rather than on "claims" about the record, seemed to make it difficult for voters to distinguish between truth and propaganda. In the stress on claims and counterclaims, the facts become elusive and, in the end, unimportant. It would appear that news media, the message carriers in a modern democracy, played a key role in the evolution of a political process in which most voters knew little about what was really going on. The winner, in this impoverished political climate, was not democracy, but the manipulative world of public relations.

Perhaps the most conspicuous success of the Bush campaign was its portrayal of Clinton as a liberal. When asked about the candidates' policy positions, voters consistently attributed positions to Clinton that were more liberal than those that he had actually endorsed, while his more conservative stances were mostly unknown.

So, for example, only 37 percent knew Clinton supported the death penalty, only 37 percent knew he supported "right-to-work" laws opposed by organized labor, and only 32 percent knew that he supported cuts in capital gains taxes. While it was true that Clinton had proposed reducing military spending by more than Bush, 73 percent agreed with the statement that Clinton had proposed a cut of 50 percent over the next five years—significantly greater than the 30 percent cut that he actually had proposed.

One of the most glaring misconceptions concerned the source of the Democrats' campaign money. Independent assessments (from groups such as the Center for Responsive Politics) indicated that both the Republican and Democratic presidential candidates relied much more on corporate and business interests than on labor for campaign money.[59] Yet when asked who contributed more to Clinton's campaign, people overwhelmingly said labor (69 percent) rather than business (16 percent). While it was true that organized labor was more supportive of Clinton than of Bush, this answer indicated an underestimation of Clinton's ties to business—and an exaggerated sense of the importance of labor to Clinton's campaign.

Just as it was attractive to GOP strategists to portray the election as a battle between liberal and conservative ideologies, it was easier for the media to emphasize the differences rather than the similarities between the two major candidates. FAIR's survey suggests, however, that such a framework was misleading to the public.

Some of the most striking gaps in voters' knowledge came in more general questions about the society they live in. Perhaps the most extraordinary finding in the entire survey concerned people's perceptions of how the federal government spends their money. Although decisions about where to spend money will be some of the most important choices any president will make, it was clear that most voters had little idea where their federal taxes are spent.

We asked respondents which the federal government spent more on in 1992: foreign aid, the military, or welfare. The most popular answer, given by 42 percent, was foreign aid. In fact, foreign aid consumes a tiny proportion of the budget—just 1 percent, according to the Senate Budget Office. (Of the developed countries, the United States spends among the least per capita on foreign aid.) The second most popular answer, at 30 percent, was welfare, which consumes just 1.5 percent of the federal budget;[60] military spending was named by only 22 percent of our respondents—even though, at 21 percent of the budget, it is by far the largest of these three items, fourteen times larger than welfare spending.

How can we explain such an extraordinary misconception? Since most people relied on television for such information, it seems that TV news has done a poor job of communicating basic facts about how tax dollars are spent. Indeed, while public perceptions bore no relation to actual spending, they may have been a rational response to the extensive coverage given to the "welfare problem" and the need for "welfare reform," and to the oft-repeated and rarely challenged statement that the United States spends "too much" on foreign aid and not enough on folks at home. Reporting on military spending, on the other hand, has tended to focus on cutbacks and the negative consequences on jobs. (Reporting on the cutbacks in the nonmilitary budget that occurred throughout the Reagan-Bush years, by contrast, rarely focused on the consequent job losses.)

Part of the problem was that media took much of their agenda from the mainstream political candidates—so if major candidates were encouraging this distorted view, the media were more likely to report it than challenge it. It was not surprising, then, that these distortions were more vivid among heavy TV news viewers, particularly when it came to overestimating welfare and underestimating military spending.[61]

The political consequences of these distortions were complex, although they would appear to favor centrist and right-wing candidates. Bush may have benefited from misconceptions about welfare spending, while Clinton may have benefited if Bush were linked with inflated perceptions of foreign aid. A candidate on the left who supported foreign aid and welfare spending, and proposed major military cutbacks, would have to fight pervasive spending myths. Since Clinton, though not a candidate of the left, drew support from that direction, it was not surprising that Clinton supporters were the least likely to be misinformed on this issue, particularly on welfare and military spending. (Among Clinton supporters, military spending was more likely than welfare to be seen as the biggest expense, whereas Bush and Perot supporters were twice as likely to believe that welfare costs more than the military.)

Welfare spending was subject to a number of misconceptions. A majority in FAIR's survey (60 percent of those who ventured an opinion) overestimated the proportion of welfare recipients who are black, and 80 percent overestimated the average number of children women on welfare have. The average number of children ascribed to women on welfare by our respondents was 3.3. The actual number is 1.9. (Only 2 percent of our respondents underestimated this figure.)

Again, these misconceptions were linked to TV news viewing: Heavy TV news viewers were more likely to overestimate the proportion of people on welfare who are black and the number of children "welfare mothers" have. Only 35 percent of people who named TV news as their primary source of information, for example, did *not* overestimate the proportion of blacks on welfare, compared to 51 percent of people who got their news from other sources.

Another myth that has taken firm hold of the electorate is the issue of the tax burden on the middle class. FAIR asked, "Which income group pays the highest percentage of their income in state and local taxes: the richest 1 percent, the middle 20 percent, or the poorest 20 percent?" Although our respondents were extremely confident that they knew the answer to this (only 1 percent chose "don't know"), the vast majority, it turned out, did not. Only 11 percent gave the correct answer (the poorest 20 percent), while an overwhelming 85 percent incorrectly identified the middle 20 percent as the main victims of local tax inequities. This response seemed to reflect the emphasis by politicians and journalists on the "beleaguered middle class"; the beleaguered poor tend to be ignored by both.

Although voters seemed to be misinformed on some issues, on others they were simply confused. Reporters and politicians have become used to talking about the influence of "special interests" on politics, but who exactly are these "special interests?" When we asked this question of our respondents, we found that, even when prompted, almost a third (32 percent) could give no answer at all, a very high proportion of "don't know" responses. TV news viewers were particularly baffled by the term: 36 percent of those who chose TV news as their primary source of information said "don't know," compared to 26 percent of those who chose other sources.

Respondents who were able to identify "special interests" gave an extraordinary array of answers. Some respondents said the term referred to groups with the financial power to influence politicians, like corporations; others said that it meant groups that had special needs, like minorities or the disabled; others cited groups that focused on particular issues, like environmentalists or activists in the abortion debate or the National Organization for Women. Given the various ideas the phrase evoked in the public—and the large number who had no idea what it meant—perhaps journalists would have done well to use a more precise term or to explain what they meant when they said "special interests."

While most scholarly research on the media emphasizes the media's tilt toward mainstream or conservative views, the most well-known criticism has come from the political right, with conservatives from Spiro Agnew to Dan Quayle accusing them of having a liberal bias. The "liberal bias" criticism surfaced again during the 1992 election campaign, particularly during the Republican convention.

What did FAIR's survey reveal about the question of bias? First of all, it was clear that the Republicans had gotten their message about bias across: Although a plurality (45 percent) felt the media are "pretty balanced," the rest were four times more likely to see the media as liberal (34 percent) than conservative (8 percent). This did not, of course, prove the Republican case; on the contrary, it may simply suggest that the media actually give more space to criticism of themselves from the right than from the left. (Journalists would rather be seen as balanced, but may prefer to be attacked from the right as overzealous watchdogs of the establishment, rather than from the left as establishment lapdogs.)

In order to ask a question about media slant whose correct answer could be verified, we asked, "Overall, in recent presidential elections, would you say more newspapers have endorsed the more liberal candidates or the more conservative candidates?" Most people said that more liberals were endorsed (57 percent) than conservatives (27 percent). But in reality, every conservative candidate from Nixon in 1968 to Bush in 1988 received between 77 percent and 93 percent of daily newspaper endorsements.[62] The notion of "liberal bias" was thus assumed even when the evidence contradicted it.

The survey also provided little data to support the conservative claim of bias. As we have indicated, the Republicans were, on many issues, quite successful in getting their message across: When asked about using family influence to avoid going to Vietnam, people thought of Clinton and not Quayle; when asked who the big spenders are, they thought of Congress rather than Bush; when asked to evaluate Clinton's tax record in Arkansas, they preferred Republican claims to the independent assessments that contradicted them.

Overall, this study, conducted only a month before election day, painted a picture of a fairly uninformed electorate who still knew little about the candidates and even less about the underlying issues. On the whole, those who watched more TV news *did not* know more about the issues and in many cases appeared to know less about the realities of the political world. The questions asked about TV's poor coverage in the wake of the 1988 campaign remain with us.

Unfair to Bush? Unfair to Clinton? Campaign Coverage Was Unfair to Voters

December 1992

JIM NAURECKAS

THE QUESTION is not whether the media were unfair to George Bush or whether the media were unfair to Bill Clinton. The question the media have to ask themselves is whether they were fair to the American people.

After 1988, an election year dominated by nonissues, deceptive attacks, substanceless one-liners, and photo opportunities, the media promised they would do better next time. Just how little has changed was illustrated by an anecdote reported by the *Washington Post*—buried in a chronology of a day on the campaign trail.

The Bush campaign had staged an event at a restaurant called the Waffle House—an attempt to convey the message that Clinton was a "waffler." The problem was that there was no reference to Clinton's waffling in Bush's speech that day; in the terminology of campaign spin doctors, there was no sound bite to go with the visual. This was seen as a crisis by one of the reporters covering the Bush campaign: "Ann Compton of ABC News moves urgently from one staffer to another," the *Post* reported. "She buttonholes Marlin Fitzwater, corners Torie Clarke, sidles up to Mary Matalin. She tells each one: If you want Waffle House, we need Bush to say something about waffling!"[63]

Bush eventually came up with a waffling allusion, but it didn't satisfy Compton, according to the *Post* account. "It's still not quite right," she complained to Clarke. Keep in mind that Compton, the journalist who was helping Bush package an attack on Clinton, was one of the journalists selected to pose questions to the presidential candidates during the debates.

Does this blatant participation in the Bush campaign mean that Ann Compton or ABC News favored Bush? Probably not. Clinton got his share of photo opportunities, with all the shots of bus trips and hay bales. What the Waffle House anecdote shows is that the press was not just a passive victim of Lee Atwater-style manipulation but was at times an active participant in turning politics into show business.

Reporters who covered the 1992 campaign need to ask themselves a series of questions about how much coverage differed from 1988 and what can be changed for 1996.

DID REPORTERS RAISE THE LEVEL OF DEBATE?

The media's hunger for staged minidramas led to an overemphasis on attack lines and "zingers"—politics that could be explained in a punchy two-minute segment or an attention-grabbing headline. Occasionally, commentators would bemoan the fact that name-calling had become the building block of campaigns, but more often pundits seemed to approve of anything they saw as "good politics": "'Ozone' is a wickedly effective nickname for Al Gore," NBC's John Chancellor said in an election eve commentary, "and there was a wonderful clarity when the president spoke of bozos who don't know as much about foreign policy as his dog Millie. More talk like that earlier this year and Mr. Bush might not be in trouble now."[64]

Political commentators also cheapened political discourse by substituting "beauty contest" judgments for discussions of what the candidates were saying. By the last presidential debate, the standards were embarrassingly low: "The president really woke up tonight and I think came alive," PBS's David Gergen said.[65] "It was much the most spirited and aggressive performance he's had in a debate so far," was the evaluation of ABC's Brit Hume. "On the Iraqgate matter, he made a strong, I thought strongly worded defense of his policy, his actions toward Saddam Hussein."[66]

It is a mark of how removed pundits are from the substance of debates that Bush could face specific charges from two opponents that he promoted a hated enemy and that this could be considered a plus for Bush—as long as he appeared "strong," or "spirited," or "animated."

These qualities did not seem to impress voters—in all three debates, polls ranked either Perot or Clinton as doing best—so Bush was not the "winner" because what he said swayed voters. He "won" because his sound bites, attacks, and one-liners were what the network spin doctors identified as good debating—an indication of how media commentary can lower the quality of debate.

WAS POLITICAL REPORTING FOCUSED ON ISSUES?

To most voters, reports on campaign strategy and candidate trivia are not as important as discussions of how the election will impact the issues that affect their lives. A FAIR analysis of campaign coverage by the three network evening newscasts (from August 21, 1992—the day after the Republican convention—until October 1, 1992), however, found that only 17 percent of their election stories focused on policy issues.[67] Reports on economic topics (including taxes, the deficit, jobs, and general economic policy) accounted for nineteen stories—7 percent of total election coverage.

Foreign policy issues were covered in only seven stories—less than 3 percent of all reports—and these were wholly focused on domestic scandals or impacts. The health care crisis was covered in four segments, and family leave was the main topic in another three.

The topic of "family values," promoted as an issue at the Republican convention, was explored in four reports. No other policy issue was dealt with as often as even three times in the six-week period—including such major topics as the environment (two segments), abortion (one segment), AIDS (one segment), and welfare (one segment). Several important topics, such as education, crime, the military budget, racism, and the banking crisis, were not the subject of any campaign reports during the six weeks studied. In that time, as many reports dealt with the candidates' alleged resemblances to Harry Truman (four segments) as with AIDS, welfare, and the environment combined.

DID THE MEDIA GET SIDETRACKED BY CANDIDATES' PERSONAL LIVES?

Even more than in 1988, the media in 1992 were absorbed by reports and rumors about candidates' personal lives. In FAIR's survey of network campaign reporting, the single topic covered most frequently was Clinton's draft record—the focus of eighteen segments, 7 percent of all campaign coverage. Although the credibility questions raised by Clinton's account of his draft record were often compared to the questions about Bush's truthfulness about Iran-contra, there was more than four times as much coverage of the draft as Iran-contra.

The fascination with the "character issue" disproves those who argue that journalists' personal views determine what stories get covered. It's likely that few reporters who focused attention on issues like the draft, marijuana, extramarital sex, and cookie-baking thought these subjects were important in themselves. Yet they followed what was essentially a New Right agenda—harping on the issues that Republican strategists decided to emphasize because they determined that they couldn't win a campaign based around the economy.[68]

DID THE MEDIA DEBUNK CANDIDATES' FALSE CLAIMS?

Perhaps the most important role that the media can play in an election campaign is debunking candidates' false claims. The media did more of this in 1992 than they did in the previous election campaign, but it was still something they seemed squeamish about. As Michael Kinsley noted in the *Washington Post,* "Eventually the press throws up its hands and declares wearily that both sides have called each other dishonest long enough and it's time to move on."[69]

Often journalists were so reluctant to appear to be taking sides that attempts to correct the record were fudged. In the vice presidential debate, Dan Quayle charged that Al Gore's book, *Earth in the Balance,* proposed that "the taxpayers of America spend $100 billion a year on environmental projects in foreign countries." As the *New York Times* accurately pointed out the next day, what Gore said was that "an effort comparable to the Marshall Plan . . . would mean the expenditure of $100 billion a year. Mr. Gore notes in the book that such levels of spending would be impossible given the country's economic distress and calls on the other industrialized countries to contribute." But the *Times,* apparently afraid of seeming to say that the vice president was making up facts, included in its description of how Quayle distorted Gore's book this inexplicable disclaimer: "There are elements of truth in the statements of both men." The passage was labeled "Truth on Both Sides."[70]

CNN's Brooks Jackson did some of the most consistent and forthright work in setting the record straight: "Judging it just on the basis of facts, Dan Quayle is the big loser here tonight," he said in a postdebate report, while also correcting some of Gore's half-truths (like the line that 17,000 people had gone off welfare in Arkansas, when the total number on welfare had actually increased).[71] But the isolated attempts to debunk political distortions did not prevent CNN, like other news outlets, from allowing those claims to continue to dominate the lead news items without challenge.

There was more analysis of misleading commercials, but much of it was ineffective. Even a strongly worded rebuttal, if only shown once, does little to counteract the endless repetition of political ads, and some coverage was merely free exposure for the ads' messages. CBS ran all of the Christian Coalition's antigay ad, which claimed that "Bill Clinton's vision of a better America includes job quotas for homosexuals." Rather than correcting this false charge, reporter Richard Threlkeld merely commented: "Some on the religious right are running a TV ad campaign targeting Clinton's ties to the gay community."[72]

DID POLITICIANS DETERMINE HOW THEY WOULD BE QUESTIONED?

To get Bush to do three live interviews on *Good Morning America,* ABC agreed to restrict questioning to three subjects: taxes, crime, and health care. "We wanted to do the economy as well as health issues," *Good Morning America* executive producer Jack Reilly told Cox News Service's Julia Malone, but the Bush campaign refused. "Reilly said the agreement for the interviews also rules out questions on Bush's role in the Iran-contra arms-for-hostages scandal," Malone reported.[73]

When Dan Rather asked to interview Bush at the Republican convention, the Bush campaign replied that Connie Chung could talk to Bush instead. CBS responsibly declined to let the Bush camp decide how the network would cover the convention. On the other hand, in order to get an interview with Bush just before the convention, ABC's *This Week with David Brinkley* agreed to campaign demands that Brinkley alone would interview the candidate, not the usual panel of Brinkley, Sam Donaldson, and George Will. According to *Brinkley* producer David Glodt, the White House "assured us the interview with Brinkley is all we're going to get." When Al Gore was interviewed by the show, by contrast, he faced Brinkley, Will, and Brit Hume, the latter a regular contributor to the conservative *American Spectator.*[74]

DID REPORTERS FOLLOW THE MONEY?

Commentators treated the failure of the predicted anti-incumbent backlash to materialize—for the third election in a row—as a puzzle. The obvious explanation for the mysterious ability of incumbents to be reelected—that they generally have much more money than challengers—went mostly unstated.

The fact that U.S. politics are shaped to a great degree by candidates' dependence on wealthy funders is the great open secret of election reporting. One media outlet that violated this taboo was PBS's *Frontline,* which ran a documentary (coproduced by the Center for Investigative Reporting) in the last stretch of the campaign. *Frontline* connected the enormous contributions flowing to candidates to the policies the contributors wanted enacted—from Cuban exiles, who gave $125,000 to Clinton when he promised to support tightening the Cuban embargo, to ARCO, which gave about $1 million in total to the two major parties in hopes of being permitted to drill for oil in Alaska's Arctic National Wildlife Refuge.[75]

One case study *Frontline* examined involved Dwayne Andreas of the Archer-Daniels-Midland (ADM) agribusiness company, which got a Clean Air Act waiver for ethanol sales after giving $400,000 to the Republicans; *Frontline* also noted that *This Week with David Brinkley* is sponsored by ADM, and that Brinkley vacations with many of the politicians who benefit from ADM's largesse—connections that begin to suggest why examinations like *Frontline*'s are so rare.

Out of Focus
September 1992

"Focus groups are obsessed with the S&L bailout and are wondering why the press isn't covering it. Back in 1988, they were obsessed with Iran-contra. . . . But the press deemed Iran-contra too difficult for the public. Instead, the media fixated on the flag-burning amendment and the Pledge of Allegiance."

—The findings of Republican pollsters, as reported by Lynda Edwards in the *Village Voice*[76]

Notes

1. *New York Times,* March 4, 1990.
2. *CBS Evening News,* July 23, 1992.
3. *CBS Evening News,* March 12, 1992.
4. *CBS Evening News,* April 18, 1992.
5. See Lawrence Soley, "Brookings: Stand-In for the Left," *The Best of Extra!* (New York: FAIR, 1994).
6. *CBS Evening News,* November 22, 1991.
7. *CBS Evening News,* March 5, 1992.
8. *Chicago Tribune,* February 25, 1990.
9. *Washington Post,* July 12, 1992.
10. *Washington Post,* July 7, 1992.
11. *Washington Post,* July 12, 1992.
12. PBS, July 15, 1992.
13. NBC, July 13, 1992.
14. *Washington Post,* July 13, 1992.
15. *Washington Post,* July 14, 1992.
16. *New York Times,* June 7, 1992.
17. *New York Times,* March 3, 1992.
18. *Village Voice,* July 14, 1992.
19. William Greider, "Bill Clinton," *Rolling Stone,* April 30, 1992, p. 33.
20. Thomas Ferguson, "The Democrats Deal for Dollars," *The Nation,* April 13, 1992, pp. 475–478.
21. John B. Judis, "Clinton's Great Leap Forward," *In These Times,* March 11, 1992, p. 14.
22. *Capital Gang,* July 11, 1992.
23. *Los Angeles Times,* July 9, 1992.
24. *New York Times,* July 22, 1984.
25. *Chicago Tribune,* July 24, 1988.
26. *New York Times,* July 15, 1992.
27. *USA Today,* July 16, 1992.
28. *Boston Globe,* July 15, 1992.
29. Minneapolis *Star Tribune,* July 15, 1992.
30. *Washington Post,* July 18, 1984.
31. *Los Angeles Times,* July 24, 1988.

32. *Chicago Tribune,* July 19, 1988.
33. *Boston Globe,* July 12, 1992.
34. *Washington Post,* June 12, 1992.
35. *Washington Post,* July 17, 1984.
36. *Washington Post,* July 20, 1988.
37. *New York Newsday,* July 27, 1988.
38. *Christian Science Monitor,* July 23, 1984.
39. *Los Angeles Times,* July 24, 1988.
40. *Newsday,* July 25, 1988.
41. *Chicago Tribune,* July 24, 1988.
42. *Meet the Press,* July 17, 1988.
43. "Fear and Loathing at the Atlanta Convention," *Extra!,* July/August 1988, pp. 4–5; "Guide to the Media Myths of Campaign '92," *Extra!,* January/February 1992, pp. 25–26.
44. *Christian Science Monitor,* July 17, 1992.
45. *New York Times,* July 20, 1984.
46. *New York Times,* July 22, 1984.
47. *Christian Science Monitor,* July 20, 1984.
48. *Washington Post,* July 19, 1988.
49. *Washington Post,* July 20, 1984.
50. *New York Times,* July 21, 1988.
51. *Chicago Tribune,* July 24, 1988.
52. *Washington Post,* July 14, 1988.
53. *Los Angeles Times,* July 24, 1988.
54. *Washington Post,* August 20, 1992.
55. The methodology and complete results of the poll are available in Justin Lewis, Michael Morgan, and Andy Ruddock, *Images/Issues/Impact: The Media and Campaign '92* (Amherst, Mass.: Center for the Study of Communication, 1992).
56. *New York Times,* April 23, 1992.
57. *Washington Post,* August 26, 1992.
58. Lance Morrow, "Family Values," *Time,* August 31, 1992, p. 22.
59. Center for Responsive Politics, "Lawyers, Wall Street, Insurance Industry, Oil and Gas Lead All Contributors in 1992 Elections," press release, October 22, 1992.
60. The figure is for federal spending on Aid to Families with Dependent Children. If all federal spending on AFDC recipients is added in—including food stamps, Medicaid, and so on—the figure would rise to 3 percent. See Sharon Parrott, Center on Budget and Policy Priorities, "What Do We Spend on Welfare?" research memo, February 7, 1995.
61. "Heavy" television viewers said that they watched more than three hours of TV in an average day.
62. "634 for Nixon—146 for Humphrey," *Editor and Publisher,* November 2, 1968, pp. 9–12; "753 Dailies for Nixon; 56 Support McGovern," *Editor and Publisher,* November 4, 1972, pp. 9–13; George Will, "411 Dailies Support Ford; 80 for Carter; 168 Newspapers Are Uncommitted," *Editor and Publisher,* October 30, 1976, pp. 5–41; John Consoli, "Reagan Backed by 443 Dailies; Carter Trails with 126; Anderson with 40, and 439 Undecided," *Editor and Publisher,* November 1, 1980, pp. 9–13; Andrew Radolf, "A Newspaper Majority for Reagan," *Editor and Publisher,* November 3, 1984, pp. 9–12. Andrew Radolf, "Majority of Newspapers Don't Endorse," *Editor and Publisher,* October 29, 1988, pp. 9–11.
63. *Washington Post,* October 23, 1992.
64. *NBC Nightly News,* November 2, 1992.

65. PBS, October 19, 1992.
66. ABC, October 19, 1992.
67. The survey, conducted by FAIR research associate Kimberly Phillips, was originally reported in FAIR's campaign newsletter, *CounterSpin,* October 28, 1992.
68. *New York Times,* July 4, 1992.
69. *Washington Post,* September 3, 1992.
70. *New York Times,* October 14, 1992.
71. CNN, October 13, 1992.
72. *CBS Evening News,* October 29, 1992.
73. Cox News Service, September 28, 1992.
74. *New York Newsday,* September 29, 1992.
75. *Frontline,* October 27, 1992.
76. *Village Voice,* June 23, 1992.

6 Race and Gender in the '92 Election

Press Finds "New Candor" in Old Stereotypes

July/August 1992

JANINE JACKSON

REPORTS AND OPINION pieces in the mainstream press heralded speeches on the urban crisis given in March 1992 by Senators Bill Bradley (D.–N.J.) and John F. Kerry (D.–Mass.) as "courageous and important,"[1] "straight talk"[2] that expressed "bravery and candor."[3] *New York Times* columnist A. M. Rosenthal saw the senators' "clear and courageous thought" as proof that American politics is not an "intellectual wasteland."[4] *Washington Post* columnist David Broder was glad that Bradley and Kerry had not "minced words" as the presidential candidates do.[5]

In the Senate, Bradley described cities as "poorer, sicker, less educated and more violent" than he could remember.[6] Kerry, speaking at Yale, called the urban environment a "violent, drug-ridden, rat-infested reality ... ruled not simply by poverty, but by savagery."[7] What was so special, so brave and courageous about these comments? Did the senators introduce new proposals to check the "downward spiral" of poverty, unemployment, underfunded or nonexistent social services, and abandonment they so colorfully evoked?

Unfortunately not. Both Bradley and Kerry spoke in vague terms about "a new politics of change" or "a new social contract." But their substantive solutions were the same programs that have floated around for years.

What was different, and what the press found so provocative, was the senators' subsuming of myriad inner-city problems under the ill-defined but highly charged rubric of "the problem of race." The speeches introduced two "new" elements into the liberal discourse on race and urban poverty. First, they evoked poor blacks' "responsibility" for their own poverty and the "inexcusability" of "self-destructive behavior" (understood to range from crime and drug abuse to "out-of-wedlock births"). Second, the senators emphasized the need to appease both white "perceptions" of "reverse discrimination" and white fear of black people generally. These were the angles that several major papers picked up on and celebrated in their coverage.

A March 29, 1992, *New York Times* editorial, for example, cited positively Bradley's "blunt reminder" that the issue of race is crucial to the future of American cities, because "the economic future of the children of white Americans will increasingly depend on the talents of non-white Americans." This narrow vision is not problematic for the *Times*; for the paper, the only "flaws" in Bradley's speech were his failure to mention the black middle class and his overemphasis on enterprise zones.

Both the March 29 editorial and an April 13 *New York Times* article recited Bradley's claim that "many white Americans" seem to be saying of "some young black males, 'You litter the street and deface the subway, and no one, white or black, says stop. . . . You rob a store, rape a jogger, shoot a tourist, and when they catch you, if they catch you . . . you cry racism.'" For reporter Sam Roberts, these remarks constituted "the most candid comments on race and its consequences."[8]

The excerpts the press selected fairly accurately reflect the crude picture Bradley drew of black welfare recipients and white taxpayers, of black criminals and white victims. But considering the obvious potential for misinterpretation, press accounts also might have included other comments he made that rang differently.

Only readers of the full speech (or the extended excerpt in the May 12, 1992, *Chicago Tribune*) would know, for example, that Bradley suggested that the "absence of meaning" he decried in the lives of the black underclass was in part "derived from overt and subtle attacks from racist quarters over many years and furthered by an increasing pessimism about the possibility of justice." Or that Bradley said that for the country's poorest, "calls to 'just say no' to drugs or to 'study hard' for 16 years so you can get an $18,000-a-year job are laughable."

In the case of Senator Kerry's comments on affirmative action, however, the spin of some coverage approached distortion. In his speech at Yale, Kerry did say that affirmative action should not be the overriding focus of a civil rights agenda, because workplace gains do not necessarily touch the lives of those most in need.

But he also said, "I want to be clear here. I do support affirmative action, not rhetorically but really." The "negative side" of the policy, for Kerry, was the "perception" it engendered in many whites: He cited a poll by People for the American Way that indicated white people believe they are more discriminated against than minorities. Congress, Kerry said, has an obligation "to correct whatever false data or preconceptions have fed the belief that is evidenced in this poll."

Affirmative action, Kerry said, has "made our country a better, fairer place to live," but public misunderstanding of the policy—which Kerry acknowledged has been "exaggerated and exploited by politicians eager to use it"—has created an "obstacle" to interracial communication.

In the press, however, Kerry was "daring to challenge the liberal dogma on . . . affirmative action."[9] An April 5 *Boston Globe* piece described the speech as Kerry's "critique of affirmative action." *The New Republic* congratulated Kerry for exposing the "liberal affirmative action obsession," but complained that he had "not bitten the bullet yet: a rejection of affirmative action."[10]

John Leo at *U.S. News & World Report* welcomed Kerry's and Bradley's speeches as signs that the liberal "orthodoxy" was breaking down. Leo called Bradley and Kerry "political harbingers" of a new school of thought about race that "assumes that old strategies have been exhausted and something new must be tried."[11] In fact, the tenor of both speeches was that many possible strategies had not been seriously tried, due to political infighting and a lack of consensus and public will. And both senators emphasized the importance of shoring up, not abandoning, existing community organizations and programs like Head Start.

Two *Boston Globe* articles went beyond unqualified celebration of this "fresh approach" to racial questions and included dissenting points of view. John Aloysius Farrell's April 3 report acknowledged that some people think the emphasis on "personal responsibility" and a "tough anti-crime message" may be just "an easy way for politicians to win votes from resentful white voters while not advancing any other alternatives."

Anthony Flint's April 5 article in the *Globe* focused mainly on proponents of what has been termed "civic liberalism"—an emphasis on poor people's responsibility for their own problems. But also included were the skeptical responses of author Andrew Hacker ("It really means veering to the right") and civil rights advocate Roger Wilkins: "These people start with the question, What can we do about the fact that so many people are upset about affirmative action? . . . The right question is: Is there still a racial question in this country, which affirmative action addresses effectively, and if so, how do we make it a more popular public policy?"

Senator Bradley mentioned "sensational news stories" as contributing to whites' fears of blacks. Indeed, skewed coverage of welfare recipients, crime, and drug addiction does contribute to racial tensions. Whether the press can shift from being part of the problem to part of the solution remains to be seen, although *New York Times* headlines like "'No Place Seems Safe'"[12] and "Race Meets Race, But Fear Is Faster"[13] do not bode well.

For a truly new dialogue about race and class, the media must make more of an effort to include disparate points of view, to critically examine such loaded terms as "black criminality" and "welfare dependency," and to make difficult but important distinctions, like that between personal prejudices and institutionalized racism. The press needs to be as interested in the crafting of urban and social policy as it is in fiery rhetoric. And they need to air the views not only of the politicians who already have easy access to the media but of the inhabitants of the "rat-infested reality" who may want to speak for themselves.

A Short Walk on the Wilder Side

April/May 1992

STEVE COBBLE

THE PUNDITS had a dream—that Virginia Governor Douglas Wilder (D.) would drive Jesse Jackson from the public stage. Doug Wilder, a self-described fiscal conservative who advocated budget cuts, supported capital punishment, and bragged of his state's "right-to-work" (antiunion) laws, was a moderate black who would, in the words of *The Almanac of American Politics 1992*, "undercut Jesse Jackson, whose radical policies and angry demeanor have hurt Democrats so much with American voters."[14]

Most of this wishful thinking came out after Wilder's 1989 gubernatorial victory. "Democratic strategists are already calculating that Mr. Wilder's victory is . . . bad news for Jesse Jackson," reported the *Baltimore Sun*.[15] "We may be seeing the sun beginning to set on 'the Jesse Jackson era,'" predicted the *Boston Globe*'s Robert Jordan.[16] "If I were Jesse Jackson," said Rowland Evans, "I'd be a little afraid of the governor of Virginia."[17]

"Does the Democratic Party finally have Jesse Jackson off its back?" asked *The McLaughlin Group*'s John McLaughlin.[18] Said George Will, "Jesse Jackson now must look around and see there are lots of other responsible office-holding black leaders, so he cannot wag the Democratic Party quite so much."[19]

Juan Williams, in the *Washington Post Magazine,* went so far as to call Wilder "arguably the most important black American politician of the 20th Century," arguing, "It is not just that Wilder is an alternative to the best-known black spokesman, Jesse Jackson: His success is a rebuke to Jackson's 1980s political vision of blacks as America's victims."[20]

Such talk almost immediately led Wilder to enter the presidential race, despite an approval rating in his home state that eventually dropped to 23 percent. Dozens of pundits had assured him that his moderate politics would attract more white support than Jackson's fiery populism, while maintaining the same African-American base Jackson commanded.

Jackson received 3.5 million votes in 1984; in 1988, he won 7 million, including almost 2.5 million white and Latino votes. In his second run, he was supported by 92 percent of African-American voters and took 29 percent of all votes cast. When he took himself out of the 1992 race, he was leading or was second to Mario Cuomo in all polls.

Wilder didn't even make it to the first primary in 1992, dropping out with 1 percent in the New Hampshire polls.

The lesson is clear: Rather than appointing leaders (only one of whom can be African American at any one time, it seems), the conventional wisdom should wait to let the voters decide.

Clinton's Willie Horton?

September 1992

BILL CLINTON'S CRITICISM of rapper Sister Souljah was part of a clear, if somewhat peculiar, political strategy: Identify those voting blocs most likely to support you, and alienate them.[21] This strategy was outlined in a David Broder and Thomas Edsall *Washington Post* piece just before the Rainbow Coalition conference: "Some top advisers to Clinton argue that . . . he must become involved in highly publicized confrontations with one or more Democratic constituencies." According to the *Post*, key aides wanted Clinton to "confront [Jesse Jackson] and his followers."[22]

Regardless of what one thinks of Sister Souljah, Clinton's focus on her was clearly one of those deliberately staged provocations, and Clinton's spin doctors were out in force, making sure that reporters did not miss the significance of Clinton "standing up" to Jackson. But as Michael Tomasky, who covered the Rainbow Conference for the *Village Voice*, accurately predicted: "Guess which one, Clinton or Jackson, will be called, as the convention approaches, 'divisive'?"[23]

Pundits nearly unanimously praised Clinton's "courage" in taking on the rap singer. (Criticizing Murphy Brown is silly; criticizing Sister Souljah is bold.) The refusal to recognize what was going on was epitomized by a June 17, 1992, *New York Times* editorial headlined "Sister Souljah Is No Willie Horton"—the distinction being that "these were hateful remarks."[24] It was as if Bush's exploitation of the Horton case was objectionable because it unfairly made the rapist seem like a bad guy.

In fact, the Horton and Souljah gambits were parallel—a politician attempted to win white votes by focusing attention on an irrelevant issue that resonated with white fears of black violence. As the Clinton handlers quoted above explained, the "confrontation" wasn't with Souljah or Jackson, but with a "constituency"—in other words, blacks. Rather than critical coverage of this calculated race-baiting, the press offered praise: "Clinton Deftly Navigates Shoals of Racial Issues," a June 17 *New York Times* news report was headlined.[25]

Jackson, on the other hand, was widely denounced as an "egotistical party wrecker"[26] who will "not sleep well if another Democrat" wins the presidency.[27] Some caricatures of Jackson were remarkably crude and vicious—a cartoon in the Portland *Oregonian* portrayed Jackson as a rapper demanding that Clinton "grovel like Mike in '88";[28] the *New York Post* showed a snarling Jackson holding a gun to Clinton's head, threatening to "waste him."[29]

One exceptionally nasty and inaccurate attack on Jesse Jackson came from CBS's Dan Rather: "There have always been two Jesse Jacksons—there's Jesse the radical, who preaches rage and black separatism . . . and there's Jesse the self-promoter, who preaches desegregation and compromise." Rather claimed that suburban voters, whom he said constituted most of the electorate, are "not in the mood to see much more money spent on the poor."[30] Yet in a May 11 CBS/*New York Times* poll, 60 percent of respondents said too little was being spent on problems of the big cities, with only 15 percent saying too much was being spent. Sixty-one percent said too little was being spent on improving conditions of blacks, while 10 percent said too much. Was the poll flawed, or was Rather parroting the line of conservative Democrats who say you can't appeal to both the poor and the middle class?

Women Candidates in 1992 Election Coverage

September 1992

TIFFANY DEVITT AND JANINE JACKSON

THE YEAR 1988, the press reported, would be a breakthrough year for women in politics. But in the end, only two additional women were elected to the House of Representatives, none to the Senate. In 1990, Americans were again told we were seeing the "Year of the Woman." But though seventy women won major party nominations that year, the numbers in Congress did not change. In 1992, the experts said, they were serious: 1992 would really and truly be the "Year of the Woman" in American politics.

The repeated recourse to the "Year of the Woman" tag was some indication of the simplistic and superficial tone of much of the coverage of 1992's female congressional candidates, as revealed by a FAIR survey of major dailies and television news. The number of women running for Congress from the two major parties was unprecedented—in the primaries, 18 aimed for Senate seats and 153 ran for the House.[31] But from the hyperbole of reporters, one would gather that women were on the verge of taking over the U.S. government.

Of all the media outlets surveyed, the *New York Times* seemed the most overheated. Characterizing 1992 as a "historic watershed,"[32] *Times* articles heralded the "political ascendancy of women,"[33] made much of women's "stunning clout,"[34] and predicted "an avalanche" of female victories.[35]

At least one letter-writer to the *Times* attempted to put things in perspective, reminding reporters and editors that "to have representative numbers of women and minorities in positions of leadership and power in this country, we will need far more than the five new women in the Senate and 20 in the House of Representatives that you project."[36] Even *multiplying* the number of women in the Senate by five (from two to ten) would have left that institution 90 percent male.

Press and TV accounts blurred individual distinctions among the nearly 200 candidates, routinely linking and effectively equating such different politicians as Carol Moseley Braun, a progressive from Illinois who ran a successful grassroots campaign against incumbent Senator Alan Dixon, and former San Francisco mayor Dianne Feinstein, who had vetoed a city ordinance extending comparable-worth laws to municipal employees, supported the death penalty, and once gave the keys of the city of San Francisco to deposed Philippine dictator Ferdinand Marcos.

Women's political orientations—unlike men's—were assumed to be defined and driven by gender. "In New York, Gender Politics Rule," according to a *USA Today* headline[37]—simply because there were two women running for the same U.S. Senate seat.

Lumping all women candidates together, the news reports FAIR surveyed frequently employed generalizations and stereotypes about women's supposed values, concerns, and abilities. Some of these stereotypes were familiar and crude, as when a *New York Newsday* headline quipped, "Will Women Pols Clean House?"[38] A *New York Times* piece by R. W. Apple referred to "former Marin County housewife" Barbara Boxer, as if that were the most germane designation for a woman who had served ten years in the House of Representatives.[39] Senatorial candidate Boxer was also dubbed a "feisty little woman,"[40] and columnist Suzanne Fields referred to the Senate contest between Elizabeth Holtzman and Geraldine Ferraro as "the cat fight at the New York corral."[41]

Stereotypes also were evident in analysis that uncritically employed the "conventional wisdom" about women candidates' supposed interests and areas of expertise. In a May 30, 1992, broadcast, ABC News's Cokie Roberts delivered the standard line that "the recent riots in Los Angeles could make it a lot harder for women to win," and suggested that women candidates' chances for success would depend on whether voters wanted "tough law and order solutions or more tender social policies."

A May 25 *New York Times* article reported that although racial violence and the economy were the "dominant issues" in California's Senate contest, candidates Feinstein and Boxer were being watched for what they said about "women and women's issues." Their contributions were important, the article indicated, "in the aftermath of several major rape trials, developments in the abortion rights debate and . . . hearings on sexual harassment."

Most accounts of women in politics tended to focus on narrowly defined "women's issues." Many issues that disproportionately affect women (such as poverty, since two-thirds of poor adults are women) were not considered women's issues, and women candidates' views on general issues of public policy were often not considered significant.

Not only were women assigned selected issues but the media very often made assumptions about what their positions on those issues were. This made it possible for 53 percent of the electorate to be spoken of—and often dismissed—as a homogeneous "special interest group," with the tacit assumption of a shared, dogmatic agenda.

A major current in mainstream coverage was overblown rhetoric about women's "anger and frustration." A May 3 *New York Times* headline read: "Another Angry Woman Wins Senate Nomination." *USA Today*'s Al Neuharth suggested that women might even win the presidency, if they "keep their dander up."[42] One article spoke of a mood of "feminine revenge."[43]

From many accounts, one would think that American women's interest in politics sprang into existence at the Clarence Thomas/Anita Hill hearings. The so-called "Thomas factor" got a mention in virtually every report about women's candidacies. Women's anger and frustration are real enough, but this sort of coverage played on a disparaging theme of women's political engagement as primarily emotion-driven and irrational.

Nowhere was the allegedly monolithic quality of women more noticeable than in the ubiquitous characterization of female candidates as "outsiders." Repeatedly—and usually unequivocally—press accounts and broadcasts described women as "ultimate" and "quintessential" outsiders, regardless of who they were or what they'd accomplished.

Most women who ran for the U.S. Senate or House in 1992 had extensive records in electoral politics. Barbara Boxer, as noted, served in the House of Representatives for ten years; Dianne Feinstein had been in public office for more than two decades; and, of course, Geraldine Ferraro was a former vice-presidential candidate.

But even articles that took note of candidates' individual histories inside the Beltway stubbornly held to the "outsider" label. For instance, an article in *USA Today* acknowledged that neither Feinstein nor Boxer was a "newcomer," but nonetheless proclaimed that their "outsider" candidacies were "shaking up the political establishment" in California.[44]

Lynn Yeakel's victory in the Democratic primary for the Pennsylvania Senate race fostered much of the "Year of the Woman" coverage. Although Yeakel had never held an elected position, it's hard to see someone whose father served three terms in the House of Representatives as the "ultimate outsider."[45]

In addition to the simple inaccuracy of labeling many of the women competing for office in 1992 as "outsiders," the assumption was that women candidates' political value was rooted more in their disengagement from the political process than in their platforms and programs.

The hype about women as "outsiders" spawned the myth that women politicians had a distinct *advantage* by virtue of their gender: "The Republicans facing Democrats Dianne Feinstein and Barbara Boxer for California's two Senate seats start with what could be a new handicap—they're men," reported *USA Today*.[46] Sexism in politics, it seems, only hurt men that year.

Reports on the supposed "gender advantage" and descriptions of women's candidacies as a "flood," "wave," or "avalanche" provided an excuse for defeated men. As Gray Davis, who lost to Dianne Feinstein, suggested, "This might not have been the best year to be a man."[47]

Some reports implied that women's candidacies somehow lacked the legitimacy of men's, as exemplified by a *Washington Times* headline that asserted, "Women Crowd Race."[48] The *New York Times* suggested insufficient gratitude on the part of women toward men who had previously defended their interests: "Old Allies Pushed Aside" ran the subtitle of one article.[49]

Rarely did press accounts acknowledge the obstacles women political candidates continue to face in raising money and securing endorsements, both because they are women and because they generally don't have the benefits of incumbency. Both Carol Moseley Braun and Lynn Yeakel, for instance, ran in the primaries without the backing of the Democratic Party. Even articles that reported the fact that their opponents were raising more money still touted these women's political "advantage."

Still more exceptional was reporting that discussed the ways that sexism undermines women's effectiveness once in office. *USA Today* published a survey of women in Congress that found "deep frustration tempered by a reluctance to criticize publicly the men whose cooperation they depend on day to day." Reporters Leslie Phillips and Patricia Edmonds summarized their findings: "Even if [women] win, victory will be far from a dream come true.... No woman has been elected to a leadership position in Congress. No woman holds a full committee chairmanship, the source of real power. The lack of seniority is to blame. But so too is the male culture on Capitol Hill."[50]

It is a trivialization of women's political involvement, as candidates and as supporters, to suggest that it is merely a trend or an anomaly, the result of a unique "confluence of factors" that may never recur.

Analysts like Ruth Mandel of the Center for the Study of American Women and Politics at Rutgers University pointed out that women were positioned to run for, and win, higher offices, not because of some sudden burst of interest or opportunity, but because of years of hard work and slow, steady gains at the local and state levels. In a May 28, 1992, *Newsday* interview, Mandel emphasized what the press usually missed, that "no single year is the year of the woman candidate."

While the press was declaring its 1990 version of the "Year of the Woman" a bust, for example, because the predicted congressional victories did not materialize, women won more than half of the eighty-five statewide seats for which they competed. The media's inconstant attentions both overhype women's potential gains and downplay real progress. Moreover, even as it might temporarily benefit women candidates and their fund-raising efforts, mainstream media's "Year of the Woman" coverage lumps and labels women's political concerns and, at its worst, threatens to deepen the same tired old stereotypes that hold women back.

Ladies' Man
September 1992

When Texas Governor Ann Richards spoke at the Democratic convention, NBC's Tom Brokaw described her as "known for her hairdo."[51] Brokaw gave a similar introduction to Geraldine Ferraro at the 1984 Democratic Convention: "The first woman to be nominated for vice president—size 6!"[52]

The Media Factor Behind the "Hillary Factor"

October/November 1992

DOROTHEE BENZ

HILLARY CLINTON became one of the most hotly debated subjects in the 1992 presidential campaign. The media eagerly focused on the battle of insults, images, and "values" that she symbolized, often characterizing her as a "lightning rod" for criticism. At the Democratic National Convention, a "new" Hillary Clinton was unveiled to much media fanfare. At the Republican National Convention, attacks on the would-be First Lady reached a fever pitch when she was derided as a "radical feminist," as "anti-family," and as unduly influential in her husband's career. Her role was one of the most charged issues in the "cultural war" declared by the Republicans, a role the media significantly helped to create.

Hillary Clinton was victimized by social expectations and political traditions that are still remarkably sexist in their prescription of what women (and especially wives) can and cannot do. While to a certain extent journalists simply reflected the prejudiced assumptions and actions of the Clinton and Bush campaigns, and of the public, the sexist biases of news organizations also helped to create and fuel this phenomenon. These biases were expressed in the fixation on a few anecdotes and quotes about Hillary Clinton's views about marriage and domestic work and in the traditional and often conservative vocabulary used to discuss these issues.

It all started, of course, with the Tammy Wynette incident. During an interview with both Clintons on the rumors of Bill Clinton's marital infidelity, Hillary Clinton told CBS's *60 Minutes* that she was not "some little woman standing by my man like Tammy Wynette."[53] Before anyone had a chance to gauge whether country music fans, or others, were offended by the remark, news outlets all over the country jumped on it, rebroadcasting and reprinting it regularly for weeks.

Similarly, reporters instantly seized upon Hillary Clinton's comment in mid-March that she "could have stayed home and baked cookies and had teas" instead of pursuing a career. That remark had been made in response to Jerry Brown's accusation of conflicts of interest arising from the Arkansas government's relations with Hillary Clinton's law firm, but it was consistently represented by the media as an affront to homemakers.

In both cases, the press immediately characterized Clinton's remarks as "gaffes" and "mistakes," a characterization that helped ensure they were perceived that way.

Cookies became a pivotal symbol in the portrayal of Hillary Clinton. In addition to the oft-repeated tea-and-cookies line, cookies figured heavily in the "new" Hillary Clinton, the one that entered her chocolate chip recipe in a bake-off with Barbara Bush. "A Conflict for the Governor? Have a Cookie" was the *Los Angeles Times* headline on an April 5, 1992, column. In an article on Hillary Clinton's commencement address to Wellesley graduates, the *Los Angeles Times*'s opening quote was her remark that women can help America "by making policy or making cookies."[54]

A *New York Newsday* July 13 article on the "new" Hillary Clinton mentioned cookies no less than five times. "Mrs. Clinton, a lawyer, talks these days about her cookie recipe" is the featured pull-out quote from the same day's *New York Times*. It got to the point where the *Los Angeles Times*'s January 1992 reference to Clinton as "one smart, determined cookie" seemed like an uncanny foreshadowing of the dominant imagery of the campaign.[55]

The cookie obsession worked to keep the issue of women's roles as homemakers up front. Whether the campaigns were projecting Hillary Clinton as "superwife" or arguing that she was not domestic enough, the cookie was the symbol of Hillary Clinton's fitness as a woman. As such, it framed debate about her in the terms preferred by the Republicans. The result was that many substantive issues, both advantageous and disadvantageous for the Clintons (e.g., her work on education reform, or the alleged conflict of interest caused by her position in Arkansas's biggest law firm), were simply not explored.

By late March 1992, Hillary Clinton's "controversial" remarks had been transformed into an "issue" in the campaign. "Will Hillary Hurt or Help?" was the title of a March 30 *Newsweek* piece, echoed by *U.S. News & World Report*'s April 27 cover story, "Hillary Clinton: Does She Help or Hurt?" "For some, she's an inspiring mother-attorney," the *U.S. News* piece began. "Others see in her the overbearing yuppie wife from hell—a sentiment that led GOP media guru Roger Ailes to quip that 'Hillary Clinton in an apron is like Michael Dukakis in a tank.'" The Ailes line was frequently repeated, and the "yuppie wife" comment was also subsequently quoted in several other publications. By summer, everyone knew what *Newsweek* meant when it put "the Hillary Factor" on its cover,[56] or when the *New York Times* headlined an item "The Hillary Clinton Issue."[57]

As Barbara Ehrenreich wrote of the "Hillary: Asset or Liability?" stories, "Of course, to ask the question, in bold black headlines, is simultaneously to provide the answer."[58]

For Hillary Clinton, the process of assimilating more to the profile of the so-called "traditional wife" began more than a decade ago, when she abandoned her last name and her wire-frame glasses. By the time of the Democratic National Convention in July 1992, the headband, the shoulder pads, and any mention of her advisory role had gone the same way. The "new" Hillary was splashed all over the front pages, cookies and all.

New York Newsday's July 13 cover story announced, "She's Come a Long Way," a phrase unmistakably reminiscent of the sexist Virginia Slims ad slogan. The article spoke of her new soft pastel image in contrast to her former "acerbic observations," "take-no-prisoners style," and "hard edges."

The *New York Times* introduced the makeover with the headline: "A Softer Image for Hillary Clinton." The July 13, 1992, story focused on the political calculus of the new image but nonetheless relied on a set of words and expectations that have been traditionally used to circumscribe women's roles. It spoke, for instance, of Mrs. Clinton's "forceful" speaking style and implied that her "fugues into technocratic prose" were off-putting. As an example of the latter, the *Times* quoted her as saying that her husband had decided to run because "the country was trending in the wrong direction on so many indicators."[59] Evidently, the *Times* thinks that economic jargon is not ladylike and should be left to the paper's economic writers.

News stories used other types of loaded language to describe Hillary Clinton. She was often characterized as "ambitious," "aggressive," and "interfering"—words that have long been considered pejorative in reference to women. *U.S. News & World Report* went so far as to say, "Much has been made of Hillary's ambition—and rightly so."[60] By contrast, the new Hillary is most often described with the word "softer," a description that again relies on long-standing gender stereotypes of women's appropriate behavior.

The sexism inherent in the role carved out for Hillary Clinton was perhaps best captured by a *New York Times* vignette from the first Clinton campaign bus tour: "Each day, Mrs. Gore and Mrs. Clinton—arms linked around each other's waists—waved at crowds and then stepped into the background to gaze adoringly while their husbands spoke."61 While this description dutifully reflected a carefully choreographed (sexist) appeal constructed by the campaign, the *Times*'s assertion that the women gazed "adoringly" at the men gave the image a sort of happy, nothing's-wrong-with-this-picture spin that served to reinforce rather than challenge its prejudice.

Hillary-bashing was a major sport at the Republican National Convention, so much so that *Nightline* did a report on it and asked whether it was fair or appropriate.62 In fact, some of the media's critiques of Republican attempts to paint Clinton as a radical feminist and turn her into a symbol of "anti-family values" were hard-hitting and accurate. The *New York Times* ran a well-researched article entitled "Legal Scholars See Distortion in Attacks on Hillary Clinton,"63 and a *New York Newsday* report bluntly asserted, "A key problem is that the Republican charges don't hold up."64

But in many ways, the media's response to Republican distortions of Clinton's views was an exercise in biting their own tails. Their coverage helped create "the Hillary Factor," even if they recoiled from the way it was exploited by the Republicans.

Playing Games with Rape and Sexual Harassment

June 1992

A MARCH 1992 *CBS Evening News* segment on "Public Figures, Private Lives" asked the question, "Where should news organizations draw the line between telling you what makes a candidate run and what the candidate's been doing with his or her personal life?"65

Correspondent Mark Phillips cast the issue of sexual politics as a bizarre board game, with spaces marked "Trouble" (illustrated with a blonde woman in a low-cut dress) and "She Goes Public." "Any politician playing the political game this year," Phillips claimed, "runs the risk of landing in trouble if he's conducted any indiscretion in the past—or if someone says he's committed an indiscretion (no proof necessary)."

Phillips wrapped up his report: "All of which begs the question as to whether presidential candidates would be better off coming straight out of monasteries or convents, whether by insisting on absolutely clean private lives, many potentially attractive candidates are being eliminated." His on-camera experts concurred: "The message we're sending out to more and more people is don't run—don't run if you have any embarrassment in your past," said the University of Virginia's Larry Sabato. "One could suggest that we should take 100 male babies and 100 female babies, remove their gonads at birth, and raise them to be future presidents," quipped Democratic Party consultant Mark Siegel.

With hyperbole like that, it's useful to look at what kind of "indiscretions" CBS had in mind: "Already we've had the damaging sexual allegations against Bill Clinton and against Washington Senator Brock Adams [D.]—this in a year where the ground was prepared by the grimy public detailing of charges against a Supreme Court nominee, and a high society rape trial in which the country was captivated by a blue blob."

CBS lumped together reports of marital infidelity on the part of Clinton with charges that Senator Adams drugged and raped at least one staff member and harassed and molested several others. It linked these cases to allegations of sexual harassment and rape against other public figures. Apparently, these are the kinds of "indiscretions" and "embarrassments" that CBS thinks are only absent from the "private lives" of monks and eunuchs.

Notes

1. "Notebook," *The New Republic,* April 27, 1992, p. 8.
2. John Leo, "Straight Talk About Race," *U.S. News & World Report,* April 20, 1992, p. 27.
3. *New York Times,* March 29, 1992.
4. *New York Times,* April 21, 1992.
5. *Washington Post,* April 5, 1992.
6. Senator Bill Bradley's quotations in this section are from "Race and the American City," *Congressional Record,* 102d Cong., 2d sess., March 26, 1992.
7. Senator John Kerry's quotations in this section are from "Race, Politics, and the Urban Agenda," a speech at New Haven, Connecticut, sponsored by Yale University, March 30, 1992.
8. *New York Times,* April 13, 1992.
9. *Boston Globe,* April 3, 1992.
10. "Notebook," *The New Republic,* April 27, 1992, p. 8.
11. John Leo, "Straight Talk About Race," *U.S. News & World Report,* April 20, 1992, p. 27.
12. *New York Times,* March 29, 1992.
13. *New York Times,* April 13, 1992.
14. Michael Barone and Grant Ujifusa, *The Almanac of American Politics 1992* (New York: Macmillan, 1991).
15. *Baltimore Sun,* November 9, 1989.
16. *Boston Globe,* December 4, 1989.
17. CNN, December 31, 1989.
18. *McLaughlin Group,* November 11, 1989.
19. *This Week with David Brinkley,* November 12, 1989.

20. Juan Williams, "One-Man Show," *Washington Post Magazine,* June 9, 1991, p. W13.

21. Clinton had attacked the rapper, whom Jesse Jackson had invited to a Rainbow Coalition conference, for saying, "If black people kill black people every day, why not have a week and kill white people?" (See *Washington Post,* June 14, 1992.) Her statement was originally published in a May 13, 1992, *Washington Post* interview. She later insisted that she was referring to the mindset of black gang members, not advocating the murder of whites: "White people, this government and that mayor were well aware of the fact that black people were dying every day in Los Angeles under gang violence," she continued in the original interview. "Do you think that somebody thinks that white people are better, or above dying, when they would kill their own kind?"

22. *Washington Post,* June 12, 1992.

23. *Village Voice,* June 23, 1992.

24. *New York Times,* June 17, 1992.

25. *New York Times,* June 17, 1992.

26. Lucy Howard and Ned Zeman, "Conventional Wisdom Watch: Clinton Veepstakes Edition," *Newsweek,* June 29, 1992, p. 4.

27. Michael Kramer, "The Political Interest: The Green-Eyed Monsters," *Time,* June 29, 1992, p. 49.

28. Jack Ohman, cartoon, *Newsweek,* June 29, 1992, p. 17; *Sunday Oregonian,* June 21, 1992.

29. *New York Post,* June 24, 1992.

30. *CBS Evening News,* July 13, 1992.

31. In the general election, eleven major-party Senate candidates and 106 major-party House candidates were women (including incumbents running for reelection). Five of the women were elected to the Senate and forty-seven were elected to the House (*Los Angeles Times,* November 6, 1992).

32. *New York Times,* June 3, 1992.

33. *New York Times,* June 7, 1992.

34. *New York Times,* June 4, 1992.

35. *New York Times,* May 29, 1992.

36. *New York Times,* June 14, 1992.

37. *USA Today,* June 22, 1992.

38. *New York Newsday,* May 27, 1992.

39. *New York Times,* June 3, 1992.

40. *New York Times,* June 1, 1992.

41. See Tiffany Devitt and Janine Jackson, "More Than We Bargained For?" *Extra!,* September 1992, p. 15.

42. *USA Today,* May 1, 1992.

43. *USA Today,* May 20, 1992.

44. *USA Today,* June 6, 1992.

45. *New York Times,* April 29, 1992.

46. *USA Today,* June 4, 1992.

47. *Los Angeles Times,* June 4, 1992.

48. *Washington Times,* April 13, 1992.

49. *New York Times,* May 29, 1992.

50. *USA Today,* April 1, 1992.

51. NBC, July 13, 1992.

52. NBC, July 18, 1984.

53. *60 Minutes,* January 26, 1992.
54. *Los Angeles Times,* May 30, 1992.
55. *Los Angeles Times,* January 29, 1992.
56. *Newsweek,* July 20, 1992.
57. *New York Times,* August 24, 1992.
58. *New York Newsday,* July 15, 1992.
59. *New York Times,* July 13, 1992.
60. *U.S. News & World Report,* April 27, 1992.
61. *New York Times,* July 23, 1992.
62. *Nightline,* August 18, 1992.
63. *New York Times,* August 24, 1992.
64. *New York Newsday,* August 21, 1992.
65. *CBS Evening News,* March 5, 1992.

PART THREE

Clinton and the Media Agenda

7 Promises to Break: The New Administration

*Pundits to Clinton:
Break Campaign Promises,
Ignore "Liberal Interests,"
Join Washington Insiders*

January/February 1993

JIM NAURECKAS

THE JOCKEYING by presidential candidates to win the support of pundits and funders is known as the "invisible primary." Bill Clinton won that primary in 1992 by presenting himself as the kind of centrist politician that political insiders are comfortable with: "tough" on foreign policy, skeptical of social programs, and friendly toward business.

In the real primaries, Clinton often ran a very different campaign. He criticized his Democratic opponents for policies he said would favor the rich at the expense of people of ordinary means. In the general election, he attacked the Bush administration for its "trickle-down economics" and for being captive to corporate lobbyists and contributors, whom he called "special interests." His promise to be a change from twelve years of Reaganism paid off, especially among women and nonwhite voters. (If only white men had voted, George Bush would have been re-elected.)

After Clinton was elected president, he had to decide which election returns he would listen to—the voice of the people or the voice of the elite. That choice was greatly shaped by feedback from the media, which immediately began calling for Clinton to abandon some of the promises he was elected on.

"The fun in the coming year will be watching Mr. Clinton juggle in the center ring," Thomas Friedman commented in a *New York Times* news analysis, "juggling Democratic supporters who will be alienated by the special interest promises he fails to keep and juggling Republican and Perot conservatives who will be outraged by the special interest promises on which he delivers."[1]

Friedman's use of the phrase "special interests" to disparage progressive constituencies like women, African Americans, and environmentalists, was a hallmark of postelection commentary. (It's ironic that these were the only "special interests" that journalists recognized, when during Clinton's campaign the pejorative term had increasingly returned to its original meaning of moneyed elites.)

A CNN report argued that Clinton need not do much for what the network called "special interest groups"—the only ones mentioned were environmentalists, women, blacks, and gays. Perennial pundit Norman Ornstein of the American Enterprise Institute was quoted as saying that Clinton "enters office with the fewest debts owed to interest groups in his own party of any Democratic president in modern times."[2] The business groups that contributed heavily to Clinton and the Democrats evidently didn't count.

Steven V. Roberts, writing in *U.S. News & World Report*, was more specific about what promises Clinton should consider breaking, on such issues as abortion, family leave, urban aid, and civil rights. Roberts presented "liberal interest groups" as greedy, demanding, and powerful, as with the groups calling for District of Columbia statehood, an issue that candidate Clinton had vowed to support: "Some of Clinton's aides fear that if he bows to black groups and pushes the measure, it could squander time and resources that he cannot afford."[3]

The last group of "liberal stalwarts" Roberts warned Clinton against were Common Cause and other proponents of campaign finance reform (which could be a "wasting battle" for the president). He then concluded: "How Clinton performs in these early battles will provide important clues to his character. Is he really a new form of Democrat? Or is he what Bush accused him of being: a free-spending liberal dressed up as a moderate?" In this Orwellian formulation, Clinton could *avoid* campaign finance reform to prove that he was a "new Democrat" who would stand up to "interest groups."

The key thing for many in the Washington political elite, including journalists, was that Clinton become part of their culture. "You have to run against 'inside Washington' to get in and you have to become inside Washington to stay in," advised Sally Quinn in the *Washington Post*. She quoted a Carter-era official who asserted that there was "nothing sinister" about the fact that "government contacts and access . . . create power." Quinn scolded Clinton for not picking corporate lawyer Mickey Kantor to run his transition team.[4]

Between the election and the inauguration, there was some strong reporting on the corporate ties of the people who were running Clinton's transition—much tougher, in fact, than the scrutiny given to the links of the Reagan and Bush administrations to big business. But there were limits to how critical media outlets could be of Clinton for, for example, relying on a corporate board-hopper like Vernon Jordan to run his transition team. After all, the media's own corporate boards are populated by exactly the same kinds of people.

What can happen when national newspapers criticize Washington insiders was illustrated by an extraordinary pair of contradictory *New York Times* editorials. One, titled "Vernon Jordan's Ethics," noted that Jordan sits on the board of RJR Nabisco, a major cigarette company; that cigarettes kill an estimated 430,000 Americans a year; and that RJR in particular has been blamed for encouraging children to smoke with its "Joe Camel" ad campaign.[5]

In light of this, the *Times* argued, Jordan should avoid "even the appearance of a conflict of interest" by resigning his directorship or recusing himself from discussions of health-related appointments. The strongest direct criticism of Jordan was pretty mild: "What's distressing is Mr. Jordan's apparent indifference to these concerns."

Unfortunately, the chair of the board of RJR Nabisco, Louis Gerstner, sits on the board of the *New York Times*'s parent company. And so the next day, the paper printed another editorial, headlined "Vernon Jordan's Integrity," that apologized for the first one. The earlier editorial "might have been read to suggest that Mr. Jordan had in some way acted unethically or in ways reflecting on his integrity," the older-but-wiser *Times* wrote.[6]

In other words, all the talk about ethics might have led readers to think that directing a company whose product kills hundreds of thousands annually might reflect on one's integrity, or that it's unethical to run advertisements that entice children to become addicted to that product. "We did not intend to convey any such impression," the *New York Times* assured.

Media Litmus Test on Clinton's Cabinet

March 1993

JIM NAURECKAS

THE *Washington Post* reported on Clinton's newly appointed economic team in an article headlined "Clinton Appointees Form a Collage of Varying Economic Views." The piece claimed that Clinton's administration would be a "tent big enough to accommodate a wide variety of viewpoints."[7]

How wide were the viewpoints represented? The article cited Lloyd Bentsen, an "old-time wheeler-dealer" who supports "tax incentives" for business; Representative Leon Panetta (D.–Calif.) and the Brookings Institution's Alice Rivlin were described as "deficit hawks"; and investment bankers Robert Rubin and Roger Altman were said to provide "real world input."

"If you're in favor of any of these things, you're represented," said Reagan administration official William Seidman—referring to tax breaks for business, cutting government programs, or having economic policy set by investment bankers. This lineup will "reassure different audiences about the steadiness of government policy," said Carter-era official Stu Eizenstadt, citing the business community, bond markets, and people interested in the deficit. The only audiences that don't seem to get any reassurance are workers and consumers—otherwise known as the "special interests."

The Clinton administration would be a big enough tent for every big business viewpoint, but not public interest perspectives—as shown by a *New York Times* article headlined "Ideology Seems to Doom Cabinet Contender." It concerned Dr. Johnetta Cole, president of Spellman College, who served as an adviser to the transition team on education, labor, and arts issues. Cole was considered a likely pick for secretary of education but was eliminated as a Cabinet possibility because she was, in the *New York Times*'s view, "associated with the far left wing of American politics."[8]

Her chief sins were her "reported affiliation with a pro-Palestinian group" and her presence on the board of a group that sponsors volunteer work in Cuba. For this, the *Times* reported, "Dr. Cole has been the subject of several critical newspaper articles and columns. . . . She found herself under intensive questioning by reporters this week while attending President-elect Bill Clinton's economic conference in Little Rock."

It's instructive to compare the media controversy over Cole's opposition to the Cuba embargo with the muted outrage over Commerce Secretary Ron Brown's public relations work for the regime of Haitian dictator Jean-Claude Duvalier. The *New York Times* reprinted without question Representative Charles Rangel's (D.–N.Y.) claim that Brown's representation of Duvalier "had helped the people of Haiti."[9]

Similarly, mainstream media showed almost no inclination to explore the extensive ties between Treasury Secretary Bentsen and the managers of corrupt S&Ls—so close that Bentsen advised Michael Dukakis not to bring up the S&L looting during the 1988 campaign because it "was not going to be a winning issue for their ticket."[10]

Nor did many outlets pick up on David Corn's report in *The Nation* that Clinton chief of staff Thomas McLarty was under investigation by the Resolution Trust Corporation, the government entity tracing where the missing S&L funds went. McLarty was connected to a failed thrift that made $300 million in questionable loans, including $5.6 million to Bentsen's son that was never paid back.[11]

When Les Aspin was picked to be Clinton's first secretary of defense, *Nightline* could have examined whether his support for the Reagan military buildup and for expensive weapons systems like the B-2 bomber would make it difficult for him to chart a new course at the Pentagon. Instead, in a report that bordered on red-baiting, *Nightline* questioned whether Representative Ron Dellums (D.–Calif.), Aspin's successor as head of the House Armed Services Committee, would be too "radical" because he had opposed such policies.[12]

While the conservative positions of Clinton appointees like Bentsen and Aspin were largely ignored or applauded by the media, commentators kept a sharp eye out for any nominee who supposedly deviated to the left—such as Donna Shalala, Clinton's choice to head the Department of Health and Human Services.

As chancellor of the University of Wisconsin, Shalala favored affirmative action and multicultural education, for which journalists dubbed her the "queen of political correctness."[13] Her efforts to prohibit hate speech on campus, while constitutionally questionable, were twisted by a *USA Today* news article into "an effort to prohibit campus free speech against liberal positions."[14] She also favored abortion rights, opposed the ban on gays in the military, and had criticized Ronald Reagan.

Because of these positions, according to columnists Rowland Evans and Robert Novak, Shalala's appointment "challenge[s] the authenticity of Bill Clinton's self-portrait as a centrist Democrat turning his party's course back to the middle of the road."[15] In other words, Clinton was just kidding when he named all those corporate lawyers and Reagan Democrats to Cabinet posts; his health and human services nominee showed where his heart really lies.

Mixed Messages
March 1993

Newsweek's December 28, 1992, cover story on "Women of the Year" presented a series of portraits of the female "power players" who are "going to reshape the way Washington does business." But the portraits themselves sent a different message: In four of the nine carefully composed photographs, the subjects are pictured with children (either their own or someone else's); in five of the portraits, the women are lying on the floor or are otherwise horizontal. Is that how *Newsweek* thinks its readers like to see powerful women?

Ask Not What Gays Will Do to the Military—Ask What the Military Is Doing to Gays

June 1993

JIM NAURECKAS

THE DEBATE OVER repealing the military's prohibition of homosexuality—not so much a question of "letting gays in," as it was sometimes described, but a matter of ending discrimination against the thousands of gay men and lesbians already in the armed forces—was peculiarly limited.

The reasons military leaders gave for maintaining the ban were usually front and center—usually couched in terms like "privacy," "discipline," and "morale." But only sometimes were advocates for gay civil rights given an adequate chance to respond.

The second paragraph of a front-page *New York Times* story on the controversy cited General Colin Powell (Chair of the Joint Chiefs of Staff) and others as saying that ending discrimination by sexual orientation "would seriously undermine morale and discipline, disrupt military readiness and threaten recruiting."[16] Twenty-one paragraphs later, on page A16, the story noted vaguely that gay rights supporters were "contending that many of the military's arguments for keeping the ban were bogus or exaggerated."

The debate almost always centered on perceptions of what out-of-the-closet gays would do to the military—and almost never dealt with what the military is currently doing to lesbians and gay men.

- Seldom did news reports mention the witch-hunts that go on in the military against those suspected of homosexuality. These purges were vividly described by Randy Shilts in his book *Conduct Unbecoming,* which was excerpted in the *Los Angeles Times Magazine*: "Routinely, military investigators tell the frightened young soldiers and sailors—most of whom are 19 years old or, at most, in their early 20s—that they will do hard labor in the military prison at Fort Leavenworth if they do not confess to being gay—and turn in others. If the subject is a single mother, investigators

sometimes threaten to turn her in to child-welfare authorities, who could take her children away."[17]
- Interviews with military personnel sometimes mentioned the fact that women in the military were much more in favor of lifting the ban than men, but less often noted a major reason for this: Charges of lesbianism are often leveled at women, both gay and straight, who fail to respond to sexual advances by men.
- The threat of violence against gay personnel was more often presented as a reason for maintaining the ban—"People are going to go after them physically," an airman was quoted in the *New York Times*[18]—than as a reason for the military establishment to stop promoting a climate of intolerance.

Part of the problem was that reporters, as usual, gave priority to official sources. While military officials and congressional leaders like Senate Armed Services Chair Sam Nunn were outspoken in defense of the ban, the Clinton administration kept a low profile, presumably out of fear of appearing "pro-gay."

But the media were selective about which official sources were quoted. Representative Ron Dellums, who heads the House counterpart to Nunn's committee, was unequivocal in support of lifting the ban, telling reporters, "This is a tempest in a teapot. America needs to get beyond its ignorance, its fear, its bigotry and its oppression and get on with it as a mature society." But this support was nowhere near as visible as Nunn's opposition. "If you read the paper, I'm not even there," Dellums complained to the *Los Angeles Times*.[19]

Most media discussions of the issue seemed unable to use words like "bigotry" or "hatred" or "homophobia." Instead, there was a tendency to put a positive gloss on the most blatant expressions of bias. In the *New York Times*, a Marine officer was quoted as arguing that the Bible said homosexuals were "worthy of death." Reporter Eric Schmitt prefaced this by reporting that "many military personnel have religious or moral objections to allowing gays in the armed services."[20] Wanting gays to be killed is a "religious or moral" position?

A former Marine was quoted in the *St. Petersburg Times*: "I can't see a guy, he's openly as queer as a three-dollar bill, and he asks me to put my life on the line? When he doesn't believe what I believe?" The reporter seemed to validate this hysteria in the next line: "Experts call it a question of group dynamics."[21]

Media commentators themselves often descended into similar macho non sequiturs. Radio talk show host Michael Reagan, a guest on CNN's *Crossfire*, made this argument in favor of the ban: "Take it back down to an 18- or 19-year-old kid that you have just trained to be a mean, lean, fighting, killing machine and tell him he has got the greatest opportunity in the world to go out and prove his manhood, prove he can go out and kill and then tell him he's got to sleep with [a] homosexual, shower with a homosexual."[22] The rationality of this argument was not questioned by nominally left host Michael Kinsley.

When Clinton "Soaks the Rich," Pundits Drip

April/May 1993

JEFF COHEN AND NORMAN SOLOMON

THE PUNDITS' DEBATE about Clinton's economic plan followed the framework of most media discussions of the Clinton administration: Conservatives attacked the plan on right-wing principle, while centrists supported it as a "bold plan" (sometimes with minor, usually conservative, criticisms). There are so few progressives with regular access to mass media that their voices went largely unheard.

Take, for example, CNN's *Capital Gang,* a talk show sponsored by General Electric that rarely features positions that offend its patron. Of the four regular panelists, rightists Robert Novak and Mona Charen predictably attacked the "tax-and-spend" plan.[23] (Novak has elsewhere suggested that it veers toward "socialism.")[24] The "leftists" on the show—Al Hunt, Washington bureau chief of the *Wall Street Journal,* and columnist Mark Shields, whose promotional literature boasts that he "is free of any political tilt"—defended Clinton's proposals, with minor reservations. Hunt apparently would have preferred more cuts in senior citizens' benefits.

Given the parameters of the debate, it was no wonder that *Capital Gang*'s guest, Clinton spokesperson George Stephanopoulos, felt the need to defend his boss by saying he's "got a pro-business slant" in the budget plan.

Left out of most mainstream debates was a progressive critique of Clintonomics: that it taxes corporations and the wealthy too timidly and middle-income people too harshly, while failing to seriously cut the bloated military budget. Virtually no one noted that the wealthiest 1 percent of Americans (with an average yearly income of $567,000) saved more than $71 billion last year—a big chunk of the budget deficit—from federal tax breaks enacted since 1978, according to Citizens for Tax Justice calculations; or that corporate income taxes supplied about 25 percent of federal revenues in the 1960s, but supply only 7 percent today.[25]

Nor did mainstream media point out that Clinton's first-year military budget, although referred to by the press as "deep defense cuts," was only 4 percent smaller than George Bush's proposed spending—achieved mainly through trimming personnel and a salary freeze. As columnist Doug Ireland argued in the *Village Voice*, costly weapons systems like Star Wars and the V–22 Osprey aircraft were likely saved from the ax because they benefited Treasury Secretary Lloyd Bentsen's home state of Texas.[26]

A good deal of media debate centered on whether Clinton's plan was tough enough in "taking on the seniors" and "going after entitlements" to reduce the deficit. On the February 22, 1993, *Crossfire*, TV's "left" (Michael Kinsley) and right (Patrick Buchanan) reversed roles, with Buchanan the one defending middle-class senior citizens.

As President Clinton prepared his economic plan, NBC's John Chancellor commented, "One group did really well from 1980 to 1990: Households headed by people over 65.... If you made a movie about who gets what, you could call it: 'Honey, We Robbed the Kids.'"[27] Chancellor could have named any number of other groups as '80s-era robbers, including S&L looters, junk bond dealers, corporate takeover artists, or even NBC's owner, General Electric, which helped write the 1981 corporate tax law that slashed its own taxes to below zero.[28]

Few pundits criticized tax increases on Social Security benefits for seniors with incomes greater than $25,000 a year (or $32,000 for couples). In fact, news reports routinely referred to such seniors as "well-to-do."

While polls show that raising taxes on the wealthy is overwhelmingly popular among the public, the most powerful pundits attacked Clinton's small, loophole-ridden tax increases on the wealthy as "soak-the-rich" tactics. After the 1992 election, ABC's David Brinkley had told a trucking industry group that raising taxes on the well-to-do was a "sick, stupid joke" and "cheap demagoguery." Brinkley accused the Democrats of practicing "long-standing class warfare."[29]

Could the whining by the megapundits have anything to do with the fact that they're in the top income brackets themselves? George Will's annual income is a reported $1.5 million;[30] Patrick Buchanan made over $800,000 in 1991, according to election filings; Rowland Evans, Robert Novak, and John McLaughlin have each earned an estimated $1 million per year.[31]

The fact that the media elite is so far removed economically from the common people they claim to speak for makes the concern they express about "class warfare" especially ironic.[32] During the 1980s, when changes in the tax code abetted a dramatic transfer of wealth from the working class to the rich, one seldom heard pundits making references to Reagan's "class war." But then, if you're making a million dollars a year—why complain?

Right-Leaning Characters
April/May 1993

A February 16, 1993, front-page *Christian Science Monitor* article by Marshall Ingwerson bluntly summed up the first weeks of Clinton's term: "The agenda Clinton has pursued so far has a more left-leaning character than his campaign had forecast." There are only three sources cited in the entire article to back up this analysis: Stephen Hess, an assistant to presidents Eisenhower and Nixon; Jeffrey Bell, described as "a political theorist who has supported Bush cabinet official Jack Kemp"; and William Brock, who's called a "former high-ranking Republican official." How could Clinton *not* seem left-leaning to sources like this?

New York Times *on Immigrants: Give Us Your Healthy, Wealthy, and 24-Hour Nannies*

April/May 1993

VEENA CABREROS-SUD AND FARAH KATHWARI

THE CONTROVERSY over attorney general nominees Zoe Baird and Kimba Wood, both of whom had to withdraw after acknowledging that they had hired undocumented immigrants to care for their children, elicited a wide response in the media, particularly in the pages of the *New York Times*.

"It's Gender, Stupid," was the headline of an Anthony Lewis column that proclaimed, "It is time to stop snickering about the politics of all this and understand the real issue, bias against women."[33] An entire *New York Times* op-ed page was devoted to analyzing "Nannygate" as a women's issue.[34]

The discussion raised a number of important issues about the double standard applied to professional women and the need for a national child care plan. Yet the definition of "women's issues" adopted by the *Times* and other media was limited to white, upper-middle-class women. It almost completely excluded the viewpoint of the immigrant child care workers themselves—most of whom are women, many with children of their own. Immigrant Latina, Caribbean, and Asian women might have asked the same question that Sojourner Truth asked more than a century ago: "Ain't I a woman?"

Much of the commentary in the *New York Times* missed this class and race angle. Author Erica Jong fumed at women's groups who didn't rush to the defense of Baird and Wood: "We should be marching down Fifth Avenue waving banners that say 'I hired an illegal alien'"[35]—as if being wealthy enough to hire cheap, exploitable labor were a mark of oppression.

The exclusion of a Third World immigrant viewpoint was not confined to opinion pieces. Of 142 news articles on the Baird/Wood controversy indexed in the *New York Times*, only two primarily focused on immigrants' lives. Many more dealt with the importance of immigrant help for professional women and the attendant legal and paperwork fusses.

A *New York Times* news article began, "While President-elect Clinton promised a Cabinet that looks like America, Zoe Baird, his nominee for attorney general, apparently behaved a bit too much like America."[36] Not only do most Americans not have a live-in nanny and driver but, as the *New York Post*'s Amy Pagnozzi declared, "On a $600,000-a-year family income, Zoe Baird could have hired one of those Mary Poppins status-symbol nannies who not only have a green card but can tutor a kid in French."[37]

Instead, Baird, like many others, opted to hire undocumented immigrants—who are often underpaid and work without health insurance, workers compensation, sick leave, or Social Security benefits, and are too afraid of deportation to complain. By viewing the issue of immigrant labor overwhelmingly from the employer's perspective, the *Times* failed to cover a sector of the population that is nearly invisible to mainstream media, one that faces widespread civil rights and labor violations, as well as racial discrimination.

The Baird flap has only made things worse for immigrants. The Center for Immigrants Rights in New York City and the Japanese American Citizens League in Washington, D.C., have received reports of employers firing immigrant workers in the wake of the controversy.

And citizens are not insulated from anti-immigrant prejudice. In 1990, the General Accounting Office reported widespread discrimination against minority citizens in the hiring process for jobs, due to stipulations in the 1986 Immigration Reform and Control Act (IRCA) that required employers to validate legal work authorization papers of prospective employees.[38]

One of the few exceptions to the *New York Times*'s blind spot on immigrants was an article by David E. Rosenbaum headlined "Usually, the Illegality in Domestic Work Is Benefits Denied." "Families who do not pay Social Security and unemployment taxes for their maids and nannies are not just breaking the law," Rosenbaum reported. "They are denying their household help the pensions and protection against disability and joblessness to which the workers are entitled."[39]

Instead of following Rosenbaum's lead and exploring the discrimination and abuse faced by immigrants, the *New York Times* more often contributed to an anti-immigrant backlash. An op-ed piece by former Foreign Service officer Lawrence Harrison blamed immigrant workers for the problems of the U.S. economy: "Illegal immigrants ... have flooded the market, kept wages low and enabled employers to avoid the cost of employee benefits," and they have been "an important contributor to the decline in real income of American workers." Harrison urged "an immigration policy based on our own needs, particularly the needs of our poor, not on the failure of other nations to meet the needs of their people."[40]

A concern for low-income U.S. workers was not evidenced when the *New York Times* pushed for a free trade pact with Mexico, editorially dismissing concerns about job losses when corporations border-hop into Mexico: "The danger is that Congress will bend to the will of these few visible losers, in the process trashing the common wealth, the huge cumulative gains for everyone else."[41] *Times* coverage demonstrated greater concern for corporations crossing borders in search of cheaper labor than for workers crossing borders in search of a better livelihood.

The *New York Times*'s callousness toward immigrants reached some kind of low with an editorial that went beyond a call for banning HIV-positive visitors: "Immigrants can come down with a wide range of costly ailments, including heart disease, cancer, stroke and end-stage renal disease. . . . Immigrants with any costly condition ought to be excluded." But the *Times* contemplated making an exception for those from the right classes: "That way infected immigrants with assets or high earnings potential could be allowed in while those apt to need publicly financed medical care could be screened out."[42]

What happened to "give me your tired, your poor"? For the *New York Times,* it's more like: give us your healthy, wealthy, and those willing to work for low pay as 24-hour nannies.

Lani Guinier: Quota Queen or Misquoted Queen?

July/August 1993

ROB RICHIE AND JIM NAURECKAS

THE CLEAREST EXAMPLE of the media serving as a political monitor over the Clinton administration was the abortive nomination of Lani Guinier, Clinton's choice for assistant attorney general for civil rights, who was abandoned in the face of widespread media distortions of her record. In the smear campaign against Guinier, her views were not only distorted but in many cases presented as the exact opposite of her true beliefs.

One of the most prominent themes of the attack on Guinier was her supposed support for electoral districts shaped to ensure a black majority—a process known as "race-conscious districting." An entire op-ed column in the *New York*

Times—which appeared on the day her nomination was withdrawn—was based on the premise that Guinier was in favor of "segregating black voters in black-majority districts."[43]

In reality, Guinier was the most prominent voice in the civil rights community *questioning* such districting. In sharp contrast to her media caricature as a racial isolationist, she has criticized race-conscious districting because it "isolates blacks from potential white allies" and "suppresses the potential development of issue-based campaigning and cross-racial coalitions."[44]

Another media tactic against Guinier was to dub her a "quota queen," a phrase first used in the headline of a *Wall Street Journal* op-ed piece by Clint Bolick, a Reagan-era Justice Department official.[45] The racially loaded term combines the "welfare queen" stereotype with the dreaded "quota," a buzzword that almost killed the 1991 Civil Rights Act.

The problem was that Guinier is an *opponent* of electoral quotas to ensure representation of minorities. In an article in the *Harvard Civil Rights Civil Liberties Law Review*, she stated that "the enforcement of this representational right does not require legislative set-asides, color-coded ballots, electoral quotas or 'one black, two votes' remedies."[46]

But once the stereotype was affixed to her, there was seemingly no way she could dispel it: "Unbelievably, the woman known as the 'quota queen' claimed she did not believe in quotas," columnist Ray Kerrison wrote in the *New York Post*.[47]

Many commentators painted Guinier as a racial polarizer who implied that "only blacks can represent blacks," as George Will put it.[48] And she was repeatedly charged with believing that only "authentic" blacks counted. But in a *Michigan Law Review* article, Guinier stated that "authentic representatives need not be black as long as the source of the authority, legitimacy and power base is the black community." But more important, she was not endorsing the concept of authentic representation; she was *critiquing* it, describing it as a "limited empowerment tool."[49]

One of the few opinions attributed to Guinier that she actually held was her support for "proportional representation"—a system in which seats in government are divided by the percentage of the vote each party or slate receives. (If 40 percent of the voters back a party, that party would get roughly 40 percent of the seats—as opposed to a "winner-take-all" system, in which 51 percent of the voters can control 100 percent of the seats.) But her position was twisted by commentators like the *Washington Post*'s Lally Weymouth into a vision of "a society in which a minority can impose its will on the majority."[50]

As Lani Guinier said in a speech to the National Association of Black Journalists:[51]

> No one who had done their homework seriously questioned the fundamentally democratic nature of "my ideas." Indeed, two conservative columnists, George Will and Lally Weymouth, both wrote separate columns on the same day in the *Washington Post*, praising ideas remarkably similar to mine.[52]

Lally Weymouth wrote: "There can't be democracy in South Africa without a measure of formal protection for minorities." George Will wrote: "The Framers also understood that stable, tyrannical majorities can best be prevented by the multiplication of minority interests, so the majority at any moment will be just a transitory coalition of minorities."

In my law review articles I had expressed exactly the same reservations about unfettered majority rule, about the need sometimes to disaggregate the majority to ensure fair and effective representation for minority interests.

The difference is that the minority that I used to illustrate my academic point was not, as it was for Lally Weymouth, the white minority in South Africa. Nor did I write, as George Will did, about the minority of wealthy landlords in New York City. I wrote instead about the political exclusion of the black minority in local, county and municipal governing bodies in America.

Yet these same two journalists and many others condemned me as anti-democratic.[53] Apparently, some of us feel comfortable providing special protections for wealthy landlords or white South Africans, but we brand as "divisive" and "radical" the idea of providing similar remedies to include black Americans, who after centuries of racial oppression are still excluded.

How could Guinier's positions be distorted so thoroughly? Part of the problem was simple laziness: Rather than doing research into Guinier's record, many journalists preferred to simply repeat the charges of ideologically motivated opponents. When the *New York Times* finally devoted an article to her views, rather than to the political firestorm that raged around them—on June 4, 1993, after the nomination had already been killed—there still was not a single quote from any of her writings.

"Almost everyone is relying on reconstructions by journalists and partisans, injecting further distortions into the process," reporter David Margolick wrote. "Everyone" included himself; Margolick admitted in an interview that he himself had not bothered to read any of Guinier's work.

The fact that Guinier is an African-American woman, a group greatly underrepresented in mainstream media, contributed to the substitution of media stereotypes for her actual views. But there was also an ideological agenda at work: promoting Clinton's media-celebrated shift "back to the center." It seemed as though Clinton's hiring of Republican spin doctor David Gergen had to be complemented by dumping a representative of the "radical left." "How he deals with Ms. Guinier in the weeks ahead may show whether Mr. Clinton is moving back to the middle of the road," the *New York Times*'s R. W. Apple wrote in a front-page news analysis of the Gergen appointment.[54]

To make her a proper sacrificial offering, however, the establishment media had to reinvent Guinier—transforming a sophisticated advocate of racial reconciliation and participatory democracy into a race-baiting enemy of the American Way.

Notes

1. *New York Times,* November 15, 1992.
2. CNN, November 14, 1992.
3. Steven V. Roberts, "A Little Self-Restraint," *U.S. News & World Report,* November 23, 1992, p. 41.
4. *Washington Post,* November 15, 1992.
5. *New York Times,* November 12, 1992.
6. *New York Times,* November 13, 1992.
7. *Washington Post,* December 11, 1992.
8. *New York Times,* December 17, 1992.
9. *New York Times,* January 7, 1993. For more on how Brown "helped the people of Haiti," see Ken Silverstein, "Ron Brown's Affair with Haiti," *CounterPunch,* December 1993, p. 1.
10. William Greider, *Who Will Tell the People: The Betrayal of American Democracy* (New York: Touchstone, 1992).
11. David Corn, "Beltway Bandits," *The Nation,* January 25, 1993, p. 80.
12. *Nightline,* December 22, 1992.
13. *Atlanta Journal & Constitution,* December 22, 1992.
14. *USA Today,* January 11, 1993.
15. *Washington Post,* January 8, 1993.
16. *New York Times,* January 26, 1993.
17. Randy Shilts, *Conduct Unbecoming: Gays and Lesbians in the U.S. Military* (New York: St. Martin's Press, 1993); Randy Shilts, "Dismissed! The Purging of Gay and Lesbian Troops from the Armed Forces," *Los Angeles Times Magazine,* April 25, 1993, p. 10.
18. *New York Times,* January 28, 1993.
19. *Los Angeles Times,* April 11, 1993.
20. *New York Times,* January 27, 1993.
21. *St. Petersburg Times,* January 31, 1993.
22. *Crossfire,* February 3, 1993.
23. *Capital Gang,* February 20, 1993.
24. C-SPAN, February 19, 1993.
25. Chris Lewis, "Public Assets, Private Profits," *Multinational Monitor,* January/February 1993, p. 8.
26. *Village Voice,* February 2, 1993.
27. *NBC Nightly News,* February 2, 1993.
28. William Greider, *Who Will Tell the People: The Betrayal of American Democracy* (New York: Touchstone, 1992).
29. *Transport Topics,* November 8, 1992.
30. Eric Alterman, *Sound and Fury: The Washington Punditocracy and the Collapse of American Politics* (New York: HarperCollins, 1992).
31. *Washington Post,* April 18, 1987.
32. E.g., "Is Clinton Pitting Class Against Class?" a *Washington Post* news article, February 21, 1993.
33. *New York Times,* February 8, 1993.
34. *New York Times,* February 10, 1993.

35. *New York Times,* February 10, 1993.
36. *New York Times,* January 15, 1993.
37. *New York Post,* January 22, 1993.
38. General Accounting Office, *Immigration Reform: Employer Sanctions and the Question of Discrimination* (Washington, D.C.: Government Printing Office, 1990).
39. *New York Times,* January 31, 1993.
40. *New York Times,* January 31, 1993.
41. *New York Times,* August 13, 1992.
42. *New York Times,* February 20, 1993.
43. *New York Times,* June 3, 1993.
44. Lani Guinier, "Second Proms and Second Primaries: The Limits of Majority Rule," *Boston Review,* September/October 1992, p. 32.
45. *Wall Street Journal,* April 30, 1993.
46. Lani Guinier, "Keeping the Faith: Black Voters in the Post-Reagan Era," *Harvard Civil Rights Civil Liberties Law Review,* Spring 1989, p. 393.
47. *New York Post,* June 4, 1993.
48. George F. Will, "Sympathy for Guinier," *Newsweek,* June 14, 1993, p. 78.
49. Lani Guinier, "The Triumph of Tokenism: The Voting Rights Act and the Theory of Black Electoral Success," *Michigan Law Review,* March 1991, p. 1077.
50. Lani Guinier, speech at Houston, Texas, sponsored by the National Association of Black Journalists, July 22, 1993. The speech was reprinted in part in Lani Guinier, "Lani Guinier's Challenge to the Press," *Extra!,* November/December 1993, p. 7.
51. *Washington Post,* May 25, 1993.
52. *Washington Post,* July 15, 1993.
53. Lally Weymouth, *Washington Post,* May 25, 1993; George F. Will, "Sympathy for Guinier," *Newsweek,* June 14, 1993, p. 78.
54. *New York Times,* May 31, 1993.

8 The Scandal Beat

Whitewater Under the Bridge: How the Press Missed the Story

May/June 1994

JEFF COHEN AND NORMAN SOLOMON

SUPPORTERS OF THE CLINTONS suggest that Whitewater, a failed real estate venture from Bill and Hillary's Little Rock days, is old news. The election campaign is over, the argument goes, and the voters chose Clinton.

But Whitewater never really became a campaign issue in 1992. Most media outlets gave a great deal of space to allegations of Bill Clinton's sexual affairs and accounts of his draft maneuverings but shied away from a story about corporate collusion with politicians—perhaps because the story wasn't pushed by an establishment party or politician.

In 1994, leading Republicans seemed to want to talk about nothing but Whitewater and the Madison Guaranty S&L. That wasn't the case during the 1992 presidential campaign, when George Bush and his allies had reason to keep quiet: Bush had his own—much more costly—bank scandals to worry about.

Taxpayers lost $47 million when Madison, owned by Clinton crony James McDougal, failed. But taxpayers lost $1 billion in the collapse of the Silverado S&L, which boasted "First Son" Neil Bush as a board member. And George Bush was implicated in the BNL bank scandal—which helped arm Iraq's Saddam Hussein with $5 billion of the U.S. public's money.[1]

One Clinton opponent who wasn't silent in 1992 about Whitewater and related issues was Governor Jerry Brown. But his calls for more investigation were silenced in much of the press.

As a media issue during the campaign, the whole affair rose and fell in about three weeks. On March 8, 1992, investigative reporter Jeff Gerth broke the story on the front page of the *New York Times*—presenting much of the essential information about the scandal that would be "exposed" more than a year later.

The article, "Clintons Joined S&L Operator in an Ozark Real-Estate Venture," asserted that Bill and Hillary Clinton "were under little financial risk" in the Whitewater venture initiated by McDougal. The implication was that this was a "sweetheart deal" offered in return for political favors. Gerth also pointed to Hillary Clinton's partnership in the powerful Rose law firm, which represented McDougal's S&L in filings before a state agency.

Gerth wrote that the McDougal/Clinton relationship "raises questions of whether a governor should be involved in a business deal with the owner of a business regulated by the state and whether, having become involved, the governor's wife through her law firm should be receiving legal fees for work done for the business."[2]

The next day's newspapers featured Bill Clinton's response to the article—including his observation that the Whitewater venture did carry risk for him and his wife, who lost thousands of dollars. But ignored was Jerry Brown's news release calling on Bill Clinton to "release all papers pertaining to his ties to the failed Madison Guaranty."

Six days later, a *Washington Post* report scrutinized the Rose law firm's representation of corporate clients, including Madison and bigger businesses, in front of state regulators appointed by Governor Clinton. "If you want something from the state," a Clinton rival was quoted, "you go to the Rose firm." The article also reported that "one of Rose's most lucrative clients is the state government."[3]

Hours after the *Post* story broke, in a Chicago debate that was the most heated of the campaign, Governor Brown accused Governor Clinton of "funneling money to his wife's law firm for state business." Clinton called it a "lying accusation."

The next day, Hillary Clinton responded to Brown's charges against her husband with a feminist appeal that would be prominently quoted for days and years to come: "I suppose I could have stayed home and baked cookies and had teas. But what I decided to do was pursue my profession."[4]

By contrast, her revealing response to a question about whether she had represented Madison Guaranty was hardly quoted at all: "For goodness' sake, you can't be a lawyer if you don't represent banks."[5]

Although Brown's criticism was aimed at Bill—not Hillary—newspapers in the next two days were full of macho posturing from Governor Clinton: "If somebody jumps on my wife, I'm going to jump them back." *Washington Post* columnist Richard Cohen even mocked Brown for being a bachelor: "One thing he knows nothing about—zilch, nada, zero—is marriage."[6]

Within a week, Whitewater was virtually dead as a campaign issue. With press attention shifting to depictions of Brown as a character assassin—and discussions about "cookies" and "teas"—the issue of candidate Clinton's links to corporate power in Little Rock disappeared.

FAIR's computer search of major dailies revealed only a couple of dozen articles in 1992 mentioning Whitewater or Madison—compared with hundreds mentioning Hillary Clinton's "cookies" remark.

In 1994, as if overcompensating for dropping the ball on what should have been a serious campaign issue, national media inflated the Whitewater story. As "presidential" scandals go, this one seemed distinctly gubernatorial. It was silly to compare it to Watergate, a presidential abuse of the U.S. Constitution, or Iran-contra, which involved the White House in secret wars and arms to terrorists.

The 1994 media onslaught on Whitewater was propelled day after day by quotes of outrage from Republican senators like Phil Gramm, who received favors from a Dallas operator of three failed S&Ls, and Alfonse D'Amato, whose dealings in support of friends and relatives were investigated and rebuked by the Senate Ethics Committee.

But in 1992, a key reason elite media dropped the story was that the only newsmaker pushing it was Jerry Brown, who often spoke out about the corrupting influence of money in politics but was considered an antiestablishment candidate, whom journalists were more prone to deride than quote.

Koppel Covers for Limbaugh's Rumor-Mongering

July/August 1994

Ted Koppel's April 1994 *Nightline Viewpoint* special on press coverage of Whitewater was a perfect opportunity to take Rush Limbaugh to task for spreading unfounded conspiracy theories. But instead, ABC journalists Koppel and Jeff Greenfield let Limbaugh off the hook.[7]

On his March 10, 1994, radio broadcast, Limbaugh had announced the following in urgent tones:

> OK, folks, I think I got enough information here to tell you about the contents of this fax that I got. Brace yourselves. This fax contains information that I have just been told will appear in a newsletter to Morgan Stanley sales personnel this afternoon. ... What it is is a bit of news which says ... there's a Washington consulting firm that has scheduled the release of a report that will appear, it will be published, that claims that Vince Foster was murdered in an apartment owned by Hillary Clinton, and the body was then taken to Fort Marcy Park.

After he returned from a commercial break, Limbaugh began referring to the story as a "rumor" but continued to claim that the story was that "the Vince Foster suicide was not a suicide."

Limbaugh was referring to an item in a newsletter put out by the Washington, D.C., firm of Johnson Smick International. The newsletter, relating a rumor with no evidence, reported that White House attorney Vincent Foster's suicide occurred in an apartment owned by White House associates and that his body was moved to the park where it was found.

Limbaugh took this baseless rumor from a small insiders' newsletter and broadcast it to his radio audience of millions, adding his own new inaccuracies: The newsletter did not report—as Limbaugh claimed—that Foster was murdered or that the apartment was owned by Hillary Rodham Clinton. Limbaugh's amplification of an unfounded rumor has been credited with contributing to a plunge in the stock market on the day it was aired.[8]

Appearing as an "expert" on the *Viewpoint* special, Limbaugh denied twisting the rumor: "Never have I suggested that this was murder," he said. ABC's Jeff Greenfield, in a taped segment, further covered for the talk show host, claiming that Limbaugh "broadcast the rumor as an example of the more wild stories circulating."

Later in the broadcast, host Ted Koppel also stuck up for Limbaugh when his role in spreading the story was challenged. "As I recall," Koppel said, "you didn't present it as accurate, did you? You represented it as one of the rumors that was going around."

But the executive producer of Limbaugh's TV show, Roger Ailes (a Republican campaign consultant and president of the CNBC cable network), didn't claim that his star had debunked the rumor—he boasted that Limbaugh's report of "a suicide coverup, possibly murder" was a scoop. On the Don Imus radio show, Ailes remarked: "The guy who's been doing an excellent job for the *New York Post* [Chris Ruddy] . . . for the first time on the Rush Limbaugh show said that . . . he did not believe it was suicide. . . . Now, I don't have any evidence. . . . These people are very good at hiding or destroying evidence."[9]

Later, Limbaugh didn't seem so proud of his scoop. When a caller to his radio show, who identified himself as a pediatrician from Memphis, articulately criticized Limbaugh for spreading false reports about Vincent Foster's death, the host seemed to take it personally: "One thing I'm not is a rumor-monger," he said.[10]

After the call, Limbaugh implied that the pediatrician had been calling from the "West Wing of the White House" (even though the caller had also criticized the Clinton health care plan and endorsed a single-payer approach). "I think that what is going to happen during the course of this year," Limbaugh said, "is that a bunch of people are going to call this show that have been given marching orders. . . . What's going to happen is there will be numerous attempts, and they've gone on all the time, to discredit what occurs on this program."

The next day, apparently still smarting from the Memphis caller's remarks, Limbaugh instructed his staff on the air: "You guys be on the lookout in there for more calls from the White House disguised as pediatricians from Memphis."[11]

FAIR associate Jonathan Eagleman tracked down the "Memphis pediatrician" and found that he was . . . a Memphis pediatrician. The pediatrician had received a number of hate calls from outraged "dittoheads"—apparently some of them hadn't believed their leader's claim that the doctor was actually calling from the White House.

Paula Jones and Sexual Harassment: The World Stayed Right Side Up

July/August 1994

LAURA FLANDERS

It seemed like May madness had hit—at least as far as sexual harassment was concerned.

Previously unreconstructed misogynists supported a working-class female who charged a powerful man with grimy sexual misconduct. *New Republic* editor and PBS pundit Fred Barnes, who once called Anita Hill's charges against Clarence Thomas "a monstrous lie,"[12] decided that Arkansas state employee Paula Jones had made a "credible" accusation of sexual harassment against Bill Clinton. Rush Limbaugh, who'd previously boasted of a sign on his office door that read, "Sexual harassment at this work station will not be reported. However, it will be graded!"[13] evinced sympathy for a woman who said she'd been harassed.

At the same time, liberal pundits often trivialized the accusation against the president. In an offhand comment that conflated consensual sex and sexual harassment, columnist Mary McGrory remarked, "This debate was held two years ago in New Hampshire, where people knew this president was not a model husband."[14] Clarence Page of the *Chicago Tribune* called sexual harassment "a vehicle for witch hunts"[15]—apparently forgetting who killed whom in Salem.

Newsweek's Joe Klein lamented on CBS's *Face the Nation* that "we're going to end up with government by goody-goodies." He went on to claim that, historically, presidents with "interesting sexual histories" have made better leaders.[16]

Klein also seemed to have a problem distinguishing sex from assault—isn't that what feminists are accused of?

One might have thought spring lunacy had taken over—especially when Rush Limbaugh started criticizing feminists for being *too quiet* about sexual harassment. But in fact, plenty of conservatives stuck to their traditional, dismissive line. William Safire called sexual harassment statutes "loosey goosey";[17] the *New York Post*'s Ray Kerrison wrote a column headed "Anita and Paula: Sisters in Sleaze."[18]

Talk show host John McLaughlin moaned about a "rush to judgment ... against the male" in sexual harassment cases, then rushed in with his own verdict: Paula Jones's suit was "largely bogus." "You can sue anybody for anything," whined McLaughlin.[19] He should know: He's been accused of sexual harassment by several female employees, settling a suit out of court with one in 1989.[20]

And feminists, contrary to media assumption, were not so silent. On his TV show, Limbaugh lined up Jones and Hill in mirror image and claimed that the National Organization for Women (NOW), which "organized marches for Anita Hill," was "just yawning" about Paula Jones.[21] Neither claim was true. NOW, which had never held a demonstration for Hill, issued a statement on the day Jones's suit was filed, stating, "Every Paula Jones deserves to be heard, no matter how old she is and how long ago the incident occurred."[22]

Feminists, wrote *USA Today* columnist Joe Urschel, "have not rushed to [Jones's] defense in ideological lockstep as they did with Hill."[23] At least Urschel interviewed leaders of women's organizations for his story. (One corrected the record in a letter the next day.) The *New York Times*'s Maureen Dowd cited no leaders of women's groups as she asserted vaguely that "some women" who supported Hill "are wishing they could cut the ground from underneath Paula Jones."[24]

Jones's lawyer, Daniel Traylor, provided phony fodder for the pundits when he claimed that his client had been refused help by the NOW Legal Defense and Education Fund (NLDEF). In fact, NLDEF hadn't been approached on the case and did send technical help once Jones's team got around to asking—which is more assistance than NLDEF ever gave to Anita Hill. Traylor later claimed that he was referring to a call made to an Arkansas chapter of NOW, a separate organization, but no one at Arkansas's NOW chapter had any record of his call.

In the absence of a hearing—or many facts at all—the Paula Jones debate took place almost entirely in the realm of politics and personalities. Participants were brought into TV studios to take sides on the basis of political loyalties.

The silenced reality is that sexual harassment comes all too often as a surprise. Most perpetrators aren't recognizable creeps but men who women dared to think might interact with them as equals. According to the National Council for Research on Women, at least *half* of all women will experience sexual harassment at some point in their lives.

But prime time left it to the afternoon talk shows to ponder the real toll harassment takes in U.S. life. Partisan debates fit better into snappy sound bites. Maybe they sell more papers, too.

Notes

1. Alan Friedman, *Spider's Web: Bush, Saddam, Thatcher and the Decade of Deceit* (New York: Bantam Doubleday Dell, 1993).
2. Gerth's own reporting has been criticized as inaccurate and overly conspiratorial. See Gene Lyons, "Fool for Scandal," *Harper's,* October 1994, p. 55.
3. *Washington Post,* March 14, 1992.
4. *New York Times,* March 17, 1992.
5. Minneapolis *Star Tribune,* March 17, 1992.
6. *Washington Post,* March 18, 1992.
7. *Nightline Viewpoint,* April 19, 1994. For more on Limbaugh's record of inaccuracy, and the mainstream media's failure to challenge him, see Steve Rendall, Jim Naureckas, and Jeff Cohen, *The Way Things Aren't: Rush Limbaugh's Reign of Error* (New York: New Press, 1995).
8. *Chicago Tribune,* March 11, 1994; Russell Watson, "Vince Foster's Suicide: The Rumor Mill Churns," *Newsweek,* March 21, 1994, p. 32.
9. *Don Imus Show* (radio), March 10, 1994.
10. *Rush Limbaugh Show* (radio), March 10, 1994.
11. *Rush Limbaugh Show* (radio), March 11, 1994.
12. *McLaughlin Group,* May 6, 1994.
13. *USA Weekend,* January 26, 1992.
14. *Meet the Press,* May 8, 1994.
15. *Chicago Tribune,* May 8, 1994.
16. *Face the Nation,* May 8, 1994.
17. *New York Times,* May 9, 1994.
18. *New York Post,* May 11, 1994.
19. *McLaughlin Group,* May 8, 1994.
20. Eric Alterman, *Sound and Fury: The Washington Punditocracy and the Collapse of American Politics* (New York: HarperCollins, 1992).
21. *Limbaugh* (television), May 4, 1994.
22. National Organization for Women, "Statement of NOW President Ireland Calling for Fair Treatment of Jones' Suit, Questioning Right Wing's Disingenuous Fervor," press release, May 6, 1994.
23. *USA Today,* May 10, 1994.
24. *New York Times,* May 8, 1994.

9 Trade: NAFTA's Manifest Destiny

Free Trade Fever Induces Media Delusions

January/February 1993

JOHN SUMMA AND PATRICE GREANVILLE

CREDIT FOR THE passage of the North American Free Trade Agreement (NAFTA), negotiated in the summer of 1992 by the United States, Mexico, and Canada, should go to the leading voices of the U.S. press—who displayed unyielding devotion to the conservative gospel of "free trade."

In the opening paragraph of a major news series that included most of the establishment press's arguments for free trade, the *New York Times* announced that NAFTA "will add jobs, wealth and economic activity throughout the continent, economists say."[1] Although a minority of people were said to face "hardship," even that caveat was contradicted the next day by an oversized subhead that trumpeted: "Better Standard of Living for All."[2] A subsequent *Times* editorial amplified the same message: Although there will be a "few visible losers," there will be "huge cumulative gains for everyone else."[3]

Similar claims were made about the free trade pact signed by Canada and the United States in 1989. But contrary to most U.S. press accounts, Canada paid a high price for its decision. The London-based *Economist* wrote that a "clear majority" of Canadians turned against NAFTA because of the negative effects of its first dose of free trade.[4]

Though it acknowledged this growing resentment, the *New York Times* still found a silver lining: Reporter Clyde H. Farnsworth, citing "some analysts," predicted that Canada "is about to outpace all major industrial nations in economic growth" thanks to the 1989 trade pact, adding that there are "signs of increased strength" in the Canadian economy, which he said suffers from world recession, not the effects of free trade.[5]

In fact, the Canadian Center for Policy Alternatives found that Canada had lost more than 460,000 jobs in manufacturing alone since 1989, due to a disastrous 23.1 percent decline in manufacturing in less than three years. "Employment in Canada has fallen two-and-a-half times as much as it has in the U.S. since the current recession began in July 1990," Doug Henwood wrote in *Lies of Our Times*.[6]

Despite Canada's experiences—and despite the fact that a free trade strategy has *never* succeeded in leading an underdeveloped country out of poverty—media commentators were optimistic about NAFTA's effects on Mexico. The *Washington Post*'s Stuart Auerbach lauded the "economic gains" that free trade measures had already brought to Mexico, noting that foreign investment had "soared."[7] "Over time, the pact would help alleviate Mexican poverty and curb illegal immigration to the U.S.," reported Kenneth H. Bacon in the *Wall Street Journal*.[8]

From south of the Rio Grande, however, the economic "gains" of free trade don't look so great. "Contrary to free-trade propaganda," William Greider wrote in *Rolling Stone*, "industrial development has not spawned a new middle class of Mexican consumers for U.S. products. In fact, real wages in Mexico have fallen by 50 percent during the last decade."[9]

The trade deal, moreover, will drive wages down even further, as millions of farmers are put out of business and forced into the swollen urban labor markets, according to John Cavanaugh and John Gershman in *The Progressive*. They argued that because cheap grain imports would destroy the market for native-grown corn, "millions of Mexican subsistence farmers would be reduced to wage earners on plantations or to urban slum dwellers if the free-trade pact goes through."[10]

There had already been a loss of five hundred engineering firms in Mexico City, resulting from unilateral moves toward trade liberalization beginning in the 1980s, according to the *Economist*, and "thousands more small and medium-sized firms are threatened" by NAFTA.[11]

While the underside of trade reform in Mexico was downplayed, the supposed benefits for the U.S. consumer were constantly played up. "The great value of free trade," editorialized the *New York Times*, "is that it can raise the living standards of most Americans."[12] According to another *Times* editorial, "consumers will save billions."[13]

The *Wall Street Journal* predicted "lower prices on a wide variety of goods as a result of lower tariffs and increased competition."[14] *Time* magazine emphasized that reduced tariffs will aid "low-income households" who "suffer" the most from import tariffs.[15]

These projections assumed that lower production costs would turn into lower retail prices, not higher profits. But most people described as "consumers" are also workers—will they really benefit from lower-priced goods if their wages have eroded, or if their jobs have vanished?

Most press accounts of NAFTA made only perfunctory mention of the issue of job loss, usually passed off as just "concerns" or "fears" of "organized labor," or worse, "protectionists" (depicted as entrenched interests opposed to the deal for purely selfish reasons).

"Most economists think fears of massive job losses are exaggerated," Kenneth Bacon reported reassuringly in the *Wall Street Journal*.[16] "The fear of companies fleeing across the border to hire dollar-an-hour labor," editorialized the *New York Times*, "is grossly exaggerated."[17]

These "fears" were usually countered by statistics from the ubiquitous, pro-NAFTA Institute for International Economics, which went unchallenged in news report after news report. A widely reported study by the industry-financed group, for instance, projected that 325,000 new jobs in the United States would more than make up for the job loss caused by the trade deal.[18]

In a rare example of evenhandedness, the *Philadelphia Inquirer* cited the rival Economic Policy Institute, which estimated a loss of 550,000 high-wage jobs.[19] Indeed, massive job losses caused by companies leaving for Mexico are not a "fear," but an ongoing fact, as news outlets have occasionally acknowledged.[20]

The focus on the supposed benefits for the U.S. consumer also ignored the threat of more pesticide-laced and irradiated foods arriving from Mexico and skirted the well-founded concern that U.S. environmental standards would be undermined as "technical barriers" to trade.[21] A *New York Times* editorial dismissed this concern: The NAFTA agreement "makes impressive strides to block the threat," the paper insisted[22]—even though the text of the agreement had not yet been released.

And a news article in *U.S. News & World Report* glibly reassured those concerned about pollution along Mexico's border by U.S.-owned factories: "President Carlos Salinas de Gortari is more determined than any predecessor to clean up pollution, suggesting a brighter future for workers and the environment."[23]

In fact, the Mexican government's own National Institute of Ecology had found that 95 percent of the 106,000 factories in Mexico "are releasing toxic waste in violation of existing rules," and that "in practice, the official attitude toward compliance was at least very lax."[24]

NAFTA prompted the emergence of a "new, broad-gauge citizen politics that is genuinely tri-national," unified by the multiple threats posed by the trade deal, William Greider reported.[25] But the broad-based U.S. coalition groups, like Citizen Trade Watch and the Fair Trade Campaign, were almost always subsumed in press accounts as nameless "critics" or "opponents" of the deal. These grassroots groups were almost never allowed to make their case: that raising labor and environmental standards in all countries, not forcing workers to compete by lowering them, should be the goal of trade agreements.[26]

In Mexico, "over 60 independent unions and democratic movements formed the United Union Front" in April 1990 to fight against government economic policies and corruption and to "exchange views with their U.S. and Canadian counterparts" about free trade and the increasing power of multinational corporations.[27] But in eight major U.S. dailies indexed by the database ProQuest, not a single story was devoted to this growing opposition inside Mexico between January 1991 and September 1992.

Instead, the *New York Times*'s Tim Golden disingenuously reported that even Mexico's poor are big supporters of NAFTA. The Mexican government's "success in ending nearly a decade of economic crisis," wrote Golden, "has also inspired many Mexicans, even among the nearly 40 million who live in poverty, to grasp its vision without reserve."[28] While not quoting a single opposition leader, the story was loaded with quotes from the U.S. Chamber of Commerce and other pro-NAFTA representatives from business and government.

The conservative *U.S. News & World Report*, looking through its anti-Communist lenses, did warn of a growing "leftist" opposition in Mexico that is drawing support from the rural poor, to whom "the market-oriented economic miracle . . . has yet to trickle down."[29] But this was as close as one got to learning about opposition to the authoritarian and pro-business policies of President Salinas, who was widely believed to have stolen the 1988 presidential election through fraud.

In endorsing Salinas's free-trade "reforms," mainstream U.S. news outlets seemed to turn a blind eye to human rights abuses committed by his government. No major U.S. news outlet noted a report by Canadian churches that called on their government to use the NAFTA negotiations to press Salinas on human rights violations—which, according to the churches' report, included "the assassination of peasant leaders, the torture of prisoners in detention, violations of labor rights, corruption in the judicial system, and virtual police and military impunity."[30]

While the opposition to NAFTA was generally ignored, also overlooked was the fact that multinational corporations were not only supporting the negotiations but actively participating in them. According to *Dollars and Sense*, the Advisory Committee on Trade Policy and Negotiations (ACTPN), which assists the U.S. government in trade negotiations, consists of forty-two representatives of corporations or trade associations, and only two representatives of labor unions.[31]

But rather than painting these corporate "advisers" as politically powerful forces who were helping to shape trade policy for their own interests, the U.S. press tended to paint unions and environmentalists as the only special interests. As Craig Merrilles of the Fair Trade Campaign told FAIR, news reports tend to "confuse the national interest with the interests of Corporate America, when they are *not* the same."

Happily Ever NAFTA?

Extra! Update, October 1993

In its January/February 1993 issue, *Extra!* reported that news coverage of NAFTA had a pronounced pro–"free trade" slant, promoting the views of government and business groups who support NAFTA over those of environmentalists, labor unions, and other critics.

Subsequently, however, the mainstream press featured claims that NAFTA foes were actually *dominating* the discussion:

- *Washington Post* columnist Hobart Rowen complained in May 1993 that "most of the voices being heard on the trade treaty, including those of labor union leaders and former presidential candidates Jerry Brown and Ross Perot, are solidly anti-NAFTA."[32]
- In July 1993, *Newsweek* decried the "new trade gospel—that America's openness to the international economy helps the world but hurts itself." The magazine asserted that "trade is good for you"—though "that may not be apparent from the headlines."[33]
- The *New York Times* reported in August 1993 that business groups were stepping up their efforts on behalf of NAFTA, "after months of letting unions and environmental groups dominate the debate."[34]

Did opponents really control the national debate about NAFTA? FAIR decided to survey two of the most important arenas for national policy debates—the *New York Times* and the *Washington Post*—to see who actually got the most opportunities to speak.

FAIR looked at news reports in the *Times* and *Post* from April through July 1993, identifying all the sources quoted by name in stories focusing on NAFTA. We categorized these sources according to whom they spoke for and whether they had an identifiable position, pro or con, on the trade agreement.

Environmentalists and trade unionists, who were said to be dominating the debate, were in fact almost invisible. Out of 201 sources in the two papers, only six (3 percent) represented the environmental movement. *No* representative of a labor union was quoted during the four-month period. (One person was quoted from the Citizens Trade Campaign, a coalition that includes labor unions.) Spokespersons for all public interest or civic action groups—including those who endorsed NAFTA—made up only 7 percent of named sources.

Who did get to speak? U.S. government representatives—including administration officials and legislators—were 51 percent of all sources in the two papers, and 62 percent of sources in the *New York Times*. These sources were overwhelmingly pro-NAFTA (81 percent), as were other government sources, mainly Mexican and Canadian, who made up another 11 percent of sources.

Corporate representatives made up 13 percent of sources, though they were much more prominent in the *Washington Post* (21 percent). These sources were also strongly pro-NAFTA (85 percent).

One gap in the four months of coverage was the absence of members of the general public—the people who will feel the effects of the trade pact. The 2 percent of sources in this category all appeared in one story, a *New York Times* piece on the impact of NAFTA on Mexican corn-farming.[35]

In all, 68 percent of quoted sources had pro-NAFTA positions, with 66 percent in the *New York Times* and 71 percent in the *Washington Post* in favor. Only 20 percent of the two papers' sources were opposed to NAFTA—24 percent in the *Times* and 17 percent in the *Post*. In other words, almost three times as many sources were defenders of NAFTA as critics in the *Times*; in the *Post*, the ratio was more than four to one.

When the two leading papers' coverage was so lopsidedly pro–"free trade," opponents of NAFTA could hardly have been said to be "dominating the debate." Although grassroots efforts by environmentalists, labor unions, and other critics were having a significant impact, they were hardly reflected in the two elite papers FAIR studied.

Defenders of mainstream media often say that government officials are quoted so frequently because they're the ones who "make news." But the *New York Times*'s and *Washington Post*'s treatment of the NAFTA issue suggests that even when grassroots groups are central to a political contest, they are still marginalized in the media debate.

Economics 101
November/December 1993

On *Crossfire*, when Michael Kinsley argued against Senator Don Riegle (D.–Mich.) in support of the North American Free Trade Agreement, he seemed to feel that he had a foolproof argument: "What are these Mexicans going to do with these dollars they're earning?" he demanded of the senator, a leading NAFTA critic. "When these plants rush down to Mexico, that you say is going to happen in huge numbers, and they earn dollars, these dollars are only good for one thing, which is buying stuff in the United States. . . . You can't spend your dollars in Mexico. You can only spend them in the United States. . . . That's the key point of free trade."[36]

Of course, workers in U.S.-owned plants in Mexico earn pesos, not dollars, and in any case dollars are freely exchanged for pesos anywhere in Mexico. But cohost

Pat Buchanan's response seemed to accuse Kinsley of being overly academic: "Michael, let's not go back to Economics 101," he said. "Well, you need to learn a bit of it, Pat," Kinsley replied.

NAFTA's Knee-Jerk Press

Extra! Update, January/February 1994

GIVEN THE OVERWHELMING support Bill Clinton received from the mainstream media on NAFTA, his annoyed comment to *Rolling Stone*'s William Greider about the "knee-jerk liberal press" seemed especially absurd.[37] "Most of the nation's brand-name commentators led the cheerleading for NAFTA in a way that clearly helped President Clinton," wrote Howard Kurtz, the *Washington Post*'s TV critic.[38]

Leading newspapers overwhelmingly used pro-NAFTA sources in news articles. Some reporters abandoned any pretense of neutrality: "Polls are showing fears of NAFTA being overcome," the *Wall Street Journal*'s deputy Washington bureau chief, Alan Murray, said in a TV interview. "So things are moving in the right direction."[39]

And the press's opinion writing was even more slanted: When Senator Byron Dorgan (D.–N.D.), a NAFTA foe, conducted a column-inch count of editorial and op-ed articles on NAFTA in the *Washington Post* in 1993, he found that the propact bias was nearly seven to one. (Other papers were even more lopsided.) The senator wrote up his findings in a column, "Getting a Word in Edgewise on NAFTA"—but the *Post* wouldn't print it.

After NAFTA passed, the *Post*'s Kurtz did mention Dorgan's findings. *Post* editorial page editor Meg Greenfield responded, "On this rare occasion when columnists of the left, right and middle are all in agreement . . . I don't believe it is right to create an artificial balance where none exists."[40] Apparently those members of Congress who voted against the treaty—including the House majority leader and 60 percent of Democrats in the House—were so marginal or ultraleft that they didn't deserve serious representation.

In the final weeks of the debate, as a NAFTA majority in Congress still seemed elusive, major media pulled out all stops to try to discredit the opposition; this largely took the form of an attack on organized labor. Anthony Lewis, who has represented the "left wing" of the *New York Times* op-ed page for years, attacked unions as "backward" and "unenlightened" because they sought to protect middle-class manufacturing jobs—which Lewis dismissed as largely "low-wage jobs."

His column also condemned the "crude, threatening tactics used by unions."[41] Unions had said they might campaign against representatives who voted for NAFTA—a democratic activity that apparently becomes a crude threat when issued by a union.

President Clinton echoed Lewis's antiunion comments on *Meet the Press*, complaining about labor's "roughshod, muscle-bound tactics." In the next breath, he complained that pro-NAFTA business owners "have not gotten their employees and rank-and-file people to call and say they're for it."[42] The pundits interviewing Clinton—and pundits in general—did not suggest it was a "roughshod tactic" for bosses to use their employees to lobby for management's political positions.

NAFTA Lockout at the New York Times

October 1993

You know a debate is skewed when one side can't even *buy* space to make its views known. That's what happened in the debate over NAFTA.

The *New York Times* editorialized strongly in favor of NAFTA, and its news coverage was heavily slanted toward NAFTA supporters. On top of that, the paper launched a series of special sections in which advertisers could buy space to talk about the trade pact—but only if they supported it.

"In an effort to educate the public and influence Washington decision-makers, the *New York Times* has planned a series of three special advertorials presenting the positive economic and social benefits of NAFTA," *New York Times* advertising executive Eve Kummel wrote to potential advertisers before the first section ran on April 20, 1993.[43] The *Times*'s house ads made it clear that only "proponents' views" would be allowed in this "unique environment" for reaching "both private- and public-sector influentials."

Few labor or other public interest groups can afford to buy many *New York Times* ads; rates for the special section topped out at $57,630 for a full-page ad. But the *Times* turned down both the Electronic Workers and Ladies' Garment Workers unions when they asked to buy space in the section to register a dissenting view.

The paper not only restricted advertising to advocates of NAFTA, it also surrounded the ads with what looked like news copy, but was actually one-sided propaganda. The second *Times* advertorial section, which ran July 21, 1993, contained a newsy-looking item attacking the NAFTA critics who were being denied space: "Special interest groups—most notably labor and environmental—have funded and organized their attempts to derail the agreement very well. . . . [But] governors, who are not overrun by special interests and who are held accountable for the welfare of their states, really see the value of NAFTA in a first-hand way."

The "special interest groups" didn't take their exclusion from the *New York Times* lying down. After labor was again denied access to the second installment of the NAFTA sections, the AFL-CIO held a protest in front of the *Times*'s New York City headquarters on July 20. AFL-CIO secretary-treasurer Thomas Donahue issued a public challenge to *Times* reporters: "We would ask journalists to answer seriously whether they are embarrassed by combining advertising and editorial content into an 'advertorial' section, which then sells access to a 'free press' to a selected few."⁴⁴

Trade Reporting's Information Deficit

November/December 1994

DEAN BAKER

IT WOULD BE hard to imagine more inaccurate and biased economic reporting than the coverage of international trade issues. Those who get their information on trade issues solely from the major media outlets are almost certainly more misinformed and confused than those who never pay any attention to trade issues at all.

This is not a situation in which reporters can claim that the complexity of the underlying issues makes it difficult for a nonexpert to follow the debate. Mainstream reporting has failed due to outright deceptions (by either reporters or their sources) and insufficient familiarity with arithmetic and simple logic.

The most basic problem with coverage is the choice of sources. News stories on trade rely almost exclusively on administration and business representatives. The information provided by these sources is almost always taken at face value, even when the individuals have an obvious interest at stake.

For example, a front-page *Washington Post* article on the impact of revoking "most-favored-nation" status with China relied mainly on business executives of firms that trade with China. Their unsurprising conclusion was that the loss of exports to China would "mean long-term damage to American workers and consumers."⁴⁵ Remarkably, there was absolutely no discussion of the possibility that reduced trade with China might increase the number of jobs in the United States since the United States currently runs a trade deficit with China that exceeds $20 billion.

The *Post* story also reported the implausible claim that imposing tariffs would cost consumers $14 billion a year. Only if the government collected a huge amount of money in the form of tariffs could prices go up that much. If the scare stories of the importers were true, the government would reap approximately $50 billion in additional revenue over a five-year period. This is ten times the size of the alleged "pork" in the crime bill, and more than four times as much as Clinton's welfare reform is slated to cost. But the windfall implied by the importers' figures went unmentioned.

The coverage of the General Agreement on Tariffs and Trade (GATT) displayed a similar uncritical acceptance of absurd numbers from partisan sources. For example, U.S. trade representative Mickey Kantor regularly stated that GATT would increase U.S. economic growth by between $1 trillion and $2 trillion over the next ten years. That amount was between ten and twenty times larger than estimates from even very pro-GATT sources, such as the multinational Organization for Economic Cooperation and Development. Yet this projection was regularly repeated in the media without question. Thomas Friedman of the *New York Times*, for example, repeated a tax revenue projection based on this growth estimate without ever noting that this number was in dispute.⁴⁶

Similar numerical tricks were played to make the case that NAFTA has been a huge success. The *New York Times* ran charts showing imports of cars from Mexico and exports of cars to Mexico to make the point that "G.M. [Is] Coloring Mexico with Chevys." In fact, car imports from Mexico have increased more than exports to Mexico since NAFTA went into effect. But the *Times* printed the charts on two different scales, making it appear that the opposite was the case.⁴⁷

USA Today went through similar gyrations to make the pro-NAFTA case. A front-page story headlined "Exports to Mexico Soar After NAFTA" was illustrated with a chart labeled "Exports Soar." The chart showed, however, that the growth rate of exports to Mexico had fallen off considerably, so that in 1993 exports to Mexico were only slightly higher than in 1992.⁴⁸

Peter Behr of the *Washington Post* tried to make the case for the benefits of NAFTA with innovative arithmetic in "NAFTAmath: A Texas-Sized Surge in Trade." "The trade figures bolster the administration's argument that NAFTA is a net job creator, [Commerce Secretary Ron] Brown noted. Based on the calculation that each $1 billion in new exports generates 20,000 jobs, a $2 billion trade surplus this year with Mexico should create 100,000 jobs."⁴⁹ Aside from multiplying correctly, Behr might have pointed out that the U.S. trade surplus with Mexico has shrunk, not grown, under NAFTA.

There are many other examples of total nonsense passing as trade reporting. *Washington Post* financial columnist James K. Glassman claimed in 1993 that "the engine that's been driving the U.S. economy for the past decade is exports."⁵⁰ But it is *net* exports (the volume of exports minus the volume of imports), not exports taken in isolation, that stimulate economic growth—and from 1984 to 1993, the United States ran a cumulative trade deficit of $858 billion.

Another *Washington Post* business columnist, Hobart Rowen, lectured union leaders that they should be humbled by the fact that car exports to Mexico had increased so much after the passage of NAFTA.[51] He either didn't notice, or didn't bother to mention, that car imports from Mexico had increased more.

Reporting on trade issues is so far from meeting minimal standards of accuracy and balance that it is usually best ignored. The quality of the media's coverage of trade issues is probably best captured by the first paragraph of a front-page *news* story written by Peter Passell in the *New York Times*: "Free trade means growth. Free trade means growth. Free trade means growth. Just say it 50 more times and all doubts will melt away."[52] This straightforward cheerleading is somewhat more concise but not significantly more biased than the bulk of the media's coverage of trade issues.

Notes

1. *New York Times*, July 21, 1992. The series continued on July 22 and July 23, 1992.
2. *New York Times*, July 22, 1992.
3. *New York Times*, August 13, 1992.
4. "No Gain Without Pain," *Economist*, August 15, 1992, p. 54.
5. *New York Times*, July 22, 1992.
6. Doug Henwood, "Nafta Thoughts," *Lies of Our Times*, September 1992, p. 12.
7. *Washington Post*, August 13, 1992.
8. *Wall Street Journal*, August 7, 1992.
9. William Greider, "Exporting Jobs," *Rolling Stone*, September 3, 1992, p. 32.
10. John Cavanaugh and John Gershman, "'Free Trade' Fiasco," *The Progressive*, February 1992, p. 32.
11. "No Gain Without Pain," *Economist*, August 15, 1992, p. 54.
12. *New York Times*, August 9, 1992.
13. *New York Times*, August 13, 1992.
14. *Wall Street Journal*, August 7, 1992.
15. "How Trade Barriers Hurt U.S. Consumers," *Time*, August 10, 1992, p. 44.
16. *Wall Street Journal*, August 7, 1992.
17. *New York Times*, August 9, 1992.
18. For more on the Institute for International Economics, see Doug Henwood, "The Media's Favorite Trade Experts," *Extra!*, January/February 1993, p. 12.
19. *Philadelphia Inquirer*, August 12, 1992.
20. See, for example, John Greenwald, "The Great American Layoffs," *Time*, July 20, 1992, p. 64; Stephen Baker, "Detroit South," *Business Week*, March 16, 1992, p. 98.
21. Walter Russell Mead, "Bushism Found: A Second-Term Agenda Hidden in Trade Agreements," *Harper's*, September 1992, p. 37.
22. *New York Times*, August 9, 1992.
23. Michael Satchell, "Poisoning the Border," *U.S. News & World Report*, May 6, 1991, p. 32.

24. "Rules Breached by Ninety-Five Percent of All Factories," *Latin America Regional Reports*, October 1, 1992, p. 8.

25. William Greider, "Exporting Jobs," *Rolling Stone*, September 3, 1992, p. 32.

26. Marc Breslow, "How Free Trade Fails," *Dollars and Sense*, October 1992, p. 6.

27. Robert Weissman, "Trade, Debt and Plunder in Mexico: An Interview with Cuahtemoc Cardenas," *Multinational Monitor*, January 1991, p. 25.

28. *New York Times*, July 23, 1992.

29. Linda Robinson and Andrea Dabrowski, "The Unfinished Revolution," *U.S. News & World Report*, July 27, 1992, p. 45.

30. "Continued Threats to Basic Freedoms," *Latin America Regional Reports*, May 7, 1992, p. 2.

31. Marc Breslow, "How Free Trade Fails," *Dollars and Sense*, October 1992, p. 6.

32. *Washington Post*, May 9, 1993.

33. Marc Levinson, "The Trashing of Free Trade," *Newsweek*, July 12, 1993, p. 42.

34. *New York Times*, August 10, 1993.

35. *New York Times*, July 12, 1993.

36. *Crossfire*, September 14, 1993.

37. William Greider and Jann S. Wenner, "President Clinton," *Rolling Stone*, December 9, 1993, p. 40.

38. *Washington Post*, November 19, 1993.

39. *Wall Street Journal Report*, October 31, 1993.

40. *Washington Post*, November 19, 1993.

41. *New York Times*, November 5, 1993.

42. *Meet the Press*, November 7, 1993.

43. Quoted in Alexander Cockburn, "Beat the Devil," *The Nation*, August 9, 1993, p. 162.

44. AFL-CIO, "Trade Unionists in Seven Cities Protest *New York Times* Ad," press release, July 20, 1993.

45. *Washington Post*, May 22, 1994.

46. *New York Times*, April 14, 1994.

47. *New York Times*, May 12, 1994.

48. *USA Today*, May 25, 1994.

49. *Washington Post*, August 21, 1994.

50. *Washington Post*, November 19, 1993.

51. *Washington Post*, August 21, 1994.

52. *New York Times*, December 15, 1993.

10 Health Care Reform: The Single-Payer Taboo

America's Health Care Crisis: A Case of Media Malpractice

January/February 1993

ROBERT DREYFUSS

I ONCE HAD the occasion to discuss health care with reporters and editors of the *Washington Post*. Entering the newspaper's conference room, I encountered as many as twenty writers on health-related issues from the *Post*'s national staff, the business pages, and the weekly "Health" section. As I looked around the room, recognizing faces and nodding to acquaintances, I thought of the collective talent in the room and commented that with the paper's resources, it ought not to be difficult to win the Pulitzer simply by documenting the dimensions of America's health care crisis.

Later, talking with a *Post* reporter not present at the earlier meeting, I recounted the story. "Not much chance of a Pulitzer here," he said, adding that the *Post*'s huge resources in health care coverage were being squandered by lack of leadership and direction.

In fact, the *Washington Post*—like most of the national media, both print and electronic—showed little or no interest in a sustained investigation into the need for health care reform. By and large, media confined themselves to workaday reporting of events, content to transcribe the arcane transactions of Washington's power elite, health care industry lobbyists, and a passel of hired-gun academics and think-tank policy wonks. Missing from the mix was reality.

Leading the pack, and setting the tone for policymakers and media bigfeet alike, was the *New York Times*. In a preelection editorial, the *Times* declared, "The debate over health care reform is over. Managed competition has won. The outcome is as wondrous as it is surprising." The new Congress, said the *Times*, "faces a delicious prospect: Come January it can start with a managed competition blueprint, dot the i's and send the president, whether his name is Clinton or Bush, a bill he'd be proud to sign."[1]

Managed competition? The new panacea with the oxymoronic name was not exactly the result of a popular groundswell. No crowds were reported chanting, "We want managed competition!" And although the phrase popped up repeatedly in media reports in virtually every newspaper and television network, few reporters managed to say exactly what it means.

In fact, "managed competition" is a nearly meaningless buzzword that, decoded, translates into completing the transformation of American medicine from one-on-one doctor-patient relationships to the establishment of Fortune 500–style corporate health conglomerates—highly profitable ones, indeed—that would monopolize an $800 billion industry.

Despite the term's obscurity, it was routinely used by reporters without even a short identifying phrase attached to it. The *Washington's Post*'s Dana Priest quoted Judith Feder, Clinton health policy adviser, saying "The campaign's position was that managed competition can work within the discipline of a global budget." The same article reported, without further explanation, that another leading Clinton adviser "is a believer in the purist 'managed competition' approach favored by conservative Democrats."[2]

Precise and specific definitions of managed competition policies for health care reform were mostly confined to the pages of academic journals and policy papers. Stripped to its core, the policy would create large-scale, corporate health care entities like health maintenance organizations (HMOs), run by a few large insurance companies. The law would define a minimum benefit package, less comprehensive than most private insurance provides. And penalties, such as higher taxes, would force most people into these plans. Consumers would lose their ability to choose a doctor or hospital, since they would be allowed to use only those providers who participate in the health care consortium.

In short, not exactly the kind of health care "solution" that most Americans would write to Congress and demand.

The first wave of media attention on health care reform began in the spring of 1991 and peaked after the November 1991 special election of Senator Harris Wofford (D.–Penn.), whose call for health care reform was a key part of his come-from-behind victory. At that point major media did two things right—and two things wrong.

First, to their credit, media began to report that the news from Pennsylvania was that the American people wanted health care reform. An editorial in the *Philadelphia Inquirer* exclaimed: "With a clarifying wallop much like the sound of a two-by-four smacking a mule between the eyes, Harris Wofford's Senate victory last week got the attention of the participants in the nation's stalled health care debate."[3]

That was the tone of the coverage in virtually every newspaper and broadcast news organization. And, as a result of the media focus on health care, President Bush and the various Democratic presidential candidates scrambled to come up with a health care "plan" of their own.

Second, again to their credit, media began to focus on the enormous lobbying clout and influence-buying of the insurance industry, drug companies, doctors, and other special interests. Typical was a piece by Tom Hamburger of the Minneapolis *Star Tribune,* entitled "Big Bucks, Politics Hinder Health-Care Reform," which explained that in 1990 the insurance industry "contributed more than $4 million to congressional candidates."[4] And Gary Lee of the *Washington Post,* who covers lobbying and public relations, wrote a number of articles about the insurance industry's clout in the nation's capital. Many other news organizations picked up on an excellent report published in *Common Cause Magazine* in January 1992 that analyzed the impact of the campaign contributions of insurers and the health care industry.[5]

This is where things began to go wrong. First, many news outlets blew it on holding presidential candidates accountable on their health plans. Early in 1992, I was asked by a reporter for a major city newspaper to analyze the "three plans" for health care reform, namely, a Canadian-style reform, the Democrats' "pay-or-play" plan to manage employer-based insurance, and President Bush's patched-together plan for tax credits and assorted other half-measures. When I commented that the Bush proposal could not really even be called a plan, since it said nothing about controlling costs and made no attempt to provide coverage for millions of uninsured, the reporter said, "I know." But in his article, he refused to say that the emperor had no clothes.

Virtually all of the reporting about Bush's health care platform throughout 1992 gave the nonplan far too much credit. (An early *New York Times* editorial did call it a "fraud, bordering on public policy malpractice."[6]) But far too many newspapers ran simple side-by-side comparisons of various plans, without taking pains to point out their glaring flaws.

Candidate Clinton's aimless drift on health care throughout 1992 was also given a free ride by the media. In the early stages of the campaign, Clinton's near-total failure to address health care was overshadowed by the media's attention to the "character issue." Then, Clinton's migration from support for the moderate Democrats' pay-or-play reform to his late-in-the-campaign endorsement for the conservative Democratic "managed competition" solution received little or no press scrutiny.

The second media flaw was that, by and large, news outlets swallowed the insurance industry's propaganda about Canada's universal health care system. In June 1991, a *Wall Street Journal*/NBC News poll found that 69 percent of Americans would support a Canadian-style system, while only 20 percent were opposed. The 69 percent also said they were willing to pay higher taxes for a system that guaranteed the best available health care for everyone.[7]

In response, the insurance industry launched a multi-million-dollar campaign to discredit Canada's system. Gradually at first, and then like a mantra that appeared in almost every article about the Canadian system, we started to hear about "waiting lines" for Canadian health care. There were unsubstantiated stories about Canadians flocking across the border to partake of America's health care cornucopia. Few and far between were stories about Canada's tremendous success in providing cradle-to-grave health care for every citizen.

While media solemnly took note of the industry's influence over U.S. political leaders, achieved via campaign contributions, they failed to report effectively on the industry's public relations war.[8] In fact, they got taken in.

Then, when a handful of insurance industry executives, big business leaders, conservative Democratic politicians, and the *New York Times* editorial board decided that "managed competition" was the deus ex machina, most media followed dutifully along.

As the Clinton administration took office, the prospects for real, sweeping health care reform were bleak. Only two outcomes were likely: Either President Clinton and Congress would succeed in enacting into law the managed competition solution that insurance industry leaders wanted, or else the sheer magnitude of putting together *any* health care reform package would cause the whole effort to self-destruct.

The slim chance for real reform depended on grassroots pressure. And that, in turn, depended on the media doing its job: exposing the inequities of America's health care system again and again. Only then could the 69 percent who wanted a Canadian-style system have been energized to make their voices heard over the insurance industry's public relations campaign.

When "Both Sides" Aren't Enough: The Restricted Debate over Health Care Reform

January/February 1994

JOHN CANHAM-CLYNE

JOURNALISTS PRIDE THEMSELVES on presenting "both sides" of a story. But if establishment media can decide which positions get to take part in debate, then telling *only* "both sides" may be a way of keeping news consumers on the outside.

Coverage of the health care reform debate provided a wealth of examples. Major news outlets went out of their way to avoid mentioning the progressive alternative to the Clinton health care program: a Canadian-style single-payer reform, which would replace private insurance with tax-financed comprehensive universal coverage.

HILLARY VERSUS THE INSURANCE INDUSTRY

In November 1993, major media focused on the White House–promoted story of "Hillary Rodham Clinton versus the insurance industry." "The First Lady came out swinging, visibly angry as she took on the health insurers industry," said ABC's John McWethy.[9] "Hillary Clinton Accuses Insurers of Lying About Health Proposal," blared a front-page *New York Times* headline;[10] the *Washington Post*'s front page followed suit with "First Lady Lambastes Health Insurers."[11] CNN's Bob Cain declared that the Clinton administration was "engaged in something close to an all-out war with the health insurance industry."[12]

These stories referred to Rodham Clinton's attack on a $6 million advertising campaign by the Health Insurance Association of America (HIAA) challenging the Clinton plan. What the news outlets didn't mention was that the "Big Five" insurance companies—Aetna, Cigna, Prudential, Metropolitan Life, and Travelers—had withdrawn from HIAA and were generally supportive of the Clintons' health policies.

These companies have invested aggressively in health maintenance organizations and other managed care networks, which stood to expand dramatically under the Clinton "managed competition" plan.[13] The "managed competition" theory, in fact, was cooked up by executives of the Big Five and other medical industry leaders in annual meetings held in Jackson Hole, Wyoming.

The *New York Times*'s Adam Clymer equated HIAA with the "insurance industry" throughout his piece—a particularly egregious error, given that the *Times* had earlier run a detailed report on the Jackson Hole Group.[14] The *Washington Post*'s Dana Priest hinted at reality, describing HIAA as a "trade group of mainly medium-sized firms," and later saying that the group "represents 270 medium- and small-sized insurers, many of whom could be put out of business by reform."[15] Insiders will recognize this as a reference to the fact that *big* insurers stood to profit greatly from the Clinton plan; other readers will remain in the dark.

Viewers of the November 2, 1993, *MacNeil/Lehrer NewsHour,* however, got a more realistic view of the dispute. The show's discussion of the HIAA ads included advocates for the Clinton plan and for the insurance group, but also Dr. David Himmelstein, codirector of the Center for National Health Program Studies at Harvard. Himmelstein, a single-payer advocate, agreed with the First Lady that the insurance industry is the problem, but he also noted that the HIAA represents the "small sharks" that will be eaten by the big sharks under the Clinton plan.

CONSERVATIVES VERSUS CLINTON

Although a bill for a single-payer health care system garnered ninety-two cosponsors in the House of Representatives, most press accounts did not acknowledge that the Clinton plan had serious competition until more conservative alternatives were unveiled.

The introduction by Representative Jim McDermott (D.–Wash.) of a single-payer bill in March 1993 was largely ignored. *ABC World News Tonight,* in fact, ran only one story that even mentioned the single-payer system in all of 1993—a political report pointing out that Hillary Rodham Clinton had already dismissed the single-payer plan, but needed to shore up her support among single-payer advocates.[16]

But in September, when Republican Senator John Chafee (R.I.) introduced his "plan"—actually a 14-page outline—it was greeted with media fanfare. The *Boston Globe* called it "the first serious response to the president's proposal."[17] ABC News's Bill Greenwood concluded optimistically: "Thirty-seven million Americans are now without health insurance. Between the President's plan and today's Republican alternative, they're certain to finally get some coverage."[18]

Actually, Chafee's proposal closely resembled the 1992 Managed Competition Act introduced by Representative Jim Cooper (D.–Tenn.), which differed from the

White House plan by not requiring employers to offer coverage and by making insurance purchasing cooperatives voluntary, not mandatory. A Congressional Budget Office analysis of 1992 health plans conservatively estimated that Cooper's bill would leave 25 million Americans uninsured.[19]

But reporters rarely challenged the assumption that conservative "alternatives"—even those offered by hard-right Republicans like Senator Phil Gramm (Texas) and Representative Dick Armey (Texas)—actually guaranteed universal coverage. "Growing Consensus on Covering All, but How?" was the *New York Times*'s headline on a summary of the debate.[20]

MacNeil/Lehrer helped puncture the consensus—in large part because instead of presenting "both sides," the debate featured members of four congressional factions: single-payer advocate Representative George Miller (D.–Calif.), Clinton supporter Senator Jay Rockefeller (D.–W.Va.), Chafee supporter Senator Nancy Kassebaum (R.–Kansas), and conservative Representative Armey.

In contrast to discussions that start with the question of cost control, host Jim Lehrer began by pressing all participants on their commitment to universal coverage. Kassebaum said she supported "the premise of access for everyone"; Armey replied that "we can achieve universal affordability." Rockefeller attacked the Republicans and conservative Democrats head on: "There are only two groups that support [universal coverage], and that is George Miller with the single-payer approach and President Clinton with his job-based approach."

BUREAUCRACY VERSUS MARKET FORCES

The *New York Times*'s Clymer also divided the debate between the Clintons and the single-payer system on one side and Cooper and the Republicans on the other. Clymer admitted vaguely that the conservative alternatives were "less generous" but also insisted that they were "less complicated"—the Republicans and Cooper "all see a virtue in less bureaucracy."[21]

In fact, the U.S. market-based health insurance system is by far the most costly, bureaucratic, and complicated health care system in the world. Peer-reviewed research published by Himmelstein and Harvard Center codirector Dr. Steffie Woolhandler found that private U.S. insurers spend 13 percent of every dollar for overhead, while Medicare and Medicaid combined average 3.5 percent overhead. Canada's single-payer system has an overhead of less than one percent.[22]

False ideological assumptions about bureaucracy and competition dominated op-ed and editorial pages. According to *Washington Post* columnist Robert Samuelson, "We need to admit that reform's twin goals—comprehensive universal insurance and cost control—are at odds."[23]

The General Accounting Office (GAO) and the Congressional Budget Office (CBO), however, both concluded that the savings on bureaucracy from switching to a single-payer system would almost immediately offset the increased cost of extending coverage to the uninsured and underinsured. Although the single-payer plan achieves universal coverage and the conservative plans don't, the CBO concluded that by the year 2000, annual national health expenditures under a 1992 single-payer proposal would total $169 billion *less* than those projected under Cooper's proposal.[24]

Despite the fact that the single-payer plan was the cheapest proposal on the table, journalists used the false equation of "cost" with federal expenditures to dismiss the Canadian-style plan. The *New York Times*'s Clymer wrote that the single-payer plan requires "unpopular taxes," causing some sympathetic Democrats to dismiss it as "politically impossible."[25] Clymer noted that these taxes would "replace" health care premiums, but he didn't note that within a few years they would likely total substantially less than the combined premiums and taxes paid under either the Clinton or Cooper plan.

When asked by a reader why the administration had not given serious consideration to the single-payer plan, *USA Today* replied that a single-payer system would have "caused great disruption to the economy, resulted in higher taxes and given the federal government vast new powers."[26]

BEYOND "BOTH SIDES"

Some mainstream outlets occasionally avoided these pitfalls. *MacNeil/Lehrer,* as noted, sometimes made an effort to include single-payer supporters on its health care reform panels. In 1992, the *Chicago Tribune*'s *Sunday Magazine* carried a long article that examined the problems facing the Canadian system, without obscuring the broader successful context.[27] The Minneapolis *Star Tribune*'s special section on health care reform compared the U.S. system to those in other countries and gave advocates of four reform approaches ample room to present their views. (Only the single-payer system, however, had a "counterpoint" placed in the middle of its argument—a distorted attack on the Canadian plan from HIAA spokesperson Ed Neuschler.)[28]

The medical press, including the *New England Journal of Medicine* and the *Journal of the American Medical Association,* has sustained a lively reform debate among medical professionals for years. Independent press highlights included special issues of *Dollars and Sense*[29] and the *Washington Monthly,*[30] an *In These Times* piece by Woolhandler and Himmelstein laying out the economic arguments for single-payer,[31] and David Corn's insightful reporting on the politics of the single-payer movement for *The Nation.*[32]

Health Care Reform: Not Journalistically Viable?

July/August 1993

In an October 10, 1992, editorial, the *New York Times* proclaimed that "the debate over health care reform is over." In fact, the debate over health care reform went on, but you might not have known it from establishment media.

While the *New York Times* and other elite outlets rallied around "managed competition"—a system in which private insurance companies provide medical care through giant HMOs—grassroots activists continued to push for a "single-payer" system, similar to Canada's, in which insurance companies would be eliminated from the health care picture and government would provide universal coverage. Single-payer proponents often referred to managed competition as the "Insurance Industry Preservation Act."

When Michael Kinsley in *The New Republic* discussed "the various alternatives" for health care reform facing Congress, he noted in parentheses that he was not talking about "the Canadian-style 'single-payer' option, which has few backers."[33] The single-payer option didn't have "few backers" among the U.S. public—in one *Wall Street Journal*/NBC poll, 69 percent of respondents supported the idea of Canadian-style, government-funded national health insurance.[34] And it didn't have "few backers" in Congress; the McDermott single-payer bill had ninety-two cosponsors in the House, more than any other health care bill. Where the single-payer plan didn't have many backers was among Kinsley's colleagues in the media elite—who seemed to go to great lengths to avoid discussing it.

While the phrase "managed competition" appeared in sixty-two *New York Times* news stories in the six months following the 1992 election, "single-payer" appeared in only five news stories during that period—never in more than a single-sentence mention.

The tilt toward the managed competition plan at the *New York Times* was so pronounced that it provoked a demonstration by single-payer advocates outside the paper's offices on May 12, 1993. Protesters pointed out a potential conflict of interest in *New York Times* health care coverage: Four of the twelve directors on the New York Times Company's board were also on the boards of health insurance companies.

The justification media managers gave for the imbalance of attention was that while managed competition was supported by the Clinton administration, a single-payer system was not "politically viable." What this means is that news judgments were based on elite preferences, not on popular opinion: The *New York Times*'s own polling since 1990 has consistently found majorities—ranging from 54 percent to 66 percent—in favor of tax-financed national health insurance.

The way elite media can marginalize opinions—even ones held by a majority of the population—was demonstrated by a May 5, 1993, discussion of managed competition on the *MacNeil/Lehrer NewsHour*. Robert MacNeil led a panel made up of three government officials—a congressman, a governor, and a state health commissioner—who were mainly supportive of managed competition, and a representative of Physicians for a National Health Care Plan, Dr. Steffie Woolhandler, who advocated a single-payer plan.

After Woolhandler argued that managed competition would increase costs and bureaucracy, and the other three guests disagreed, MacNeil said to her pointedly, "Dr. Woolhandler, that's three against one on the cost reduction thing"— as if this were a random sample of opinion, rather than a panel assembled by *MacNeil/Lehrer*. Near the end of the discussion, MacNeil said he was asking the last question of Woolhandler "since you're in the minority"—to which she responded: "Robert, I'm not in the minority. Polls are showing two-thirds of the American people support government-funded national health insurance."

MacNeil continued: "If this [managed competition] is the program that has political consensus and the other one that you advocate [single-payer] is considered impossible politically at the moment, why are you then against the one that is viable and would produce a large amount of reform?"

Woolhandler responded by rejecting the assumption that managed competition would provide meaningful health reform. But the other assumption of the question—that a proposal supported by up to two-thirds of the population should not be seriously debated if it doesn't have a "political consensus"—speaks volumes about the health of American journalism.

Health Debate in Quarantine
July/August 1993

In 1990, the grassroots group Neighbor to Neighbor called for a boycott of Folgers coffee to protest human rights abuses in El Salvador, where some Folgers beans were grown. When Neighbor to Neighbor tried to run ads publicizing this boycott, however, nearly every TV station turned the group down.

The reason stations were reluctant to air the ad soon became apparent. One of the few stations that did accept the spot was Boston's WHDH, a CBS affiliate. In response, Folgers's parent company, Procter & Gamble, canceled the $1 million it spent annually on advertising at the station.[35]

Three years later, Neighbor to Neighbor tried to run another ad on WHDH—this time promoting a Canadian-style single-payer health care plan. At first, according to Neighbor to Neighbor spokesperson Rob Everts, the response was at least honest: "It looks as if all the substantiation is here," the station's public affairs director reportedly said. "However, many of our advertisers are health insurers, and we don't want to take any hits from the health insurance companies."[36]

But after station executives had time to think it over, their line changed. They rejected the ad, issuing this statement: "The station management feels that the issue is not addressed in a comprehensive manner in a 30-second format and will address it itself in a longer form sometime in the future."[37]

Other TV stations had equally disingenuous reasons for rejecting the Neighbor to Neighbor ads: The spots were said to be "confusing," "simplistic," or lacking in "documentation." Presumably these stations believe that the commercials for detergent and beer that they run every ten minutes are clear, complex, and well documented. (Two of the ten stations approached by Neighbor to Neighbor did accept the ad: KGTV and KNSD, both in San Diego.)

But the most obvious hypocrisy is that the TV ads by the "Coalition for Health Insurance Choices" appeared across the country, promoting "a plan supported by consumers, businesses and health care professionals." Only the fine print at the end of the ads informed viewers that they were actually funded by the Health Insurance Association of America, part of the industry's $4 million public relations campaign.[38] When the other side of the debate can't even buy time to have its say, what kind of debate do you really have?

NPR Health Care Reform "Debate" Needed Second Opinion

Extra! Update, June 1994

LISTENERS TO National Public Radio's (NPR) *Morning Edition* were provided with two regular pundits—former U.S. Representatives Tom Downey (D.–N.Y.) and Vin Weber (R.–Minn.)—who were supposed to present contrasting viewpoints on congressional events.

But on the health care issue, NPR's point/counterpoint team was working for the same side—the health insurance industry and health care companies, which have a strong interest in preventing any meaningful health care reform.

According to *Legal Times*, Downey was a lobbyist for the Metropolitan Life Insurance Company, one of the largest providers of health insurance, and for US Healthcare, a large Pennsylvania-based HMO. Both HMOs and the large health insurance companies stand to benefit from a "managed competition" approach to health care, different versions of which were pushed by President Clinton, Representative Jim Cooper (D.–Tenn.), and Senator Chafee (R.–R.I.). Downey also represented a division of the Merck pharmaceutical corporation.[39]

Legal Times reported that Weber, for his part, was a consultant to the Alliance for Managed Competition, a coalition of the "Big Five" health insurance companies (including Metropolitan Life). Another client Weber consulted for was the United Healthcare Corporation.

Weber and Downy "debated" the health care reform issue on *Morning Edition* at least three times in late 1993 and early 1994.[40] In none of these debates did they mention their extensive ties to the health care industry.

Nevertheless, their clients had reason to appreciate the positions they took on health care reform. For example, on the October 28, 1993, program, Weber declared: "At the end of the day, there are two ways to pay for universal service. One is through some big increase in taxes somewhere and the other is through some serious, rigorous restriction of choice."

Actually, both the Congressional Budget Office and the General Accounting Office had found that there was a way to provide universal service while cutting costs, without rationing: a Canadian-style single-payer system, in which all medical bills are paid by the government. This plan would eliminate the health insurance companies that Weber and Downey both work for, however.

Neither of NPR's congressional analysts treated the single-payer option as a serious alternative. In fact, Downey actively encouraged Clinton to avoid seeking the support of the single-payer advocates, who made up a large bloc of votes in Congress. During the September 21, 1993, NPR discussion, Downey said, "There are not enough Democratic votes" to pass a health care plan, because "the Democrats in the House and the Senate are split between those who would like a Canadian single-payer system and the more moderate and conservative Democrats who would like to try a managed competition approach."

Downey advised Clinton to "play a bipartisan game" and "isolate the far left and the far right"—that is, single-payer Democrats and Republicans who insisted there's no health care crisis.

After questions were raised about Weber and Downey's conflict of interest, *Morning Edition* began noting that Downey was a "lobbyist" and Weber was a "consultant." But even though both worked for corporate clients that have an interest in any number of issues, no more specific identifications were given. NPR seemed to feel that everyone knows that former members of Congress go on to become corporate lobbyists. "Do you think our audience is so naive that they think people trained in a specific line of work are now out there making pizza?" *Morning Edition* senior producer Ellen McDonnell asked *Legal Times*.[41]

A Couple of Mentions of Single-Payer September/October 1994

On ABC's *Nightline*, from July 1993 until the November 1994 election, there were only two mentions of the Canadian single-payer health care system: On a March 1994 show, an insurance representative made dire, unsupported predictions that with single-payer "there will definitely be limitations on your selection options in your future."[42]

On a September 1993 broadcast that featured an interview with Bill Clinton, Ted Koppel pressed the president about "frenzied" Canadians swarming over the border for U.S. health care. Canadians, Koppel told Clinton, were saying, "Whatever you do, don't exchange what you've got for what we've got."[43] According to a Gallup poll taken only a few days earlier, just 2 percent of Canadians believed that the U.S. health care system was better than their own.[44]

Notes

1. *New York Times,* October 10, 1992.
2. *Washington Post,* November 23, 1992.
3. *Philadelphia Inquirer,* November 10, 1991.
4. Minneapolis *Star Tribune,* November 21, 1991.
5. Vicki Kemper and Veveca Novak, "What's Blocking Health Care Reform?" *Common Cause Magazine,* January/February/March 1992, p. 8.
6. *New York Times,* January 7, 1992.
7. *Wall Street Journal,* June 28, 1991.
8. E.g., *Wall Street Journal,* November 27, 1992.
9. *ABC World News Tonight,* November 1, 1993.
10. *New York Times,* November 2, 1993.
11. *Washington Post,* November 2, 1993.
12. CNN, November 3, 1993.
13. President Clinton acknowledged this in a February 1994 speech in Connecticut, where four of the biggest insurance companies are based. "I frankly quite appreciate the fact that most of your big insurance companies here who write health insurance ... have not been participating in financing the misleading campaign against the administration's health plan," he said. "The companies that operate here will actually do quite well if our plan passes." (*Washington Post,* February 25, 1994).
14. *New York Times,* February 28, 1993.
15. *Washington Post,* November 2, 1993.
16. *ABC World News Tonight,* June 23, 1993.

17. *Boston Globe,* September 16, 1993.

18. *ABC World News Tonight,* September 15, 1993.

19. Congressional Budget Office, *Estimates of Health Care Proposals from the 102nd Congress,* 103d Cong., 2d sess. (Washington, D.C.: Government Printing Office, 1994).

20. *New York Times,* November 14, 1993.

21. *New York Times,* October 17, 1993.

22. Steffie Woolhandler and David U. Himmelstein, "The Deteriorating Administrative Efficiency of the U.S. Health Care System," *New England Journal of Medicine,* May 2, 1991, p. 1253; S. Woolhandler, D. U. Himmelstein, and J. P. Lewontin, "Administrative Costs in U.S. Hospitals," *New England Journal of Medicine,* August 5, 1993, p. 400.

23. *Washington Post,* October 20, 1993.

24. General Accounting Office, *Health Care Spending: Trans-Contributing Factors and Proposals for Reform* (Washington, D.C.: Government Printing Office, June 10, 1991).

25. *New York Times,* October 17, 1993.

26. *USA Today,* September 27, 1993.

27. Storer H. Rowley, "Prescription from Canada: Would Universal Health Care Work in This Country?" *Chicago Tribune Sunday Magazine,* May 31, 1992, p. 14.

28. Minneapolis *Star Tribune,* October 25, 1993.

29. "Health Care Emergency: Who's Paying? What's Wrong?" special issue, *Dollars and Sense,* May 1993, pp. 6–21.

30. "You're Not Going to Feel a Thing," special issue, *Washington Monthly,* September 1993, pp. 27–41.

31. Steffie Woolhandler and David U. Himmelstein, "Socialized Medicine is Good Business," *In These Times,* January 25, 1993, p. 18.

32. David Corn, "Must We Take the Clintons' Medicine?" *The Nation,* October 18, 1993, p. 409.

33. *The New Republic,* December 13, 1993, p. 4.

34. *Wall Street Journal,* June 28, 1991.

35. "Corporate Censorship," *Extra!,* May/June 1990, p. 13.

36. *CounterSpin,* May 22, 1993.

37. *Boston Globe,* May 25, 1993.

38. Coalition for Health Insurance Choices, advertisement, 1993.

39. *Legal Times,* March 28, 1994.

40. NPR *Morning Edition,* September 21, 1993; October 28, 1993; March 8, 1994.

41. *Legal Times,* March 28, 1994.

42. *Nightline,* March 1, 1994.

43. *Nightline,* September 23, 1993.

44. UPI, September 13, 1993; *Toronto Star,* September 13, 1993.

11 War and "Peacekeeping": Intervention in the Clinton Era

Media on the Somalia Intervention: Tragedy Made Simple

March 1993

JIM NAURECKAS

THE FIRST QUESTION national media should have asked themselves about Somalia is: Why did we ignore the story for so long? In January 1991, six leading relief agencies warned that 20 million people in Africa faced starvation unless food aid was forthcoming—mainly in Somalia, Sudan, and Ethiopia.[1] In the fall of 1991, U.N. officials estimated that 4.5 million Somalis faced grave food shortages. In all of 1991, Somalia got three minutes of attention on the three evening network news shows. From January through June 1992, Somalia got five minutes.[2]

By July 1992, when the news media began to pay attention, 25 percent of Somalia's children under five may already have died, according to one international aid group.[3]

Although some people have cited the intervention in Somalia as an example of the power of TV pictures to compel governments to act, the fact is that the TV networks were hardly interested in Somalia until *after* the U.S. government started using military planes to airlift supplies there. Instead of waiting for the U.S. government to lead the way, the media should have been reporting on all countries where food aid was urgently needed, including Sudan, Mozambique, and Liberia.

There was a constant sense in news coverage that a full-scale U.S. military operation was the only way to save lives. "The American troops are the only solution. Every other solution has been tried," one relief worker was quoted in the *New York Times*.[4] In fact, many in the relief community believed that while military intervention may have been necessary, it should have been done with a U.N. force, not by the United States acting virtually alone.

The U.N., these experts believe, could have carried out an effective relief mission months earlier with a much smaller force. But U.N. peacekeeping forces were never fully deployed, largely because the U.S. mission to the U.N. obstructed full-scale peacekeeping efforts in Somalia (and other countries such as Angola, Namibia, and Mozambique), on the grounds that it would cost too much.

The United States is chronically behind in its payments to the U.N.; in late 1992, it owed some $415 million, including $120 million for peacekeeping missions. This reluctance on the part of the U.S. government to carry its share of the peacekeeping burden contrasts sharply with the frequent media portrayal of the United States as the only country willing or able to help in humanitarian causes. This perception resulted in self-congratulatory commentary reminiscent of the Persian Gulf War, as when columnist Murray Kempton wrote, "A visitor could walk the corridors of the United Nations fairly swollen with the majesty of the United States that could at last glory in its conscience instead of its might."[5]

Since the United States had not consistently acted in an altruistic manner toward starving people in Africa, why did it ultimately dispatch troops to Somalia? There have been frequent media denials that geopolitical considerations might have entered into the decision. The *Washington Post* reported that "unlike previous large-scale operations, there is no U.S. strategic or economic interest in the Somalia deployments."[6]

But *The Nation* referred to Somalia as "one of the most strategically sensitive spots in the world today: astride the Horn of Africa, where oil, Islamic fundamentalism and Israeli, Iranian and Arab ambitions and arms are apt to crash and collide."[7] Given that the United States and USSR jousted over the Horn of Africa for years, *The Nation*'s assessment may have been more realistic.

There was also little discussion of the fact that northern Somalia contains mineral deposits and potential oil reserves. Considered geologically analogous to oil-rich Yemen across the Red Sea, it has been the site of oil exploration by such companies as Amoco, Chevron, and Conoco.[8] Not until six weeks into the operation did a journalist for a major media outlet, Mark Fineman of the *Los Angeles Times*, report on the "close relationship between Conoco and the U.S. intervention force," which used Conoco's Mogadishu headquarters as a "de facto U.S. embassy."[9]

If the solutions to Somalia's crisis and the reasons for the U.S. reaction were generally given simplistic treatment, the root causes of famine were seldom dealt with in any more depth. Until the 1970s, Somalia was self-sufficient in grain, and its agricultural land is productive enough that the country should have been able to feed itself despite the drought.

Often, references were made to warfare as the cause of famine in Somalia, but usually the political context was ignored or distorted, as in the *New York Times*'s Elaine Sciolino's comment that "countries crumble without the stabilizing glue of the Cold War to hold them together."[10] In fact, of course, the Cold War is largely to blame for Somalia's plight, as Bread for the World's Sharon Pauling pointed out: "The current humanitarian crisis has its origins in deposed dictator [Mohamed] Siad Barre's militarized approach to subduing Somali factions. For over 20 years, Barre's regime used Soviet and U.S. weapons to ruthlessly repress the Somali people through divide-and-rule tactics. The country has been left with a legacy of clan fighting, death and starvation."[11]

The 1969 to 1991 Siad Barre dictatorship bears direct responsibility for the 1991–1993 famine. The Somali clan hardest hit by the famine, the Rahanweyn, was the group living adjacent to the lands of Siad Barre's clan, the Marehan, and consequently had much of its fertile land stolen during the dictatorship.[12] It was this political conflict, not natural disaster, that created the desperate condition of many of the starvation victims seen on TV.

The U.S. responsibility for supporting and arming Siad Barre was seldom acknowledged by U.S. mass media. One of the noteworthy exceptions was a report by ABC's Peter Jennings, who stated that Siad Barre had received "almost $200 million in military aid and almost half a billion in economic aid." Jennings explained why the U.S. ignored Siad Barre's corruption and human rights abuses: "To Washington's satisfaction, he was more than willing to keep [Soviet-allied] Ethiopia tied down in a debilitating war. . . . Millions of innocent civilians paid the price."[13] Jennings's report, from his New York anchor desk, was more informative than anything produced by anchors Tom Brokaw and Dan Rather, who felt a need to travel to Somalia to greet the Marines.

Even more useful was a segment on the Somalia crisis reported by Charlayne Hunter-Gault for the *MacNeil/Lehrer NewsHour*. Hunter-Gault brought on Human Rights Watch's Holly Burkhalter, who noted that at the same time that Washington was claiming it was trying to moderate Siad Barre with $50 million in "security-related assistance," the dictator "engaged in a counterinsurgency effort against the North that by our calculations left about 50,000 Somali civilians dead, [and] forced a half million . . . Somali civilians across the borders into the desert of Ethiopia."[14]

More typically, mainstream media viewed Somalia's problems as indigenous and eternal: "Limited natural resources and internal disputes have historically kept stability at a distance. And the clans of Somalia have regularly battled one another into a state of anarchy," *Time* reported.[15]

Another underexplored issue was the economic causes of famine—in particular, the way the United States and international agencies like the International Monetary Fund (IMF) pressure underdeveloped countries to shift agriculture from local subsistence to export crops. To take a non-Somali example, Zimbabwe cut corn planting from 895,000 acres to 245,000 acres because the U.S. Agency for International Development encouraged them to grow, of all things, high-grade tobacco. The IMF told Zimbabwe that its Grain Marketing Board had to be run to make a profit, so it sold much of the grain it was storing. The result was that Zimbabwe, which used to be the breadbasket of southern Africa, ended up facing major famine.[16]

Although news accounts stress the aid Western nations give to Africa, the amount of money taken from sub-Saharan Africa in the form of profits and income on loans (an average of $22 billion a year) is greater than all Western aid to Africa ($10 billion a year). This disparity has contributed to Africa's debt burden, which now stands at $235 billion.[17] These structural economic problems were seldom addressed as part of the cause of Africa's chronic hunger.

Food aid itself is a controversial subject, though the debate seldom made it into mainstream forums. Donations of food are generally used by the West as a way of reducing agricultural surpluses, a practice that tends to discourage local food production. One former relief worker, Michael Maren, argued in the *Village Voice* that "hundreds of billions of dollars in food aid over the last 30 years have left the continent more famine-prone and dependent on outside relief than ever."[18]

Much coverage of Somalia has reflected a colonial mindset, arrogant about U.S. power and disparaging of Somalis. CBS's Alan Pizzy compared the U.S. intervention to the Marine presence in Lebanon: "As in Beirut, it's just a few good men trying to help another nation in need, another treacherous country where all the members of all the murderous factions look alike."[19]

The *New York Times*'s Elaine Sciolino went so far as to suggest, citing U.S. officials, that Somalia should be turned into a colony: "One state could govern Somalia in a formal 'trusteeship' until it is ready to govern itself, in the same way that Italy administered much of what is now Somalia until it became independent in 1960"[20]—a benign view of Italy's role that probably would be shared by few Somalis.

The Somali people were generally depicted as either passive victims waiting for U.S. help or as drug-crazed thugs. Actually, as Rakiya Omaar and Alex de Waal, former officials of Africa Watch, have written, most of the famine relief efforts were being carried out by Somalis themselves. Yet television's relief heroes were almost all Americans or Europeans. In an op-ed piece in the *Los Angeles Times,* Omaar and de Waal wrote that Somalis had been "reduced to nameless extras in the shadows behind Western aid workers or disaster tourists."[21]

News reports tried so hard to create an idyllic image of Somalis embracing U.S. help that one reporter was startled by the contrast between the real Somalia and the TV version. "I searched the once-grand streets of Mogadishu for signs of what had appeared to be a cute little made-for-TV military operation," wrote Andrea Peyser in the *New York Post*. "I expected scenes of rugged troops embracing happy, affectionate and grateful natives. Here's the reality: In Mogadishu, you're more likely to see a soldier shove a kid out of the way than hug him."[22]

The political factions in Somalia were discussed in cartoon-like stereotypes: *Time* referred to them as "Mad Max characters,"[23] and *Newsweek*'s Joe Klein called them "thugs, warlords and micro-messiahs."[24] Despite the dismissive treatment of the so-called warlords—"Taking on the Thugs" was the swaggering *Time* headline[25]—little attention was given to the complaints by relief groups and Africa experts that the U.S. forces lent credence to military leaders like Mohamed Farrah Aidid and Ali Mahdi Mohamed by recognizing them as local authorities.

One detail of Somali culture that seemed to fascinate journalists—perhaps because it tied in with domestic stereotypes—was the chewing of a plant called khat. Reporters constantly pointed out that the young men with guns are especially dangerous because they're "high on khat": "Youth, guns and khat—it's a deadly combination," reported ABC's Jim Laurie in an especially sensationalistic segment.[26]

People familiar with Somalia and with khat give a different picture of the drug. "It's used as a social drug in much the same way that we would use coffee," Dr. Andrew Weil told NPR. "I think that khat is a relatively mild stimulant. . . . As with any stimulant, if you take too much of it, it can make you jittery and anxious. But I can't see it as a major factor in what's going on over there."[27]

Reporters, however, couldn't seem to get enough of it. CBS's Dan Rather, interviewing a Somali clan leader, pressed him: "I have heard people tell me that when the American troops come, they must be very careful in the afternoon because many people chew on khat and get reckless." The leader laughed and replied: "No, it's not like whiskey."[28]

A tragic situation in Somalia, with complex political, economic, and historical roots, came across in the bulk of media coverage as a simple situation—helpless victims menaced by thugs—with an obvious solution: Send in the Marines. This melodramatic depiction of events meshed with the need for commercial media to tell exciting, easily grasped stories but did not do justice to the reality of the Somalian situation. It did nothing to help the U.S. public understand either the causes of or the realistic responses to the famine that threatened millions across Africa.

Rather than dealing with their failure to treat seriously the context of the Somali famine, the media seemed most preoccupied with the issue of whether camera crews should have used lights in taping the landing of Marines at the Mogadishu airport. Rather than arguing about what amounted to a Pentagon photo op that got out of hand, media self-critics might better have shone a light on the overall failure of mainstream media to educate viewers so that tragedies like Somalia's might be averted.

Somalia: Shifting Stereotypes

Extra! Update, December 1993

THE RENEWED MEDIA attention on Somalia in October 1993 did not result in more substantive coverage. What was new in the media's return to Somalia was a new dominant stereotype: changing from one-dimensional victim to one-dimensional villain.

From the beginning, coverage of Somalia was dominated by lack of context. When U.S. troops began suffering serious casualties, the stereotyping got worse. Dan Rather led off CBS's October 5, 1993, broadcast with a reference to "the hellhole that is Somalia." Jeff Gralnick, executive producer of *NBC Nightly News*, was quoted by the New York *Daily News* calling General Mohamed Farrah Aidid "an educated jungle bunny." "The rest of the jungle bunnies are not like this at all. They're illiterates," Gralnick told an NBC editorial meeting.[29]

One need not romanticize Aidid to feel that the U.S. public was denied information that would explain why many Somalis did not see U.S. and U.N. forces as benevolent providers of humanitarian aid. When Pakistani troops massacred unarmed demonstrators,[30] or U.S. helicopter gunships fired into a crowd that included many women and children, killing some 100 Somalis,[31] the U.S. press dropped the stories almost immediately.

Seldom have U.S. troops been taken to task for the deaths of innocent bystanders in Somalia. Indeed, the *New York Post* took the opposite position: "The president would do well to shed his excessive concern over the fate of Somali civilians—the desire to avoid spilling innocent Somali blood has caused the U.S. to leave American troops woefully exposed and lacking in air support."[32]

The language used to describe the intervention was decidedly slanted. Even while U.N. forces were actively engaged in search-and-destroy missions, they were still frequently referred to as "peacekeepers." A U.S. soldier captured by opposing forces was a "hostage"; Somali fighters captured by U.N. troops were "prisoners."

Major media outlets went out of their way to avoid casting doubt on the U.S. role in Somalia. The Associated Press (AP) put out a story that referred in the second paragraph to "U.S.-backed dictator" Siad Barre. Twenty-five minutes later, AP dispatched a new version of the story that deleted "U.S.-backed"—arguing that "Siad Barre received backing at various times from [the] United States and Soviet Union."[33]

But Pentagon efforts were set back when U.S. news outlets ran graphic images of U.S. troops who had been killed or captured. The Clinton administration's reaction suggested it was following the lessons of the Bush era: The White House announced it was sending a top press aide, Jeff Eller, to Somalia to help "coordinate" press coverage of the U.S. mission, by forming reporters into official "press pools." According to an AP report, "Eller was chosen in part because he did a similar job for the Pentagon during the 1989 Panama invasion."³⁴ In Panama, as in the Gulf War, the press pools were used to control what information and images the press could report; the pools, along with a compliant press, kept the U.S. public from seeing disturbing pictures of war casualties. No wonder the Clinton administration wanted Eller to do a "similar job" in Somalia.

Enemy Ally: The Demonization of Jean-Bertrand Aristide

November/December 1994

JIM NAURECKAS

USUALLY WHEN THE U.S. military intervenes overseas, the U.S. press demonizes the enemy. But in the case of the Haiti occupation, many media reports spent more time demonizing the U.S.'s ostensible ally, deposed President Jean-Bertrand Aristide.

Newsweek described Aristide as "an anti-American demagogue, an unsteady left-wing populist who threatened private enterprise and condoned violence against his political opponents."³⁵

An editorial in the liberal *New York Newsday* proclaimed: "Aristide seems bent on proving his critics' claims: that he's a fickle ideologue, a rabble-rouser with a messianic complex essentially uninterested in the pragmatic realities and possibly incompetent to be chief exec."³⁶

Fred Barnes on the *McLaughlin Group* dismissed the fact that two-thirds of the Haitian population voted for Aristide: "The notion that because Aristide was once elected, that we now have to impose him, carries democratic formalism to an extreme.... Hitler was elected."³⁷

Aristide has long been the target of a disinformation campaign, with CIA distortions sourced to the Haitian military being disseminated through the media by public relations agents paid for by the Haitian elite.³⁸ The key elements of the campaign have long been disproven, but they still kept coming up in coverage of the Haitian occupation.

On the *McLaughlin Group,* John McLaughlin provided one of the shriller summaries of the claims: "Aristide has been charged by eyewitnesses with criminal horrors, including assassination; complicity in the humiliation of the Papal Nuncio ... and, most horribly, Aristide's exhorting of mobs to use necklacing, Haitian slang for gang execution with a gasoline-soaked tire put around the neck and set aflame, also called Père Lebrun." McLaughlin then showed a video clip that he said showed "Aristide inciting a mob to Père Lebrun with his lunatic singsong chant."[39]

The assault against the Papal Nuncio, who was suspected of supporting an attempted coup, occurred before Aristide came to power, and Aristide was not involved. As for the alleged "Père Lebrun" speech, it nowhere mentions necklacing, and seems in context to be referring to the Haitian Constitution as a "beautiful tool." Despite the constant repetition of the claim that the spellbinding Aristide "exhorted mobs to use necklacing," there were no documented cases of necklacing during all of Aristide's residence in office.

While the old charges lingered (*Newsweek* merged quotes from two different statements into "one angry speech" to make it seem like Aristide had called for necklacing),[40] new disinformation surfaced—often based on the flimsiest of reporting.

Time ran an item on "a series of uncorroborated but sensational allegations that Jean-Bertrand Aristide, Haiti's erstwhile President, took hundreds of thousands of dollars in look-the-other-way money from Colombian drug cartels while in office."[41]

Not even *Time* claimed that they had credible evidence for this: "None of the claims have been supported, and the sources may have suspect motives," the magazine admits. In reality, far from looking the other way, the ascetic Aristide instigated the first-ever serious crackdown on drug trafficking by the military—whose involvement in the cocaine trade was well documented.[42]

What could motivate *Time* editors to print such a dubious charge against Aristide? *Time*'s standards were quite different when a reporter there tried to do a story in 1987—based on substantial documentation—about drug smuggling by Oliver North's contra resupply network. The reporter told *Extra!* that after the article was repeatedly sent back for rewrites, a senior editor leveled with him: "*Time* is institutionally behind the contras. If this story were about the Sandinistas and drugs, you'd have no trouble getting it in the magazine."[43]

Another Aristide smear involved his administration's Port-au-Prince police chief, Colonel Pierre Cherubin, whose human rights record compares very favorably with others who have held that post—particularly next to his self-appointed successor, the notorious Colonel Michel François.

But while Cherubin was in charge, five alleged "bandits" were murdered by Port-au-Prince police—a crime for which a subordinate of Cherubin's was arrested. Because of the new seriousness about human rights under Aristide, an investigation was launched to see if Cherubin himself had anything to do with the killings, an investigation aborted by the 1991 coup.

This incident resurfaced in distorted form. The *Washington Post*'s version of the charge was that Cherubin was "authorizing torture and killing of Aristide's opponents." The *Post*'s evidence was not exactly conclusive: An anonymous U.S. government official provided a "classified assessment" that "concludes there is circumstantial evidence to suggest it could be true."[44]

As with the children's game of Telephone, the charge became wilder with each retelling: John McLaughlin referred to him as "Cherubin the torturer and the murderer."[45]

Why was this somewhat obscure incident reexamined? Because Cherubin was Aristide's representative in planning the formation of a new police force. If Cherubin could be discredited, Aristide's influence over the new force would be greatly limited.

It was difficult to whitewash the murderous Haitian military and police, who savagely beat demonstrators in plain view of U.S. cameras. (CBS's Dan Rather did make a serious effort at whitewashing when he conducted a series of interviews with coup leader General Raoul Cedras—whom Rather once referred to as "President Cedras"—that concentrated on his patriotism, honor, and love of family, and that avoided any serious mention of his human rights abuses.) Instead, reporters adopted the "balanced" approach of condemning equally the violence of Aristide and the military.

"For two centuries, political opponents in Haiti have routinely slaughtered each other," wrote R. W. Apple in the *New York Times*. "Backers of President Jean-Bertrand Aristide, followers of General Cedras and the former Tontons Macoute retain their homicidal tendencies, to say nothing of their weapons."[46] "Everybody in both factions down there, both factions are shot through with slavering murderers," Jack Germond declared on the *McLaughlin Group*.[47]

This equation of the military and Aristide would seem ridiculous if news reports had accurately reported Aristide's human rights record. The number of killings dropped dramatically during Aristide's tenure: There were fifty-three murders of all sorts in Haiti in the seven months he held office, including common nonpolitical murders, lynchings of criminal suspects, and killings by the military. A comprehensive Human Rights Watch report did not attribute direct responsibility for any of these murders to Aristide.[48] Compare that with the estimated 3,000 to 5,000 killings by the military that followed Aristide's 1991 overthrow.

Still, violence was treated as an endemic quality in Haitian life. "Vengeance, not voting, has been the Haitian way," reported *Newsweek*.[49] Morton Kondracke gave the same sentiment more of a racist spin: "Nobody is going to bring democracy to Haiti any time soon. This is a country soaked in blood—primitive, backward, you know."[50]

An unnoted fact: The per capita murder rate in the United States in a normal year is roughly nine times what it was in Haiti under Aristide's administration.

The *New York Times*'s Apple suggested vaguely that Clinton's occupation would be "another futile attempt to reshape a society that has long resisted reform."[51] This was typical of the absence of any real historical context in most U.S. coverage of the occupation.

Occasionally, reporters mentioned the 1915–1934 U.S. occupation of Haiti as a "previous attempt to support democracy." But how many mentioned that the U.S.

occupation dissolved the Haitian Parliament, forced Haiti to accept a U.S.-written constitution that allowed foreign ownership of land, and reinstituted virtual slavery?[52]

Reporters could have quoted the words of the commander who led the Marines ashore in 1915, Colonel Littleton W. T. Waller: He wrote that the Haitians were "real niggers and no mistake—there are some fine-looking, well-educated polished men here but they are real nigs beneath the surface."[53]

How often did reporters mention that the United States had intervened militarily against Haiti at least twenty-seven times before 1915;[54] or that the first U.S. intervention was in 1791, when the United States sent troops and $750,000 to Haiti to try to *suppress* a slave revolt against the French colonizers?[55]

Or reporters could have recalled a more recent intervention, when Marines landed in Haiti in the 1960s during the dictatorship of Jean-Claude "Papa Doc" Duvalier. Their orders, according to Colonel Robert Heinl, the officer in charge, were "to help keep Duvalier in power so he can serve out his full term in office, and maybe a little longer than that if everything works out."[56]

The U.S. military's fondness for dictatorship was not a thing of the past, as a timely article by Allan Nairn in *The Nation* documented: "You're going to end up dealing with the same folks as before," Major Louis Kernisan, a Defense Intelligence official involved with "retraining" Haitian police, explained, "the five families that run the country, the military and the bourgeoisie. They're the same folks that are supposed to be the bad guys now, but the bottom line is that you know you're always going to end up dealing with them because they speak your language, they understand your system, they've been educated in your country. It's not going to be the slum guy from Cité Soleil."[57]

"Given Haiti's bloody history and President Jean-Bertrand Aristide's own dubious record," right-wing columnist Mona Charen predicted, "the chance is slim that the 15,000 U.S. troops in Haiti will bring either lasting peace or political freedom to the island."[58] Maybe it was the U.S. military's "dubious record," not Aristide's, that should have given journalists cause for pessimism.

Haiti: The Crisis Is Not Over

Extra! Update, December 1994

THE NEW YORKER magazine wrote an editorial to mark President Aristide's return to Port-au-Prince. "Political murders," the liberal weekly stated, "have practically ended [since the U.S. occupation].... Haiti's extreme human rights emergency—the reign of torture, terror and death ... is for the moment over."[59]

In fact, as the *Weekly News Update on the Americas* (published by the Nicaragua Solidarity Network) pointed out, human rights violations actually continued at nearly the same rate following the U.S. occupation. The total reported killings by "attachés" and others associated with the military regime was between thirty-one and forty-six during the first three weeks of the U.S. occupation, or about ten to fifteen murders each week.[60] The U.S. government estimates that 3,000 people were murdered during the three years of the coup—roughly nineteen murders a week.

Despite the actual record in Haiti, mainstream news outlets pushed the idea that the human rights crisis in Haiti was over. The real threat, journalists suggested, was from "popular vengeance" or "mob violence"—overlooking the continuing violence coming from the very sectors that the U.S. military had picked to keep "order" in Haiti.

Some major media—including the *Washington Post, New York Times*, CBS, and NBC—did pick up on Allan Nairn's reporting in *The Nation* about U.S. ties to the Haitian death squad, FRAPH (Front for the Advancement and Progress of Haiti).[61] But an interesting pattern was noted by *Village Voice* press critic James Ledbetter: Most outlets covered Nairn's revelation that FRAPH leader Emmanuel Constant was a paid informant of the CIA. But Constant's statement that he was encouraged to form FRAPH by the U.S. military intelligence attaché, who wanted a "balance" to forces seeking the return of ousted President Aristide, was reported only "sporadically." And Constant's charge that this same U.S. intelligence official, along with the top-ranking CIA officer in Haiti, were both present in Haiti's military headquarters the day that Aristide was overthrown was almost totally ignored.[62]

This pattern suggested that the mainstream press was not ready to fully discuss U.S. intelligence involvement with the forces that the U.S. military was supposedly in Haiti to displace: It was OK to admit that the CIA is getting information from unsavory organizations, but looking into whether those unsavory organizations were set up by the CIA?—they left that to *The Nation*.

The unwillingness to see the U.S. role in Haiti's politics was taken to an extreme in a *Washington Post* piece by Ken Ringle, headlined: "The Spirit of Haiti: Haunted by a Dark History, It Remains an Island in the Sun." It was presented as a lesson in Haitian history, but the history had some obvious gaps: It skipped the period from 1915 to 1957, for example, completely omitting the U.S. occupation from 1915 to 1934. The piece didn't mention any of the countless foreign interventions that have plagued Haiti since its independence. And even its descriptions of the horrors of French colonialism were an opportunity for Ringle to tout the comparatively enlightened slaveowners in the U.S. South, where "slaves' value as property mitigated to a great extent mistreatment that endangered their lives."[63]

Ringle demonstrated how far Haiti had sunk into "poverty, terror and superstition" by quoting Sir Spenser St. John, a British diplomat, on supposed Haitian cannibalism. Ringle might have quoted a longer passage from St. John's writings, to illustrate the caliber of the sources on which the *Post* relies: "I know what the black man is," St. John declared, "and I have no hesitation in declaring that he is incapable of the art of government, and that to trust him with framing and working the laws for our islands is to condemn them to inevitable ruin."[64]

Someone who was a bit more willing to examine the real historical role of the United States in "our islands" was George Bergman, who at ninety-six was one of the last living veterans of the last U.S. occupation of Haiti. Interviewed on NPR's *Morning Edition,* Bergman said that he spent most of his time there hunting down rebels: "It was our job to rootem out. I don't know why, but that's the job we were given. That's what we did. See, in retrospect, you see a lot of things in retrospect you never see immediately. In retrospect, to me right now, if you ask me, I say they were the patriots and . . . we were the intruders. But that comes 75 years later, that thinking."[65] We shouldn't have to wait seventy-five years to get honest reporting on the latest intervention in Haiti.

Is Koppel Running for Secretary of State?
July/August 1994

The May 18, 1994, edition of *Nightline* looked at the Clinton administration's foreign policy, a subject sorely in need of examination. *Nightline*'s balance, however, left a great deal to be desired.

Nightline did point out the differences between President Clinton's and candidate Clinton's foreign policies: A taped segment showed Clinton on the campaign trail making sharp criticisms of Bush administration policies toward Haiti, Bosnia, and China—policies that Clinton largely continued after taking office.

But the discussion on *Nightline* was confined to Madeleine Albright, Clinton's ambassador to the U.N., and Dick Cheney, Bush's secretary of defense. If a big issue was that Clinton had broken campaign promises and adopted the Bush policies he had denounced, shouldn't someone besides a member of Bush's Cabinet have been part of the discussion, someone who disagreed with both the Bush and Clinton policies?—or at least someone besides Cheney, who was considering a run for president and made a predictably partisan attack on Clinton.

Koppel, who once indicated that he'd like to be secretary of state, also seemed to be making partisan attacks on Clinton. "The Clinton administration has taken a bad situation and made it worse," Koppel said of foreign policy. Imagine Koppel making a similarly blatant put-down of a Republican president—about, say, Bush's economic policies.

At one point, while talking to Cheney, Koppel acknowledged the one-sidedness of *Nightline*'s approach: "We have focused only on the negative aspects of [Clinton's] foreign policy. As you know from your own experience, that's the way we are in the media, and that's the way political critics are."

Actually, Cheney probably remembered that Koppel generally celebrated Bush's foreign policy—especially when it involved U.S. military intervention.

Notes

1. See Jane Hunter and Steve Askin, "Hunger in Africa: A Story Untold Until Too Late," *Extra!*, July/August 1991, p. 8.
2. "Post Cold-War Hot Spots," *Tyndall Report*, January 1993, p. 1.
3. Medicins Sans Frontières, cited in Steve Askin, "Hunger in Africa: A Story Still Untold," *Extra!*, September 1992, p. 5.
4. *New York Times*, December 6, 1992.
5. *New York Newsday*, November 29, 1992.
6. *Washington Post*, December 6, 1992.
7. "Rescue Somalia?" *The Nation*, December 21, 1992, p. 7.
8. John Prendergast, *Peace, Development and People of the Horn of Africa* (Silver Spring, Md.: Bread for the World Institute, 1992). Northern Somalia had declared itself independent under the name Somaliland—a political factor almost never noted in media accounts. See *Oakland Tribune*, December 21, 1992.
9. *Los Angeles Times*, January 18, 1993.
10. *New York Times*, December 6, 1992.
11. Sharon Pauling, Bread for the World, "Statement on the Proposed Intervention in Somalia," press release, December 1, 1992.
12. Alex de Waal and Rakiya Omaar, "The Lessons of Famine," *Africa Report*, November/December 1992, p. 62.
13. *ABC World News Tonight*, December 7, 1992.
14. *MacNeil/Lehrer NewsHour*, December 2, 1992.
15. Sophfronia Scott Gregory, "How Somalia Crumbled," *Time*, December 14, 1992, p. 34.
16. Carol B. Thompson, "Beware the Hand That Feeds You: U.S. Aid in Southern Africa," *Southern Africa Perspectives*, No. 2, 1992, p. 1.
17. "Developing by Region: Current Account Transactions," *World Economic Outlook*, October 1992, p. 130.
18. *Village Voice*, January 19, 1993.
19. *CBS Evening News*, December 9, 1992.
20. *New York Times*, December 6, 1992.
21. *Los Angeles Times*, December 10, 1992.
22. *New York Post*, January 5, 1993.
23. Strobe Talbott, "America Abroad: Dealing with Anti-Countries," *Time*, December 14, 1992, p. 35.
24. Joe Klein, "When Everyone's an Amateur," *Newsweek*, December 14, 1992, p. 42.
25. Bruce W. Nelan, "Taking on the Thugs," *Time*, December 14, 1992, p. 26.
26. *ABC World News Tonight*, December 7, 1992.
27. NPR, December 8, 1992.
28. *CBS Evening News*, December 8, 1992.
29. *Daily News*, October 15, 1993. Gralnick later claimed he was merely illustrating the racist way many people in the United States view Somalia—a statement that shows a striking lack of respect for his viewers, millions of whom have gotten their ideas about Africa from news outlets Gralnick has led.
30. *New York Times*, June 14, 1993.
31. *New York Times*, September 10, 1993.
32. *New York Post*, October 6, 1993.
33. Associated Press, October 7, 1993.

34. Associated Press, October 13, 1993.
35. Russell Watson, "Our Man in Haiti," *Newsweek,* September 26, 1994, p. 33.
36. *New York Newsday,* September 21, 1994.
37. *McLaughlin Group,* September 20, 1994.
38. "CIA/CBS Smear Aristide," *Extra! Update,* December 1993, p. 1.
39. Sheldon Rampton, "Hustling for the Junta: P.R. Fights Democracy in Haiti," *P.R. Watch,* No. 1, 3d quarter 1994, p. 8.
40. Russell Watson, "Is This Invasion Necessary?" *Newsweek,* September 19, 1994, p. 36.
41. "Inside Washington: Accusations About Aristide Put Justice in a Bind," *Time,* September 26, 1994, p. 9.
42. *Chicago Tribune,* October 27, 1993.
43. "*Time* Suppresses Contra Drug Story," *Extra!,* November/December 1991, p. 14.
44. *Washington Post,* September 18, 1994.
45. *McLaughlin Group,* September 20, 1994.
46. *New York Times,* September 20, 1994.
47. *McLaughlin Group,* September 20, 1994.
48. Anne Fuller, "Haiti: The Aristide Government's Human Rights Record," *Americas Watch Report* (New York: Human Rights Watch, November 1991).
49. Evan Thomas, "Here We Go Again," *Newsweek,* September 26, 1994, p. 20.
50. *McLaughlin Group,* September 20, 1994.
51. *New York Times,* September 20, 1994.
52. Paul Farmer, *The Uses of Haiti* (Monroe, Maine: Common Courage Press, 1994).
53. Farmer, *Uses of Haiti.*
54. Farmer, *Uses of Haiti.*
55. Farmer, *Uses of Haiti.*
56. Farmer, *Uses of Haiti.*
57. Allan Nairn, "The Eagle Is Landing: U.S. Forces Occupy Haiti," *The Nation,* October 3, 1994, p. 344.
58. *USA Today,* September 21, 1994.
59. Hendrick Hertzberg, "Haiti So Far," *The New Yorker,* October 17, 1994, p. 7.
60. Nicaragua Solidarity Network, "Right-Wing Violence Continues in U.S.-Occupied Haiti," *Weekly News Update on the Americas,* October 16, 1994, p. 1.
61. Allan Nairn, "Beyond Haiti's Paramilitaries: Our Man in FRAPH," *The Nation,* October 24, 1994, p. 458.
62. *Village Voice,* October 18, 1994.
63. *Washington Post,* October 13, 1994.
64. Farmer, *Uses of Haiti.*
65. *Morning Edition,* October 12, 1994.

PART FOUR

In Search of Scapegoats

12 Teen Mothers and Other Young Monsters

The "Crisis" of Teen Pregnancy: Teenage Girls Pay the Price for Media Distortion

March/April 1994

JANINE JACKSON

A RECENT ROUND of media attention focused on the "tragedy" of teenage pregnancy, casting the unmarried teenage mother as the source of virtually all of society's ills. Papers and pundits were moved to florid prose on teen mothers' "world of warped morals and wasted lives that affects the quality of life for all of us."[1]

Various indicators on birth rates and poverty rates were tossed around to document the "social catastrophe."[2] No serious analysis was needed, since it was obvious to bipartisan politicians and media alike that the "soaring birth rate among welfare mothers"[3] was "the smoking gun in a sickening array of pathologies—crime, drug abuse, physical and mental illness, welfare dependency."[4] *USA Today* reported in a near-panic, "Beyond the drugs and the gunfire lies what is perhaps the most shocking of social pathologies: rates of out-of-wedlock births."[5]

This round of finger-pointing was largely touched off by an October 1993 *Wall Street Journal* op-ed piece by the American Enterprise Institute's Charles Murray, which contended that "illegitimacy is the single most important social problem of our time—more important than crime, drugs, poverty, illiteracy, welfare or homelessness, because it drives everything else."[6]

Murray's call for denial of all government support to any unmarried woman who has a child (and orphanages for children whose parents can't support them) fits a familiar conservative pattern of blaming poverty on the character faults and bad decisions of the poor themselves. He harks back to "the old way, which worked," and calls for making "illegitimate birth the socially horrific act it used to be."

What was chilling was how easily the mainstream media latched on to Murray's ideology-laden notions, presenting the condemnation of poor unwed mothers as a fresh policy approach—"given the failure of all other remedies."[7]

In fact, the assumptions of the conservatives' argument are demonstrably false, but they successfully play on cultural (and racial) tensions and fears, along with the need for scapegoats in times of economic strain. Unfortunately, mainstream media have done a poor job of separating moralistic arguments from economic ones.

Journalists speak of "teen pregnancies and the underclass" as "entwined social pathologies."[8] But few question why this should be. Substantial evidence shows that though single motherhood is associated with poverty, it does not *cause* poverty. Most teenagers who become mothers were living at or below poverty levels to begin with. Explaining their choice to researchers, these women speak of factors associated with socioeconomic status: educational failure, low self-esteem (often connected with sexual abuse), and a lack of job opportunities. These factors, not "the sex-me-up songs on radio and television,"[9] can make early motherhood appear to be a rational option.

After becoming mothers, young women are confronted with a lack of affordable child care and a job market that pays women (especially minority women) inadequate, disproportionately low wages. That many are pushed below the poverty level is not surprising. Nor is it surprising that single fathers are less than half as likely to live in poverty as single mothers.

In an earlier round of the "unwed mothers" discussion, this overlooked economic context was pointed out by family historian Stephanie Coontz in a *Washington Post* op-ed piece. Most poverty in the United States, Coontz wrote, is related not to family structure but to work force and wage structures, including the "growth of low-wage work that makes one income inadequate to support a family."[10] "The United States tolerates higher levels of child poverty in *every* family form than any other major industrial democracy," Coontz wrote. "The fastest growing poverty group in America since 1979 has been married-couple families with children."

Nevertheless, the notion that cutting women's welfare benefits will discourage them from having children is finding new receptivity among the press and policymakers, including President Clinton, who called Charles Murray's idea "essentially right."[11]

"What many experts suspect, and fear," *Newsweek*'s Joe Klein told readers, "is that nothing short of [Murray's] draconian solution . . . will change the culture of chronic dependency."[12] The *Milwaukee Sentinel* called Murray's idea "the only real way to send the message that illegitimacy doesn't pay."[13]

Murray's basic theory—that women have children because of the "economic incentive" of welfare—has been thoroughly disproven by research, most recently in a study by the Urban Institute. The study found that "generosity [of welfare payments] has at best a very modest impact on a woman's initial childbearing decision and virtually no effect on subsequent births."[14] What did have significant impact, the researchers found, were education, race, and income. FAIR saw no major media reporting on these findings.

The ubiquitous media label for teen motherhood, "children having children"—or even "babies having babies," as syndicated columnist Charles Krauthammer put it[15]—evokes the cultural discomfort the phenomenon stirs, but it's more evocative than accurate, since roughly two-thirds of teenage births are to women eighteen or nineteen, not thirteen or fourteen.

Many women's and welfare rights advocates also believe the "children having children" label infantilizes adolescent mothers, helping to justify policies that treat them as incapable of making decisions. Punitive proposals that compel teenage mothers to live with their families and stay in school in order to receive public assistance (no analogous rules are suggested for fathers) are justified by the press because unwed mothers are, "especially if they're teenagers, plain ignorant," as a *New York Times* editorial declared.[16]

But labeling pregnancies of women under twenty a "teen" problem is itself questionable, since 70 percent of such pregnancies result from sex with a man over twenty. Some 50,000 teen pregnancies a year are the result of rape, and two-thirds of teen mothers have a history of rape or sexual molestation, with a perpetrator averaging twenty-seven years of age.[17] You won't find mention of this in editorials decrying "teenagers shouting about their 'right' to become mothers."[18]

With so many articles about the "crisis of teen pregnancy," it might surprise most people to learn that the number of teenagers having babies has *dropped* significantly: from 9.1 percent of 15- through 19-year-old girls in 1958 to 6.2 percent in 1991. (The teenage birth rate has risen slightly since 1986, when it hit a low of 5.1 percent.)

The birth rate for *unmarried* teenagers has risen gradually over the last fifty years—from .74 percent in 1940 to 4.25 percent in 1990. However, the birth rate of unmarried *adult* women has risen somewhat faster. In the early 1970s, roughly half of all "out-of-wedlock" births were to teens; today, it's less than three in ten.

In order to make these numbers sound more alarming, news accounts usually report the percentage of births in which the mother is not married—a number that has less to do with the "soaring" birth rate of unmarried women than with the falling birth rate of married women.

Some in the press mourned the loss of the "stigma" of teen pregnancy. *Newsweek* asked, in an interview with President Clinton: "Should we reattach a stigma to those who are having children out of wedlock?"[19] In an *NBC Nightly News* report, Betty Rollin complained, "The stigma of being an unwed mother is history." She then went on to harangue teenage girls about their pregnancies: "Did you feel any shame about this?"[20]

This nostalgia for "stigma" suggests that what many politicians and their supporters in the media find troubling is not so much teen pregnancy as teen sexuality, and that their intention is not so much to offer young women better choices as it is to socially engineer the "right" kind of families.

While they hyped the urgency of the crisis, mainstream media simultaneously constricted the range of debate, such that simplistic "solutions" crowded out years of relevant research. Charles Murray was cited at least fifty-five times by major dailies and newsweeklies in the two months following his *Wall Street Journal* column; his ideas appeared in many more. On the ABC network alone, Murray was featured on *This Week with David Brinkley*,[21] *ABC World News Tonight*,[22] and *Good Morning America*.[23]

On the other hand, social service agencies and research groups that actually work with pregnant teens and young mothers, who might point out the fallacies and omissions in conservative proposals, were largely missing from stories concerned with moralizing and "New Democrat" rhetoric.

Of the many newspaper and magazine articles in the last few months of 1993 on the topic of teen pregnancy, only a handful contained comments from actual teen mothers, whose motivations and beliefs are the subject of so much speculation. As the object of high-minded harangues and the target of endless programs, teens' voices were easily drowned out both in the media and in the policy debate.

The talk about Clinton's stand on teenage pregnancy as proof that he'll "get tough on entitlements" was evidence of another distressing media trend: the tendency to see complex socioeconomic issues primarily as political footballs. That was illustrated when *Time* magazine confronted President Clinton: "There's a story in the paper today saying that the stigma has been removed from teenage pregnancy and that Democrats are responsible."[24]

The Cleveland *Plain Dealer* summed up the significance of welfare "reform" proposals that may disrupt the lives of millions of people: "Riding on the outcome are Clinton's claim to be a 'new Democrat' and the hopes of dozens of moderate and conservative House Democrats hoping to pocket a politically popular vote in time for next year's elections."[25]

By allowing symbolic politics to outweigh reasoned research and by focusing attention on individual teens and their morals, media accounts of teen pregnancy sidestep just those issues politicians of both parties want to avoid: the role of structural economic forces that condemn single mothers—and many others—to poverty.

Blame It on Mom
Extra! Update, February 1995

Teen mothers are often treated as scapegoats in the media, but Jonathan Alter's December 12, 1994, *Newsweek* column set some kind of record for sweeping generalizations: "Every threat to the fabric of this country—from poverty to crime to homelessness—is connected to out-of-wedlock teen pregnancy." In a future column, Alter will explain how unwed teenaged moms are responsible for toxic waste, the S&L bailout, and the export of manufacturing jobs.

Too Many Kids and Too Much Money: The Media's Persistent Welfare Stereotypes

July/August 1992

RENU NAHATA

"THERE IS NOW a fairly widespread feeling, justified or not, that some welfare recipients are not doing enough to get off the dole." Thus began *ABC World News Tonight*'s "American Agenda" segment on welfare reform.[26] Although Peter Jennings's opening statement acknowledged that there may be disparities between public perception and reality, this segment and many others continued to rely heavily on widely held misconceptions about welfare.

With few exceptions, the corporate media have portrayed the issue of welfare in terms and images not too far removed from Ronald Reagan's "welfare queens." Following news coverage, one might believe that most welfare recipients are black, unwed, unemployed, teenaged mothers of several children, living in the inner city. Such a recipient might be, as one article suggested, "a walking statistic: a single welfare mother of five who dropped out of high school at 17, pregnant with her first child."[27] But the statistic she represents is quite small, since most AFDC recipients have high school diplomas, most have had their first children after age 19, and only 3.5 percent have had five or more children.[28]

In fact, as reporter Jack Smith acknowledged on *This Week with David Brinkley*, "most welfare recipients are white, not black; most live in the suburbs, not the inner city; most want to work and stay on welfare less than two years."[29] According to a Health and Human Services report, the average number of children in Aid to Families with Dependent Children (AFDC) families is only 1.9—roughly the same as the national average.[30]

Whether "justified or not," several states have based their reform measures on the perception that the welfare system's failures derive from women abusing its benefits. In response, state legislatures have taken aim at those receiving assistance, and media have further fueled these concerns by offering up a parade of mothers—unwed, unrepentant, and most often black.

The Wisconsin program, considered a model for other states, reduces benefits for a second child and eliminates them for a third, on the assumption that increased benefits will encourage women to have more children. However, according to the House Ways and Means Committee's 1991 *Green Book,* the average size of AFDC families has been decreasing steadily for twenty years.[31] More to the point, the Center on Budget and Policy Priorities has demonstrated that there is no significant relationship between AFDC benefit levels and birth rates.[32] Although these statistics are readily available, most news reports about such welfare "reforms" fail to use them.

ABC News' "American Agenda" segment on welfare relied on the "decline in values" critique made by many of welfare's detractors. Correspondent Rebecca Chase tried to demonstrate the corrosive social impact of welfare by interviewing several black mothers, most of them unwed and in their teens, one a mother of six who has been on welfare for the past twenty years. The two questions put to these women were "How many of you are married?" and "Do you feel like you owe the taxpayers anything for them helping you support your children?"[33]

Chase seemed to find the moral dilemma of unmarried motherhood, and the issue of gratitude for public support, far more compelling than soaring black unemployment (particularly for males), absence of affordable child care, and discriminatory hiring practices. Instead of addressing these kinds of issues, Chase looked at poverty and welfare through the narrow lens of individual responsibility and moral double standards.

The same lens was used by *U.S. News & World Report*'s David Whitman, who approvingly described the latest attitude toward those on welfare as the "new paternalism," that is, "rewarding them for doing right and fining them for doing wrong." Given these absolute terms, Whitman's condemnatory conclusion was not surprising: "No federal intervention . . . is likely to prompt legions of unwed, chronic welfare mothers to marry the fathers of their children."[34]

This Week with David Brinkley, in a lengthy segment on Wisconsin's reform experiment, made an effort to dispel long-standing myths. But the show managed to undermine those facts by loading both the taped segment and the discussion that followed with repeated images of and references to urban blacks. Despite one guest's effort to raise the question of incentive in the absence of employment opportunities, larger societal factors lost ground to George Will's concern over "illegitimacy in our cities."[35]

Even as she attempted to dispel "social myths" about welfare, columnist Ellen Goodman focused on poor women with a sense of "entitlement" as the main problem with welfare. "Americans instinctively believe that the welfare poor should play by the same rules as the rest of us. A family that works does not get a raise for having a child. Why then should a family that doesn't work?"[36]

The headline chosen by the *Boston Globe* for Goodman's column, "Welfare Mothers with an Attitude," played up the worst aspects of the piece. And the "satirical" graphic that accompanied the article—an Afroed woman with several children, being showered with money—could just as easily be read as endorsing the stereotype of the African-American welfare mother with too many kids and too much money. At some point, repetition of stereotypical imagery merely hardens perceptions, rendering corrective caveats effectively useless.

Although most polls show that Americans still support public spending on the poor, James Patterson, a historian of social policy at Brown University, pointed out in the *New York Times* that "people support programs when they imagine the beneficiaries look a lot like themselves."[37]

Lending credence to this premise was an article the *Times* had run just one month earlier: "From Middle Class to Jobless: A Sense of Pride Is Shattered."[38] The primary concern of that article was the suffering, fear, and loss of pride felt by recently unemployed white-collar workers (illustrated by a photograph of a white accountant). Mounting welfare rolls in predominantly middle-class areas like New York's Westchester County inspired the writer to feel compassion. In this case, the rise in chronic unemployment, family breakdowns, vanishing spouses, substance abuse, and domestic violence were seen to stem from economic circumstances rather than from vaguely defined social pathologies.

However, most welfare recipients we see in the media are black. And most efforts to reform welfare are directed at inner cities. There is little room for compassion here. The panacea generally offered for inner-city poverty and family breakdowns comes most often in the form of imposing "values."

Lawrence Mead, the author of an influential 1992 book, *The New Politics of Poverty: The Nonworking Poor in America*, demonstrated this tendency. One of the main sources in the *U.S. News & World Report* article about the "new paternalism," Mead argued in a *New York Times* op-ed piece that "if poor adults behaved rationally, they would seldom be poor for long in the first place. Opportunity is more available than the will to seize it." Child care, he believes, can usually be found if one only looks for it, and the ghetto mentality, more than racism or any other factor, is the main cause of unemployment. His solution to these personal failings is "a more authoritative social policy in which the needy are told how to live instead of merely being subsidized."[39]

The official view was not far from Mead's, as President Bush demonstrated when he blamed the 1992 riots in Los Angeles on Lyndon Johnson. Stories like "White House Links Riots to Welfare" displayed a certain skepticism,[40] yet media assumptions about welfare and poverty—which focus on inner-city black women, their supposed unchecked fertility, and their lack of "individual responsibility"—differed little from those of the Bush administration. Despite the fact that most media outlets recognize the prevalence of stereotypes, few seem willing to give up those stereotypes as the basis for their coverage.

"Sexually Incorrect"— or Just Inaccurate?

Extra! Update, December 1993

IN THE WAKE of Katie Roiphe's *The Morning After,* a much-publicized book about "date rape hysteria,"[41] a new backlash of antifeminist articles hit the newsstands. *Newsweek* took its swipe at the women's movement in an October 1993 cover story, blaring, "Sexual Correctness: Has It Gone Too Far?"[42] Like Roiphe, *Newsweek* writer Sarah Crichton described a world in which feminist activists are clamping chains on human sexuality and turning personal relations into misery, out of a hysterical fear of violence against women.

Crichton, an assistant managing editor at *Newsweek,* began the article by describing a Brown University student who was suspended for a year for sexual misconduct; when he returned to campus, anonymous posters publicized his offense. "Who is the victimizer here and who is the victim?" Crichton wondered. Is the victimizer the sex offender or the one who publicizes sex offenses? To Crichton, that's a tough question. Toward the end of her treatise, Crichton quoted another male Brown University sophomore: "Women," he says, "have all the power here on sexual conduct. . . . It's very dangerous for us."

"In the ever-morphing world of Thou Shalt Not Abuse Women, it's getting mighty confusing," said Crichton. What's confusing is why she thinks the danger to women is exaggerated. Like Roiphe, Crichton mocked and distorted the research of Dr. Mary Koss as finding a "bloated" number of rape victims. Yet Crichton went on to cite as the "most conservative, yet trustworthy, numbers" a study that found a rate of forcible, completed rape (13 percent of all women) similar to that found by Koss's study (11 percent of female college students). Eighty-three percent of rapes occur to women age twenty-four or younger.[43]

FBI figures, which even Crichton noted are "conservative," show rape reports rising for the past ten years.[44] The figures for 1992 were up 2.3 percent over those of 1991. Crichton said campus rape activists are not "creating a society of Angry Young Women. These are Scared Little Girls." Perhaps they're just informed.

Crichton also belittled reports of sexual harassment by distorting them. As an example of how not all complaints merit "attention or retribution—or even much sympathy," she cited two charges of verbal abuse made by New York state representative Earlene Hill and dismissed them as trivial, with a sarcastic "Oh, please." Crichton completely ignored another charge that Hill had made—that a fellow assembly member had "yelled a racial epithet and threatened to throw her out a window in 1989 after she asked him to leave her office."[45]

Crichton's story is filled with opinion, not fact. "Feminist politics," she wrote, "have now homed in like missiles on the twin issues of date rape and sexual harassment." In reality, it is mass media, not feminist theorists, who are most responsible for defining feminism in terms of a few narrow issues. Not coincidentally, these are issues that mainstream media outlets associate with sex (although most feminists would describe them as issues of power). After all, if you had a cover story on the real core issues of feminism—the unequal distribution of political and economic power—it would be hard to illustrate it with a picture of two attractive nude models, like those featured on *Newsweek*'s "Sexual Correctness" issue.

Bashing Youth: Media Myths About Teenagers

March/April 1994

MIKE MALES

UNPLANNED PREGNANCIES. HIV infection and AIDS, other sexually transmitted diseases. Cigarettes, alcohol and drug abuse. Eating disorders. Violence. Suicide. Car crashes."[46] The twenty-one-word lead-in to a *Washington Post* report sums up today's media image of the teenager: 24 million 13- through 19-year-olds toward whom any sort of moralizing and punishment can be safely directed, by liberals and conservatives alike. Today's media portrayals of teens employ the same stereotypes once openly applied to unpopular racial and ethnic groups: violent, reckless, hypersexed, welfare-draining, obnoxious, and ignorant.

And like traditional stereotypes, the modern media teenager is a distorted image, derived from the dire fictions promoted by official agencies and interest groups. During the 1980s and 1990s, various public and private entrepreneurs realized that the news media would circulate practically anything negative about teens, no matter how spurious. A few examples among many:

- In 1985, the National Association of Private Psychiatric Hospitals, defending the profitable mass commitment of teenagers to psychiatric treatment on vague diagnoses, invented the "fact" that a teenager commits suicide "every 90 minutes"—amounting to 5,000 to 6,000 teen suicides every year.[47] Countless media reports of all types, from the Associated Press[48] to *Psychology Today*,[49] continue to report this phony figure, nearly three times the true teen suicide toll, which averaged 2,050 per year during the 1980s.[50]

- In a 1991 campaign to promote school-based clinics, the American Medical Association (AMA) and the National Association of State Boards of Education published a report that inflated the 280,000 annual births to unmarried teenage mothers into "half a million" and that claimed a "30-fold" increase in adolescent crime since 1950.[51] In fact, 1950 youth crime statistics are too incomplete to compare, and later, more comprehensive, national reports show no increase in juvenile crime rates in at least two decades.[52] The facts notwithstanding, the national media dutifully publicized the organizations' exaggerations.[53]

- In the early 1980s, officials hyping the "war on drugs" orchestrated media hysteria about "skyrocketing" teenage drug abuse, at a time when, in fact, teenage drug death rates were plummeting (down 70 percent from 1970 to 1982). In the late 1980s, the same media outlets parroted official claims of a drug war "success" when, in reality, youth drug death rates were skyrocketing (up 85 percent from 1983 to 1991).[54]

Today, official and media distortions are one and the same. Who's to blame for poverty? Teenage mothers, declared Health and Human Services Secretary Donna Shalala in uncritical news stories that failed to note that teenage mothers on welfare were poor *before* they became pregnant.[55]

Who's causing violence? Kids and guns, asserted President Clinton, favorably quoted by reporters, who neglected to mention that six out of seven murders are committed by adults.[56] Who's dying from drugs, spreading AIDS, committing suicide? Teenagers, teenagers, teenagers, the media proclaimed, at the behest of official sources, even though health reports show that adults are much more at risk from all of these perils than are adolescents.

MEDIA MYTH: "TEENAGE" SEX

The strange logic of the modern media's attack on adolescents is nowhere stranger than their portrayal of "teen" sexuality. Consider their jargon: When a child is born to a father over age twenty and a teenage mother (which happened 350,000 times last year), the phenomenon is called "children having children." When an adult pays a teenager for sex, it is "teenage prostitution." Some 2 million sexually transmitted diseases and a quarter-million abortions every year that result from adult/teen sex are headlined as "teenage" VD, AIDS, and abortion. The causes of these "epidemic social problems" are teenage immaturity, risk-taking, and peer pressure. Their cure is more preaching, programming, and punishment, aimed at "teenage sex."

According to California and National Center for Health Statistics reports, 71 percent of all teenage parents have adult partners age twenty or over. California and U.S. vital statistics reports show that men age twenty or over cause five times more births among junior high school–age girls than do boys their own age, and 2.5 times more births among high school girls than high school boys do. Even though many more pregnancies among teenage females are caused by men older than twenty-five than by boys under eighteen, media reports and pictures depict only high schoolers. With their choices of terms and images, the media blame the young and female while giving the adult and male a break.

This is exactly the image desired by thousands of agencies and programs, which profit politically and financially from the issue—for example, the Centers for Disease Control, which blamed "teenage AIDS" on promiscuous "kids . . . playing Russian roulette."[57]

The media have followed the official lead: The three leading newsweeklies have all run cover stories featuring the same formulaic reporting. *Newsweek*'s "Teens and AIDS,"[58] *Time*'s "Kids, Sex and Values,"[59] and *U.S. News & World Report*'s "Teenage Sex: Just Say Wait"[60] all featured surveys of "kids," photos of suburban schools, sidebars lambasting sexy movies, and dire commentary on sexual irresponsibility among schoolboys and girls. Both *Time* and *U.S. News* blamed "teenage sex" on "confused" kids and held up sex and abstinence education as the cure.

Imagine how different these stories would be if the media told the decidedly unsexy truth about pregnant teens: The large majority are impoverished girls with histories of physical, sexual, and other abuses by parents and other adults, and most are impregnated by adult men. When the *Los Angeles Times*, in an exceptional report, actually showed the bleak childhoods of pregnant, disadvantaged teens, the accompanying official rhetoric blaming MTV and "peer pressure" looked silly.[61]

MEDIA MYTH: "TEENAGE" VIOLENCE

On "teenage" violence, the media picture is similarly skewed. *Newsweek*'s "Teen Violence: Wild in the Streets"[62] and "Kids and Guns,"[63] *U.S. News & World Report*'s "When Killers Come to Class,"[64] and *Time*'s "Big Shots"[65] all followed a standard format. The lead-in detailed the latest youth mayhem, followed by selected "facts" on "the causes of skyrocketing teen violence": adolescent depravity, gun-toting metalheads, TV images, rap attitude, gang culture, and lenient youth-court judges—and perhaps (in a few well-buried sentences) such small matters as poverty, abuse, racial injustice, unemployment, and substandard schools.

Given the emphasis on "teen" violence, a California Department of Justice report came as a shock: It found that 83 percent of murdered children, half of murdered teenagers, and 85 percent of murdered adults are slain by adults over age twenty,[66] not by "kids"—or, in President Clinton's stock phrase, "13-year-olds . . . with automatic weapons."[67] In fact, FBI reports show that people Clinton's age are twice as likely to commit murder as are 13-year-olds.[68]

But while the media champion official rhetoric on violence *by* youth, they rarely provide similar attention to the epidemic of adult violence *against* youth.

The National Center on Child Abuse and Neglect reported that every year at least 350,000 children and teenagers are confirmed victims of sexual and other violent abuses, by adults whose average age is thirty-two years.[69] Comparison of these figures with crime reports shows that for every violent and sexual offense committed by a youth under eighteen, there are three such crimes committed by adults against children and teens.

The reporting on the 1992 National Women's Study of 4,000 adult women, *Rape in America,* was a case study in media bias. The report found that 12 million American women have been raped; of these, 62 percent were raped before age eighteen. The half-million-plus children and teenagers victimized every year averaged ten years of age; their rapists' average age was twenty-seven.[70]

The media unrelentingly spotlight "children having children" and "killer kids" and endlessly wonder what is "out of control when it comes to the way many teens think."[71] Surely the widespread adult violent and sexual attacks against youths that *Rape in America* documents are a compelling answer. Research consistently shows such abuses are the key factors in violence, pregnancy, drug abuse, and suicide among teenagers.[72]

But the same media outlets with plenty of space to dissect sexy videos and dirty rap lyrics couldn't find room to examine the real rapes of hundreds of thousands of children and teenagers every year. *Time* gave *Rape in America* three paragraphs,[73] while *U.S. News & World Report* didn't mention it at all; neither did *Newsweek,* although in four years it has devoted five cover stories to the dangers of rock and rap music.[74] Similarly, the media have largely ignored the rising number of prison studies, which show 60 percent to 90 percent of all inmates—and nearly all of those on death row—were abused as children. The most conservative study, by the National Institute of Justice, projects that 40 percent of all violent crimes (some half-million every year) are associated with offenders having been abused as children.[75]

In a similar vein, news outlets have generally failed to examine (other than a flurry of coverage of the National Commission on Children's report) the enormous increase in youth and young-family poverty, which rose by 50 percent from 1973 to 1991.[76] Nor have mainstream media seriously addressed the devastating effects of racism, rising poverty, and unemployment on a generation of young people of color.

The media portrait reflects politicians' unadmitted priorities: Condemning violence by youth is a guaranteed crowd-pleaser; focusing on adult violence against kids isn't as popular. (Most news consumers are adults, and kids can't vote.)

In a rare exception—a report that devoted more space to poverty and child abuse than to TV sex—*Time*'s October 8, 1990, cover article pointed out a truth long known to prison wardens and juvenile court judges: "If children are not protected from their abusers, then the public will one day have to be protected from the children."[77] But most outlets continue to treat violent youth as mysterious freaks of nature. A lead item in the Sunday *Los Angeles Times* opinion section blared: "Who are our children? One day, they are innocent. The next, they may try to blow your head off."[78]

Perhaps the *Los Angeles Times* (whose landmark 1985 survey indicated that childhood sexual abuse is epidemic, affecting one-fifth of all Americans)[79] should instead question its own media escapism. From July through September 1993, that newspaper carried thirty-four articles and commentaries on the effects of violent media, rap music, and video games on youth—but not one inch on the effects of child abuse in promoting youth violence.

The *Los Angeles Times* gives prominent coverage to charges of child abuse involving the rich and famous—like singer Michael Jackson and the Beverly Hills Menendez brothers. But when the Los Angeles Council on Child Abuse and Neglect reported that 140,000 children were abused in the county in 1992, the *Times* relegated the story to an inside section, with no follow-up or comment.[80]

TWO SIDES, SAME BIAS

The extraordinary lack of context and fairness in media coverage of youth stems from two elemental difficulties. First, the standard media assumption is that fairness is served by quoting "both sides"—but on youth issues, "both sides" frequently harbor adult biases against teenagers.

In the much-publicized debates over school programs to reduce "teen" pregnancy, for example, the press quoted "liberal" sources favoring condom handouts, balanced by "conservative" sources demanding abstinence education.[81] However, both lobbies based their arguments on the same myth—that heedless high school boys are the main cause of "teen" pregnancy—and avoided the same disturbing fact: that even if every high school boy abstained from sex or used a condom, most "teen" pregnancies would still occur.

The second difficulty is that "teenage" behavior is not separate from "adult" behavior. Such hot topics as "teen pregnancy," "teen suicide," and "youth violence" are artificial political and media inventions. In real-world environments, teenagers usually act like the adults of their family, gender, race, class, location, and era, often because their behaviors occur *with* adults.

For example, *Vital Statistics of the United States* shows that white adults are twice as likely to commit suicide as black adults, and white teens are twice as likely to commit suicide as black teens. From 1940 to 1990, unwed birth rates rose from 7.4 per thousand to 42.5 per thousand among teenage women and from 7.0 per thousand to 44.0 per thousand among adult women.[82] The FBI's 1992 *Uniform Crime Reports* show that men commit 88 percent of all adult violent crime; boys commit 88 percent of all juvenile violent crime.[83]

Why are adult contexts, common to media reports on youth prior to the 1970s, only rarely cited today? Because that would prevent adolescents from serving as the latest scapegoats for problems that affect society in general.

And there is a subtler reason: The interests circulating negative images of teens want the source of malaise located *within youth,* where it can be "treated" by whatever solutions the publicizing interest groups profit from, rather than in unhealthy environments whose upgrading will require billions of dollars in public spending. Thus short-term political and corporate profit lies not in fixing environments, but in fixing kids.

The treatment industry's message is clear: "Our teenagers have lost their way," declares the AMA.[84] The press has been a key element in the campaign to persuade the public that the cause of youth pregnancy, violence, suicide, and drug addiction lies within the irrational psychologies and vulnerabilities of adolescents.

A standard news and documentary feature is the "troubled teen" rescued by the teamwork of "loving parents" and "get-tough" professionals.[85] Despite melodramatic media splashes advertising the "success" of this program or that therapy (often based on testimonials or the promoter's own "study"), controlled, long-term research finds efforts to "cure" troubled teenagers generally ineffective.

Although the cures themselves don't work, the publicity campaigns for such treatments—disguised as news—have been quite successful. During the 1980s, the number of teens forced into intensive psychiatric treatment quadrupled, and adolescent commitments to drug and alcohol treatment tripled. If institution and treatment industry claims are valid, we should have seen dramatic improvements in youth behavior.

Exactly the opposite is the case. In the past five to ten years, intense media and government attacks on various behaviors—chiefly drug abuse, violence, and pregnancy—have been followed by *rising* problems among teenagers. Stable violence rates and rapidly declining birth rates and drug death levels prior to 1985 have suddenly reversed: All three rose rapidly from the mid-1980s to the early 1990s. The media's unwillingness to question official policy and its failures helped make these reverses possible.

A few journalists refuse to kowtow to official myths and instead publicize the enormous racial disparities inherent in campaigns against "youth violence"; the fundamental sexism of the current debate over "teen" pregnancy; the realities of millions of raped, beaten, and neglected children; the skyrocketing rates of youth poverty imposed by ever-richer American elites; and the futility of modern behavior modifications, laws, and treatments aimed at forcing the young to "adjust" to intolerable conditions.

Ron Harris's *Los Angeles Times* series on juvenile crime analyzed the crucial factors of racism, poverty, and abuse in creating today's youth violence and exploded the popular fiction of lenient sentencing. (Teens, in fact, serve prison terms 60 percent longer than adults do for equivalent crimes.)[86] From *Time* magazine, Kevin Fedarko's perceptive eulogy to postindustrial Camden, New Jersey, "a city of children" relinquished to poverty and prostitution, may stand as the decade's finest illustration of 1990s America's abandonment of its young.[87]

Jamie Talan's *New York Newsday* exposé of the profiteering behind the skyrocketing rate of fraudulent adolescent psychiatric commitments to "fill empty beds" in "overbuilt hospitals" was one of the few articles to question official "treatment" claims.[88] *Time*'s indictment of the "shameful" selfishness, abuses, and uncaring attitudes of adults toward "America's most disadvantaged minority: its children" also stands as an indictment of today's media obsequiousness.[89]

These articles' debunking of conventional wisdom didn't stop the same children-blaming myths from showing up in day-to-day coverage of youth problems. But these occasional exceptions do suggest how media responsibility could halt today's political assault on youth and heal spreading intergenerational hostilities.

Smells Like Teen Stereotype
Extra! Update, June 1994

The death of Kurt Cobain, lead singer of Nirvana, sparked media speculation about possible "copycat" suicides among young people. *Newsweek*'s sidebar, "Teen Suicide: One Act Not to Follow" was typical. "What makes teens especially vulnerable is the tendency—by the healthy and the troubled alike—to view life as an all-or-nothing proposition. Unlike adults, they haven't had the ability or experience to see that every defeat isn't permanent. The young also tend to view suicide itself as impermanent, glamorizing how pain-free their existence might be afterward."[90] A few pages later, *Newsweek* published a chart listing suicide rates by age, which indicated that the "especially vulnerable" teenagers have a significantly *lower* suicide rate than any adult age group. Out of one hundred thousand 15- to 19-year-olds, about eleven will commit suicide in a given year; age groups between 20 and 54 all have suicide rates of roughly 15 per 100,000. The age group that is really most susceptible to suicide is those aged 75 to 84 (almost 25 per 100,000)—not a group especially noted for listening to Nirvana.

Notes

1. Cleveland *Plain Dealer,* December 5, 1993.
2. *Detroit News,* December 19, 1993.
3. *Chicago Sun-Times,* December 11, 1993.
4. Joe Klein, "The Out-of-Wedlock Question," *Newsweek,* December 13, 1993, p. 37.
5. *USA Today,* December 14, 1993.
6. *Wall Street Journal,* October 29, 1993.
7. *Detroit News,* December 19, 1993.
8. *Atlanta Journal and Constitution,* December 21, 1993.
9. Cleveland *Plain Dealer,* December 5, 1993.
10. *Washington Post,* May 9, 1993.
11. *NBC Nightly News,* December 3, 1993.
12. Joe Klein, "The Out-of-Wedlock Question," *Newsweek,* December 13, 1993, p. 37.
13. *Milwaukee Sentinel,* December 13, 1993.
14. Gregory Acs, "The Impact of AFDC on Young Women's Child-Bearing Decisions," *Urban Institute Policy and Research Report* (Washington, D.C.: Urban Institute Press, August 1993).
15. *Washington Post,* November 19, 1993.

16. *New York Times,* January 17, 1994.
17. Mike Males, "Infantile Arguments," *In These Times,* August 9, 1993, p. 18.
18. Cleveland *Plain Dealer,* December 5, 1993.
19. Eleanor Clift, Bob Cohn, and Jonathan Alter, "I Tried to Do So Many Things," *Newsweek,* December 13, 1993, p. 35.
20. *NBC Nightly News,* November 29, 1993.
21. *This Week with David Brinkley,* November 28, 1993.
22. *ABC World News Tonight,* December 1, 1993.
23. *Good Morning America,* December 28, 1993.
24. Margaret Carlson and James Carney, "President Bill Clinton: 'That's What Drives Me Nuts,'" *Time,* December 13, 1993, p. 42.
25. Cleveland *Plain Dealer,* December 26, 1993.
26. *ABC World News Tonight,* April 14, 1992.
27. Long Island (N.Y.) *Newsday,* (Long Island, New York), September 23, 1990.
28. Aid to Families with Dependent Children, *Characteristics and Financial Circumstances of AFDC Recipients* (Washington, D.C.: U.S. Department of Health and Human Services, 1993); U.S. Department of Health and Human Resources, "AFDC Program Overview," Fact Sheet, July 1993.
29. *This Week with David Brinkley,* April 12, 1992.
30. U.S. Department of Health and Human Services, Division of Program Evaluation and AFDC Information and Measurement Branch, *Characteristics and Financial Circumstances of AFDC Recipients* (Washington, D.C.: Government Printing Office, 1992).
31. House Ways and Means Committee, *Green Book 1991,* 102d Cong., 1st sess. (Washington, D.C.: Government Printing Office, 1991).
32. Sharon Parrott and Robert Greenstein, "Welfare, Out-of-Wedlock Child Bearing, Poverty: What Is the Connection? (Washington, D.C.: Center for Budget and Policy Priorities, January 1995).
33. *ABC World News Tonight,* April 14, 1992.
34. David Whitman, "War on Welfare Dependency," *U.S. News & World Report,* April 20, 1992, p. 34.
35. *This Week with David Brinkley,* April 12, 1992.
36. *Boston Globe,* April 16, 1992.
37. *New York Times,* May 17, 1992.
38. *New York Times,* April 13, 1992.
39. *New York Times,* May 19, 1992.
40. *New York Times,* May 5, 1992.
41. Katherine Roiphe, *The Morning After* (Boston: Little, Brown, 1993). See also Paula Kamen, "Erasing Rape: Media Hype an Attack on Sexual-Assault Research," *Extra!,* November/December 1993, p. 10.
42. Sarah Crichton, "Sexual Correctness: Has It Gone Too Far?" *Newsweek,* October 25, 1993, p. 52.
43. National Victim Center, *Rape in America: A Report to the Nation* (Washington, D.C.: National Victim Center and Crime Victims' Research and Treatment Center, 1992).
44. Department of Justice, Bureau of Justice Statistics, "Estimated Number and Rate (per 100,000) of Offenses Known to Police" (Table 3.107), *Sourcebook of Criminal Justice Statistics 1993* (Washington, D.C.: Government Printing Office, 1994).
45. *New York Times,* January 12, 1993.
46. *Washington Post,* December 22, 1992.

47. National Association of Private Psychiatric Hospitals, "Emerging Trends in Mental Health-Care for Adolescents," testimony before the Select Committee on Children, Youth and Families, *Congressional Record*, 99th Cong., 1st sess., June 6, 1985.
48. Associated Press, April 4, 1991.
49. David Elkind, "Waaaa!" *Psychology Today*, May/June 1992, p. 81.
50. U.S. Department of Health and Human Services, National Center for Health Statistics, *Vital Statistics of the United States*, Vols. I and II (Washington, D.C.: Government Printing Office, 1989).
51. National Commission on the Role of the School and the Community in Improving Adolescent Health, *Code Blue: Uniting for a Healthier Youth* (Alexandria, Va.: National Association of State Boards of Education, 1990).
52. Contrast, for example, the FBI Uniform Crime Reports for 1970 and 1992 in U.S. Department of Justice, Federal Bureau of Investigation, *Crime in the United States* (Washington, D.C.: Government Printing Office, 1993).
53. E.g., Associated Press, June 8, 1990.
54. U.S. Department of Health and Human Services, National Center for Health Statistics, *Vital Statistics of the United States*, Vol. II (Washington, D.C.: Government Printing Office, 1990).
55. E.g., *Los Angeles Times*, December 12, 1993.
56. Associated Press, November 14, 1993.
57. Associated Press, April 10, 1992.
58. "Teens and AIDS," cover story, *Newsweek*, August 3, 1992.
59. Nancy Gibbs, "How Should We Teach Our Kids About Sex?" *Time*, May 24, 1993, p. 60.
60. Joseph P. Shapiro, "Teenage Sex: Just Say Wait," *U.S. News & World Report*, July 26, 1993, p. 56.
61. *Los Angeles Times*, March 14–15, 1993.
62. "Teen Violence: Wild in the Streets," cover story, *Newsweek*, August 2, 1993, p. 40.
63. "Kids and Guns," *Newsweek*, March 9, 1992.
64. Thomas Tuch, Ted Gest, and Monika Guttman, "Violence in Schools," *U.S. News & World Report*, November 8, 1993, p. 30.
65. Jon D. Hull, "A Boy and His Gun," *Time*, August 2, 1993, p. 20.
66. Law Enforcement Information Center, *Willful Homicide Crime, 1992: Age of Victim by Age of Offender* (Sacramento, Calif.: California Department of Justice, 1993).
67. Associated Press, November 14, 1993.
68. U.S. Department of Justice, Federal Bureau of Investigation, *Crime in the United States* (Washington, D.C.: Government Printing Office, 1993).
69. U.S. Department of Commerce, Bureau of the Census, *Statistical Abstract of the United States*, Tables 340 and 341 (Washington, D.C.: Government Printing Office, 1993).
70. National Victim Center, *Rape in America: A Report to the Nation* (Washington, D.C.: National Victim Center and Crime Victims' Research and Treatment Center, 1992). See also Debra Boyer and Daird Fine, "Sexual Abuse as a Factor in Adolescent Pregnancy and Child Maltreatment," *Family Planning Perspectives*, January 2, 1992, p. 4; *Los Angeles Times*, August 25, 1985.
71. Thomas Tuch, Ted Gest, and Monika Guttman, "Violence in Schools," *U.S. News & World Report*, November 8, 1993, p. 30.
72. Debra Boyer and Daird Fine, "Sexual Abuse as a Factor in Adolescent Pregnancy and Child Maltreatment," *Family Planning Perspectives*, January 2, 1992, p. 4.

73. "Unsettling Report on an Epidemic of Rape," *Time*, May 4, 1992, p. 15.

74. *Newsweek* cover stories on the dangers of rock and rap include "Rap Rage," March 19, 1990; "Art or Obscenity?" July 2, 1990; "Rap and Race: Beyond Sister Souljah—The New Politics of Pop Music," June 29, 1992; "The New Voyeurism: Madonna and the Selling of Sex," November 2, 1992; and "When Is Rap 2 Violent?" November 29, 1993.

75. See Childhelp USA, *Breaking the Cycle of Child Abuse* (Woodland Hills, Calif.: Childhelp USA, 1993).

76. U.S. Department of Commerce, Bureau of the Census, *Poverty in the United States 1992* (Washington, D.C.: Government Printing Office).

77. Nancy Gibbs, "Shameful Bequests to the Next Generation," *Time*, October 8, 1990, p. 42.

78. *Los Angeles Times*, December 9, 1993.

79. *Los Angeles Times*, August 25, 1985.

80. *Los Angeles Times*, November 4, 1993.

81. E.g., *USA Today*, November 19, 1991.

82. U.S. Department of Health and Human Services, National Center for Health Statistics, *Vital Statistics of the United States*, Vol. II (Washington, D.C.: Government Printing Office, 1990).

83. U.S. Department of Justice, Federal Bureau of Investigation, *Crime in the United States* (Washington, D.C.: Government Printing Office, 1993).

84. National Commission on the Role of the School and the Community in Improving Adolescent Health, *Code Blue: Uniting for a Healthier Youth* (Alexandria, Va.: National Association of State Boards of Education, 1990).

85. For an example of media justifying the abduction of youth by "therapeutic programs," see the *Los Angeles Times*, June 2, 1993.

86. *Los Angeles Times*, August 22–25, 1993.

87. Kevin Fedarko, "Who Could Live Here?" *Time*, January 20, 1992, p. 20.

88. "Using Scare Tactics to Fill Adolescent Wards," *New York Newsday*, January 7, 1988.

89. "Suffer the Little Children," *Time*, October 8, 1990, p. 40.

90. Harry F. Walters, "One Act Not to Follow," *Newsweek*, April 18, 1994, p. 49.

13 The Crime Scam

New York Post: *Militant White Daily*

January/February 1993

An op-ed piece in the November 11, 1992, *New York Post* worried that 25 percent of African-American New Yorkers relied on the black-owned radio station WLIB and "militant black weeklies" for their news—not on "mainstream media whose perspective could counter extremist views."

While FAIR encourages news consumers to seek out the widest possible range of information sources, we're also worried about white New Yorkers who rely on "militant white dailies"—like the *New York Post*—for all of their news. Opposite the op-ed warning that WLIB was trying to stir up racial fear and divisions, the *Post* ran an editorial headlined "Target: Suburban Women."

Commenting on a gruesome crime in New Jersey, the editorial maintained that there was something particularly "depraved" about crimes against "middle-class people, many of whom are refugees from urban crime." These victims aren't "courting danger"—they're people who "used to feel safe by virtue of their geographical separation from the inner-city." The *Post* urged President Bill Clinton to focus his attention on crimes that "tend to victimize people who live in suburbs," since they have "reached epidemic proportions."

It's clear that "suburban," as used by the *New York Post*, is a barely veiled code word for "white." The paper went out of its way to mention that the suspected killer was "wearing an 'X' sweatshirt"—the shirts honoring Malcolm X were popular with black youth at the time—and noted insinuatingly that similar crimes often have "racial implications, although there's an obvious reluctance on the part of the media and public officials to note this circumstance." Apparently the *Post* wants to return to the days when newspapers routinely identified suspects by race.

A report by Katherine McFate of the Joint Center for Political and Economic Studies (described by Michel McQueen in the *Wall Street Journal*)[1] shows that the *New York Post* is engaged in racial fear-mongering. Although media present crime as being at a new height, the number of victims of violent crime actually decreased by 9 percent from 1981 to 1990. The most common victims are black men, who are 50 percent more likely than white men and two and a half times more likely than white women to be the victim of a violent crime.

And crime seldom has what the *Post* calls "racial implications." Only 18 percent of white victims of violent crime reported that their assailant was black. The real racial bias in the system is against African Americans: Blacks account for 29 percent of arrests but are 47 percent of prison inmates. If all you read is the *New York Post*, you probably won't read about that.

Crime Contradictions: U.S. News *Illustrates Flaws* in Crime Coverage

May/June 1994

JANINE JACKSON AND JIM NAURECKAS

"A SCARY ORGY of violent crime is fueling another public call to action." That's how *U.S. News & World Report* opened its January 17, 1994, cover story on "Violence in America." It also encapsulates the tone of much of the overheated and overhyped reporting on crime in the mid-1990s.

Despite the impression one would have gotten from news coverage, the incidence of crime did not rise dramatically in 1993. The most reliable research suggests, in fact, that there was no more violent crime that year than there was twenty years ago.

What there was more of—much more—was crime coverage. Crime took up 157 minutes a month on network news from October 1993 until January 1994—more than two and a half hours every month. In the thirty-six months ending with January 1992, by contrast, the networks spent only 67 minutes a month on crime stories.[2] And the reporting took on a shrill tabloid tone, designed to evoke fear, as with *NBC Nightly News*'s regular feature, "Society Under Siege."

This type of coverage seems to have had an effect. In June 1993, 5 percent of respondents to a *Washington Post*/ABC poll named crime as the most important issue facing the country. By February 1994, after months of saturation media coverage of crime, 31 percent said it was the most important problem—far outstripping any other issue.[3] When a January 1994 *Los Angeles Times* poll asked people where these feelings about crime came from, 65 percent said that they learned about crime primarily from the media.[4]

How did mass media give people the false impression that crime was climbing drastically? How did they justify portraying steady crime rates as a "scary orgy" that demands immediate action? An examination of *U.S. News & World Report*'s special report on crime is revealing, illustrating the major themes, distortions, and contradictions that characterized mainstream crime coverage in 1993 and 1994.

A recurring theme in *U.S. News*'s crime report, headlined "The Truth About Violent Crime" on the cover, was that crime was up. "Violence in modern America began its upward climb in 1960," we were told. "Nothing has stemmed the upward spiral of reported violent incidents." The coverage—which consisted of a main article, four companion pieces, and several sidebars—was sprinkled with casual references to the ongoing "wave of violence" and the "escalating crime numbers." A graph charted the crime statistics' "relentless growth."

The claim that crime in the United States was on the rise was based on the FBI's Uniform Crime Reports, which show collected data on reported crimes from police agencies across the country. The rate of violent crime, according to FBI statistics, had risen by 81 percent since 1973 (and has more than quadrupled since 1960).[5]

But there is another source for crime statistics, the Bureau of Justice Statistics (like the FBI, a branch of the federal Department of Justice). This agency conducts the annual National Crime Victimization Survey (NCVS), which asks people across the country whether they or members of their household have been victims of crime in the past year (tabulating unreported as well as reported crimes). According to the NCVS, the crime rate has been basically flat since the survey began: There were 32.6 violent crimes per thousand persons (twelve years old and up) in 1973, and 32.1 per thousand in 1992.[6]

Of the two surveys, the NCVS is considered the more reliable. The Uniform Crime Reports "are widely mistaken as indicators of the 'real' level of crime, rather than merely rough, and flawed, estimates," Tony Pate of the Police Foundation, an independent crime research institute, told an *Extra!* interviewer. There is "enormous variation in reporting procedures and policies" among the thousands of police agencies that take part in the survey, Pate said. "Not all agencies follow the reporting instructions properly."

This variation makes it extremely difficult to compare the FBI statistics from different years, since there is no way to say whether local police are classifying and reporting crimes consistently. Although the NCVS is not a perfect gauge of crime rates—it is notoriously bad, for example, at counting rapes—Pate called it the "preferable indicator," since it is "applied in a standardized fashion over time."

U.S. News was well aware that an alternative measure of crime exists—it used NCVS figures more than once to show that the number of all crimes is much greater than the number of reported crimes. But the magazine never mentioned that this alternative measure contradicts its picture of "relentless growth in crime."

To be sure, *U.S. News* did have a disclaimer toward the front of the article, noting that "the latest evidence is that crime levels actually fell last year [1993]"—because even the FBI figures showed a drop in reported crimes. There was even an implicit criticism of "the drumbeat of news coverage [that] has made it seem that America is in the midst of its worst epidemic of violence ever. That sense is not supported by the numbers," the magazine acknowledged.

U.S. News immediately followed that statement, however, with an assertion that the numbers don't matter: "But that doesn't mean that last year [1993] wasn't the scariest in American history." The implication was that the perception of danger from crime is as important as the reality—even if the perception is a product of media hyperbole.

The magazine seemed to realize, however, that media-inspired worry about crime couldn't justify another cover story on the crime threat. "Overriding the statistics," the article continued, "is the chilling realization that the big crime stories of recent months have invaded virtually every sanctuary where Americans thought they were safe."

This theme of "invading sanctuaries," prominent in much current crime coverage, ran throughout *U.S. News*'s crime report: "To many, this wave of violence is ominous because safe havens are violated," a caption declared. "The nature of some of the crime is changing," the main article stated, "making some people more vulnerable and bringing the worst kinds of problems into communities that many thought were safe."

The "some people" whose communities are no longer safe were apparently supposed to be (white) suburbanites, an assertion that is usually implicit but occasionally overt: "Middle-sized and small towns . . . are now experiencing some of the same trends in the violence contagion that cities have faced for a generation," the magazine stated. Writing about "cold-blooded kids" from "America's mean streets," a companion piece declared that "their malign ethos has metastasized to the suburbs, where youthful murder is increasingly common."

In both these references, urban crime was compared to a disease—a "contagion" or a "metastasized" cancer—that city-dwellers carried into previously uninfected suburbia. But the reality of crime distribution is very different from this pathological imagery.

As *U.S. News* briefly noted in a sidebar, crime was not rising in suburbs, it was falling. According to the latest statistics available from NCVS, a suburban resident was 13 percent more likely to be a victim of violent crime in 1973 than in 1992. Crimes like theft and burglary have declined substantially in the suburbs, and in rural areas as well.

The magazine did note that black people are disproportionately victims of crime. But when African Americans figure in *U.S. News*'s crime report—as in most U.S. crime coverage—they appear as "them," not as "us."

U.S. News avoided appearing overtly racist by focusing not on violence against whites but on "random" violence. The message is the same: You, the reader, whom we assume to be a white, middle-aged suburbanite, are in danger.

Thus *U.S. News* gave us "safety tips" that began: "No safety rules can protect the law-abiding from being hit by random fire from crazed gunmen." "Many are terrified by the random nature of current violence," a caption asserted. "A holiday-season burst of multiple killings showed . . . how random the slaughter can be," the magazine reported.

This focus on "random" violence resulted in strained logic. Under the heading of "Murder," the magazine noted, "While the absolute numbers fluctuated in the past decade, an increase in random murder was especially ominous. Decades ago, most murders were committed by relatives or acquaintances of the victim. Now, the proportion committed by strangers may have risen to one third, fueling the growing fear that there's no place where anyone is really safe."

Since the murder rate wasn't really changing much—it had fluctuated between 8.3 per 100,000 people and 10.2 per 100,000 for the past twenty years—*U.S. News* was searching for another way to make the numbers seem scary. Actually, the FBI classifies 13.5 percent, not one-third, of murderers as strangers to their victims, while 47 percent are relatives or acquaintances. (The remaining 39 percent are unclassified.)[7] Even if there had been a significant change, it's unclear how a *drop* in the proportion of murders committed by family and friends would make people feel *less* safe in their homes.

As if that weren't illogical enough, two paragraphs later, *U.S. News* was telling us that "contrary to conventional wisdom, random slaughters like last month's [December 1993] Long Island Railroad massacre and recent shooting sprees at postal facilities are not increasing sharply." The writers seemed not to notice that they had been reporting on the "increase in random murder" just moments earlier.

U.S. News's report, like crime coverage in general, was filled with such contradictions. The magazine seemed to be torn between the impulses to alarm and to reassure. Usually, it was the frightening boldface assertions—particularly in captions—that ended up being contradicted in the text.

Thus the pictures that accompanied the main article of *U.S. News*'s report featured the Long Island Railroad slaughter, two examples of revenge killings at workplaces, the suspect in the killing of 12-year-old kidnapping victim Polly Klaas, and the site of a random killing at a Dallas mall—all of which were presented as evidence of disturbing new trends ("Angry disputes often end in gunfire," "Impulsive violence is also on the rise," etc.).

In the text, however, we were told that mass murders in public places were not becoming more common, that child snatchings likewise continued to be very rare, and that workplace killings were "hardly at epidemic proportions." Although *U.S. News & World Report* said it is "a common error of citizens and policy makers

... to mistake big news stories for big trends," the magazine's own report made that mistake over and over again.

Although the central article of *U.S. News*'s report had little to say about the causes of crime, a companion piece on youth violence dealt with the question with more seriousness than most mainstream accounts. Writer Scott Minerbrook stressed the fact that violent offenders are often victims of severe child abuse, a connection well documented by social scientists but little noted in the media.

Minerbrook's attempt to find explanations for violence had its blind spots: Is it a "tragic trend," for instance, that the number of single-parent families is growing, or is it tragic that single mothers are given only the barest level of support in this country? Scandinavian countries, noted for progressive welfare and child care systems, have high rates of out-of-wedlock births, along with very low murder rates.

Minerbrook wrote, while listing contributing factors to crime, that "not least, there's the loss of millions of urban manufacturing jobs that are no longer available to kids willing to work to avoid lives of crime." If that's not the least important factor, isn't it worth more than one sentence?

If underlying issues of poverty and job loss didn't figure much in *U.S. News*'s explanation of the causes of crime, economic issues were entirely left out of its discussion of solutions. According to the main article, "massive spending on social programs for the poor" is just one example of previous efforts to stem crime that have failed.

But *U.S. News*'s descriptions of crime remedies were as convoluted as its discussion of the problem. For example, money for more police officers was cited as "the most important item" in new crime legislation. But in the next paragraph, *U.S. News* cited its own survey that "found that more police does not necessarily mean lower crime rates."

Similarly, the "massive buildup of prison cells" and the imposition of mandatory minimum sentences were cited as anticrime strategies that have been tried and have failed. Yet the article praised the "heightened anti-crime fervor" of local officials, as represented by one Kansas City state prosecutor who was quoted as saying, "We've got to lock them up for as long as we can."

Ultimately, what came across as the preferred solutions to crime were not programs that would require government investment but those of "grassroots organizations"—that is, those that residents of the poorest and most crime-ridden areas carry out themselves.

Political solutions may help in the "larger community," as Michael Barone argued in an accompanying column, but "something more is required to reduce the sickening violence in poor communities where violence and sexual predation can be overwhelming."

Barone contended that those who are most frequently the *victims* of crime are the ones ultimately responsible for it, because by allowing it to happen to them, they "sanction" it. Because they "take pains to avoid and never anger" the sus-

FIGURE 13.1 Two Crime Measures

Reported violent crimes per 1,000 people		Violent crimes per 1,000 persons 12 or older	
1973	4.174	1973	32.6
1974	4.611	1974	33.0
1975	4.878	1975	32.8
1976	4.678	1976	32.6
1977	4.759	1977	33.9
1978	4.978	1978	33.7
1979	5.489	1979	34.5
1980	5.966	1980	33.3
1981	5.943	1981	35.3
1982	5.711	1982	34.3
1983	5.377	1983	31.0
1984	5.392	1984	31.4
1985	5.566	1985	30.0
1986	6.177	1986	28.1
1987	6.097	1987	29.3
1988	6.372	1988	29.6
1989	6.637	1989	29.1
1990	7.318	1990	29.6
1991	7.581	1991	31.3
1992	7.575	1992	32.1

SOURCE: Uniform Crime Reports in Department of Justice, Bureau of Justice Statistics, *Sourcebook of Criminal Justice Statistics* 1993 (Washington, D.C.: Government Printing Office, 1994); National Crime Victim Survey in Department of Justice, Bureau of Justice Statistic, *Sourcebook of Criminal Justice Statistics* 1993 (Washington, D.C. : Government Printing Office, 1994).

pected criminals among them, Barone stated, residents of poor neighborhoods tell "the criminal that his misdeeds are expected, assumed, in some sense understood and approved."

Having told readers who it believes ought to fear crime—white suburbanites, or "us"—*U.S. News* then reminded readers who's really to blame for crime—black city dwellers, or "them." Having argued that now "crime can strike anywhere," the magazine—like much of U.S. crime coverage—still traced the roots of crime back to the same old place, poor urban neighborhoods, whose residents need not more jobs, but more morals.

Crime Hysteria's Illogical Conclusion
May/June 1994

THE GREATEST DANGER of crime wave stories is that the resulting hysteria will lead to criminal assaults on the Bill of Rights. Columnists like A. M. Rosenthal and Dennis Duggan have declared that freedom from the fear of crime is "the most important civil right"—implying that other rights might have to take a backseat.[8]

Probably the most extreme response to the crime hype in mainstream media came from Anne Roiphe, a columnist for the weekly *New York Observer*, who called for "martial law" in her January 10, 1994, column. "Perhaps it's time for democracy to admit that there are limits to its space," Roiphe wrote.

> At the edge of the wilderness, we may truly need martial law. We could take a cold look at our jails smelling of rotting lives and wasted minds, we could count the dead bodies and the ruined lives and say to ourselves: Enough. Bring in the Army and let them clean the place out. Let them shoot the dealers and the armed gang members; let anyone found with a gun on his or her person be killed as in a war in which we take no prisoners.

The idea of civil rights was briefly raised and dismissed by Roiphe: "Yes, there are constitutional issues here. But when a man has his hand on your throat, you don't Mirandize him, you fight back."

The racism inherent in Roiphe's hysteria was manifest in her fantasy of "our G.I.s" stationed "in Bed-Stuy, in El Barrio, up in Washington Heights"—all easily recognized by New Yorkers as black or Latino neighborhoods. (She went on to imagine the Army setting up "headquarters in the Apollo Theater" in Harlem and passing out "chocolate bars and condoms to the cheering crowds.")

This may sound like satire, but Roiphe seemed to be completely serious, even as she suggested that armed force can keep people from becoming pregnant or failing to learn to read. She closed her column: "Drugs and guns, teenage pregnancies and illiteracy are not private indulgences—they are the stuff of class warfare, they are termites feeding on civil society, they are the calamity of modern America and I don't think we should take it anymore. Send in the Army while there's still time. Uncle Sam, we want you."

Roiphe's frankly fascistic vision evoked little response in the rest of the press, although *New York Post* columnist Scott McConnell praised Roiphe's call for martial law, saying "she has managed to find clear words to express what many are surprised to find themselves thinking."⁹

Hearing What They Want to Hear: Media on Jesse Jackson on Crime

May/June 1994

JANINE JACKSON

REVEREND JESSE JACKSON's late 1993/early 1994 comments about how blacks could take action against crime in their communities received an unusually favorable response from mainstream media outlets that are usually cool, if not hostile, toward the civil rights leader.

But the selective emphasis of many press accounts distorted the content and context of Jackson's remarks, revealing more about media priorities than about Jackson's ideas.

Of particular fascination to reporters was a comment Jackson made to an Operation PUSH group in Chicago in November 1993: Jackson said that he has sometimes felt "relieved" to find that the footsteps following him on a dark street are those of a white person. There is, he said, "nothing more painful" to him.

There was something "new, explosive and, perhaps, liberating" in that November "confession," claimed *U.S. News & World Report*.[10] Jackson's focus on urban violence has been a long-standing part of his civil rights work, yet journalists praised it as a "decided departure."[11] "Having built a career fighting the powers that be," *Newsweek* declared, "Jesse Jackson has now found a new foe."[12]

And although it seems we hear about urban black crime on virtually every newscast, some pundits congratulated Jackson for tearing away the "protective shroud of secrecy" surrounding "blacks being terrorized by other blacks."[13]

The media spin on Jackson's Washington, D.C., African-American leadership conference in January 1994 was captured in the *Washington Post* headline: "Blacks Are Urged to Take Responsibility for Violence."[14]

In even the more measured accounts, Jackson's appeal to African Americans to "take the lead" in helping their communities was rhetorically pitted against calls for government investment, making these approaches seem mutually exclusive. In this framework, anyone calling for federal aid to cities or the redressing of racism and socioeconomic imbalances is painted as "making excuses" for violent crime.

In fact, Jackson has long insisted that both government help and self-help are needed for the African-American community. At the January conference, Jackson proposed a "domestic Marshall Plan" for inner cities, involving low-interest mortgages and loans, youth mentoring programs, and a meaningful jobs bill. "What is needed," Jackson told reporters, "is some combination of more demands upon ourselves but also more demands upon our government."

But such subtleties were ignored by many journalists. In November 1993, columnist Mike Royko reported (approvingly) that Jackson believes it's "a waste of time to expect government to reduce . . . urban mayhem."[15]

Some journalists interpreted Jackson's comments as putting an acceptable face on their own long-held opinions. In his December 21 column, the *Washington Post*'s Richard Cohen declared that Jackson's remarks "pithily paraphrase what I wrote" in 1986. The reference is to Cohen's assertion in a column that if he were a shopkeeper, he would lock his doors "to keep young black men out."[16]

For Cohen, Jackson's comments proved that "it is not racism to recognize a potential threat posed by someone with certain characteristics." The difference between recognizing violence as a problem for black communities and advocating discrimination against young black men was evidently lost on Cohen.

Columns and reports like this seemed to celebrate the notion that black people's difficulties are due above all to self-destructiveness. If even Jesse Jackson says African Americans should take action on crime in their communities, it must follow that racism and economic injustice have nothing to do with the problems of those communities.

For some, merely acknowledging blacks' "responsibility" is not enough. *New York Times* columnist Sam Roberts credited Jackson with "belatedly exposing" what Roberts called the "propensity toward violence among black Americans," but warned that "by focusing on genocidal black-on-black crime, to some people Mr. Jackson may seem to be suggesting that white lives are cheaper."[17]

"Some people" would include former Klan leader David Duke, whose expert opinion on the January leadership conference was quoted by *New York Newsday*. "There are white victims of black crime," Duke complained, sounding remarkably like Sam Roberts.[18]

The media's preoccupation with scapegoats rather than solutions was evident in *U.S. News & World Report*'s piece. By saying he sometimes fears young black men, Jackson "seemed to be offering sympathetic whites something for which they hungered: absolution," the article declared. "Yet rather than grant such absolution—and reap the enormous good will and political cooperation such a move might bring—Jackson has pulled back."[19] What *U.S. News* was looking for, apparently, was a statement that whites' fear of blacks has nothing to do with racism.

The message for black spokespeople is clear: They will be deemed "mature" and "responsible" when they seem to be mainly blaming black people for poor urban blacks' situation. Mention of any other factors is cause to dub them "divisive" and difficult.

Many civil rights leaders, and Jackson himself, expressed fear that his ideas would be misconstrued by media looking for "acceptable" targets of outrage and blame, media that find gun-wielding teenagers front-page material but systemic socioeconomic problems boring. The media response indicates that such concern was fully warranted.

Notes

1. Katherine McFate, *Black Crime, White Fear: Recent Trends in Victimization, Arrests and Incarcerations in the United States* (Washington, D.C.: Joint Center for Political and Economic Studies, 1992); *Wall Street Journal,* August 12, 1992.

2. Andrew Tyndall, "Crime Panic," *Tyndall Report,* February 1994, p. 6.

3. *Boston Globe,* April 4, 1994.

4. *Los Angeles Times,* February 13, 1994.

5. Department of Justice, Bureau of Justice Statistics, *Sourcebook of Criminal Justice Statistics 1993* (Washington, D.C.: Government Printing Office, 1994).

6. Department of Justice, Bureau of Justice Statistics, *Sourcebook of Criminal Justice Statistics 1993.*

7. Department of Justice, Bureau of Justice Statistics, *Sourcebook of Criminal Justice Statistics 1993.*

8. A. M. Rosenthal, *New York Times,* February 25, 1994. Dennis Duggan wrote in *New York Newsday* (February 27, 1994): "If you're dead as a result of a drive-by shooting, then what good are your other civil rights—voting or housing or protection from job discrimination? How in hell can you live in this or any other city and not realize that the freedom to go on living is the cornerstone of all your other freedoms?"

9. *New York Post,* January 14, 1994.

10. "The Truth About Violent Crime: What You Really Have to Fear," cover story, *U.S. News & World Report,* January 17, 1994.

11. *Houston Chronicle,* January 17, 1994.

12. *Newsweek,* January 10, 1994.

13. *New York Newsday,* February 27, 1994.

14. *Washington Post,* January 17, 1994.

15. *Chicago Tribune,* November 30, 1994.

16. *Washington Post,* September 7, 1986.

17. *New York Times,* November 15, 1993.

18. *New York Newsday,* January 7, 1994.

19. Paul Glastris and Jeannye Thornton, "A New Civil Rights Frontier," *U.S. News & World Report,* January 17, 1994, p. 38.

14 Economic Losers

No Hope for the Homeless at the New York Times

March/April 1990

JIM NAURECKAS

THE *New York Times*'s campaign against the homeless, begun in 1988 with an article charging beggars with "hardening New Yorkers against their fellow citizens,"[1] heated up at the beginning of the 1990s.

The barrage began with a January 26, 1990, op-ed column by Myron Magnet, a *Fortune* magazine editor, who was given nearly half the page to make the point that growing numbers of homeless do not reflect "rising injustice and inequality in the social order." "Anyone who goes home by train or subway and trusts the evidence of his senses," Magnet wrote, "knows this just isn't so. What you see, if you stop to look, is craziness, drunkenness, dope and danger."

Magnet's piece, and others with a similar viewpoint that followed, were not balanced by others expressing sympathy for street people. A January 31, 1990, *New York Times* editorial attacked federal judge Leonard Sand, who had ruled that the city could not ban begging in the subway. Referring to the homeless as "wild-eyed vagrants who just might be loony enough to push someone in front of a train," the paper said that it was not callous to ban beggars from the subways because of the "officially tolerated exercise of begging rights in the streets above."

The editorial was echoed by an op-ed piece appearing a week later, also criticizing the judge's ruling. "What Judge Sand is urging upon us," wrote Samuel Lipman, publisher of the neoconservative *New Criterion*, "is the use of constant public irritation, provocation and threats, not for the ostensible purpose of alleviating suffering, but to cast radical doubt on the entire structure of society."[2]

Taking a somewhat different tack, in a *New York Times* February 2, 1990, op-ed article, Bernard Goldberg, a correspondent for CBS's *48 Hours,* attacked the media for always sympathizing with the homeless and other underdogs. "So what if many of the homeless are truly drug addicts or alcoholics or simply lazy?" Goldberg asked.

He also chided the press for a supposed excess of compassion for AIDS patients and the unemployed. "When there's a recession and workers get laid off, the press and television often portray them as innocent victims," he wrote. "But how many stories have you seen on TV or read in the newspaper—in your entire life—that attempt to find out how many of these laid-off workers took school seriously? How many thought kids who studied were wimps, and worse?" (Is Goldberg perhaps gloating that the kids who used to call him a geek have been thrown out on the streets?)

One of the more bizarre examples of the *New York Times*'s assault on street people was a February 15, 1990, news story on the front page of the metropolitan section. It focused on the first person to apply for a "permit" to beg at Manhattan's Port Authority bus terminal, James Benagh, who turned out to have taken the permit in hopes of preventing other people from collecting money. (Benagh is, of all things, a *New York Times* copy editor!)

"Might not his scheme seem callous?" asked the *Times* reporter. "Not, he said, after his teen-age son was threatened at knife point by a beggar at the terminal and his younger son suffered an ugly insult from a panhandler." "I'm not against helping people," Benagh is quoted. "But I am against people pestering you."

It might take a psychoanalyst to explain what drives the *Times*'s writers to see homeless people less as victims deserving of compassion than as victimizers deserving of contempt. The *Times* did consult a psychoanalyst in that first story back in 1988. The homeless population "provides a new target for my homicidal fantasies," he said, proving that doctors sometimes need more care than patients.

Geezer-Bashing:
Media Attacks on the Elderly

July/August 1991

JOHN HESS

BUDGET OUT OF CONTROL, banks going bust, states and cities going broke, children going hungry—who's to blame? For major media, no problem. It's elderly Americans.

In their drive to punish gray hair, big media give no quarter. There is no trial, no defense. "Elderly, Affluent—and Selfish," snarled a typical op-ed piece in the *New York Times*.[3] "The 800 Pound Gorilla Vs. the Hungry Baby," growled a *Washington Post* column, referring to the invisible geezer lobby as an ape.[4] *Time* magazine said the country could work its way out of the hole it's in "by spending less on the elderly and more on preschoolers," but alas, "the elderly vote and preschoolers don't."[5] Columnist Lars-Erik Nelson of the New York *Daily News* proposed a cure for that: a Constitutional amendment denying the vote to everybody who gets a government check, like Social Security.[6]

Nelson happens to be one of the more liberal members of the Washington press corps. What could have caused him to utter such a cruel jest? It is that he and others like him have been taken in by vicious and preposterous propaganda—and have never heard the truth of it.

For instance, a *New York Times* report was headlined "Political Might of Elderly Is Felt Again in Senate: Dole Complains That Medicare Has Become Untouchable."[7] The news? The Senate had agreed to cut Medicare spending by only $43 billion, rather than the $60 billion slash that was in the original budget deal.

Earlier, the House had done likewise, terrified no doubt by that same 800-pound gorilla. A *New York Times* news report called it "another demonstration of the power of entitlements for the elderly and lobbyists of the elderly." *New York Times* reporter Jason DeParle went on to write that Social Security and Medicare "cost more than four of every 10 federal dollars"—after, of course, "subtracting military spending and interest."[8]

A similar numbers game was played by the White House in its 1992 budget proposal, which called, incidentally, for another $13 billion cut in Medicare. *New York Newsday* bit on this one, in color charts published February 5, 1991.

One chart showed "Social Security and other social insurance receipts" as making up 30 percent of revenues. The other put "Social Security and other benefit payments to individuals"—whatever in the world that might include—at 41 percent.

What the two charts—sourced to the White House Office of Management and Budget—concealed was that Social Security and Medicare taxes take in far more than they pay in benefits, thus subsidizing the federal deficit by $1 billion a week.

But in the *New York Times*, DeParle still wrote that spending under these programs "cramps other social spending, leaving less to build housing, fight infant mortality, provide better schools, battle drug abuse and otherwise invest in the future."[9] From this point of view, Nelson's proposal to take the vote away seems like modest punishment for baby killers.

Over the years, many liberals like Nelson, Tom Wicker, and Anthony Lewis have been taken in by this sort of propaganda. If the elderly were indeed well off and were indeed bankrupting the republic and depriving the needy, why shouldn't liberals object?

Well, perhaps they should have been a teensy bit skeptical. They should have realized that when a typical worker retires, his or her income drops precipitously. A call to Social Security would have turned up the news that most of the elderly depend on it for most or all of their income, that fully half would fall below the poverty line were it not for Social Security, that Social Security and Medicare help millions of children and the disabled as well as the elderly, and that no more than 3 percent of the elderly may be described as affluent.

Anyway, the notion that either Congress or the Bush administration would have used money cut from programs for the elderly to feed hungry babies was as absurd as the other basic postulates of geezer-bashing: that the elderly as a class are rich (they are of course poorer than any other segment of adults); that they are especially selfish (they are more supportive of a cradle-to-grave health care system than any other group); and that they have overwhelming political clout.

In the 1980s, while taxes on the rich were being cut by more than half, old age benefits took repeated hits. Early 1980s bankruptcy scares allowed for sharp cuts in pensions and heavy increases in payroll taxes, touted to assure the solvency of Social Security into the twenty-first century.

Senator Daniel Patrick Moynihan (D.–N.Y.), one of the perpetrators of these cuts, has since acknowledged that the insolvency of Social Security was a hoax, but it enabled the media to present the cuts and hikes as a "Social Security rescue."[10]

That 1983 act also pushed back the retirement age from sixty-five to sixty-seven, in phases beginning in the year 2005. That meant that baby boomers and the generations that followed—the real targets of the geezer-bashing campaign—would pay more and get less over a lifetime. Indeed, this very argument was then used by William Buckley and other conservatives to urge repeal of Social Security.

One might think that the early cutbacks (there were others, like trimming pension pennies back to the next lower dollar and chipping away at Medicare and Medicaid) would have mollified the geezer bashers. But the continuing growth of the national debt, the savings and loan debacle, the crisis in local government, and the decline in real wages maintained a serious need for scapegoats. Who better than the geezers, especially if they could not answer back?

The beneficiaries of the propaganda campaign can be seen from those who sponsored it. One of the outfits that served as a major guide to mainstream journalists was Americans for Generational Equity (AGE). In 1987, Common Cause published a partial list of AGE donors: General Dynamics, Rockwell, TRW, U.S. Steel, ITT, Metropolitan Life, Massachusetts Mutual—and the U.S. League of Savings Institutions, the lobby of the S&Ls. Such were the interests that were accusing elderly Americans of robbing babies.

It must be emphasized that the principal target of this campaign is not the elderly but all segments of the public being hurt by retrenchment, rollbacks, and unfair taxation. All are being told that the elderly are hogging what is rightfully theirs. All are victims of bad reporting. All need to realize that the battle for fair play must begin in the news media.

Alarming Drops in Unemployment! Why the New York Times *Wants Your Job*

September/October 1994

DOUG HENWOOD

THE MANTRA "jobs, jobs, jobs" has been used by politicians and pundits to justify everything from the Gulf War to NAFTA to mass owl death. The need to preserve that same holy trinity is offered as a reason why we can't afford universal health care.

The U.S. economy's ability to generate new employment made Bill Clinton "the envy" of his Group of Seven peers, NBC's Irving R. Levine reported from the Naples economic summit.[11] The reason for Europe's sluggish employment growth, Levine explained, was generous social policies. So our mean-spirited and meanly financed welfare system is really a good thing because it creates jobs, jobs, jobs.

So you might think the news that the "jobless recovery" of the early 1990s had given way to moderate job growth by spring 1994 would be met with cheers. But that would be too simple.

Take, for example, this item from a report by Kenneth N. Gilpin in the July 11, 1994, *New York Times*. Gilpin quotes a J. P. Morgan banker as saying: "We have created one million jobs in the last three months alone. And various [private] surveys . . . tell us this is going to continue."

Great, right? No. Gilpin turns to another banker, Paul Kasriel of Northern Trust, who tells us that this very strength "warrants some sort of tightening" by the Federal Reserve—an upward nudge in interest rates that would slow the economy, and, more bluntly, destroy jobs.

In the looking-glass world of Wall Street, bad news—slower income growth, for example—is good, and good news—lower unemployment—is bad. The language gets pretty surreal at times. In a June 6, 1994, story, the *New York Times*'s Keith Bradsher, who has served as a frictionless transmitter of leaks from the Federal Reserve, noted that three of the central bank's five governors "said that they did not believe that unemployment had dropped to an alarming extent." An alarming drop in *un*employment?

The reasoning behind this inversion is fairly simple. If growth gets too rapid and unemployment gets too low, the economy will "overheat," with prices and wages rising, and a generalized inflation is set into motion. If we want to prevent a rerun of the 1970s—goes this reasoning—the process cannot even be allowed to start: The Fed must tighten now, even though there is no evidence of inflation, because if it doesn't, there's bound to be trouble down the road.

Underlying this argument is an economic concept known as the "natural rate of unemployment," developed by Milton Friedman in the late 1960s. Friedman argued that attempts to push the economy below this magic level would only result in higher inflation, not more employment. Actually, as Friedman himself admitted, the level is not a fact of nature but is rather a function of demographics, technology, government regulation, international trade, labor skills, and other mutable social phenomena.

The natural rate, assuming it exists, can't be seen; it can only be guessed at using statistical techniques. An effort at doing that, by Federal Reserve analyst Stuart Weiner,[12] attracted wide attention on Wall Street and was turned by Weiner into an op-ed piece in the *New York Times* Sunday business section.[13]

Examining the relation between unemployment and inflation since 1961, Weiner estimated that the natural rate is now around 6.2 percent, well above what most economists had been assuming. (For technical reasons having to do with the redesign of the Bureau of Labor Statistics' monthly employment survey, Weiner's *New York Times* article puts the natural rate at 6.7 percent; in an interview with *Extra!*, he withdrew this increase, meaning 650,000 workers can now breathe easier.)

But while "nature" treats the sexes pretty equally, at least when it comes to unemployment, Weiner's estimates of the natural rate by race and age show huge gaps: The white rate is 5.5 percent, less than half of the nonwhite rate of 11.8 percent, with nonwhite youth clocking in with a natural rate of unemployment of 33 percent.

Weiner, like Friedman, does concede that policy changes can change the natural rate, and that the racial gap in the "natural" rate is not really a fact of nature but a result of "discrimination and differences in family background, quality of education, and job information networks."[14] Weiner and Friedman also concede that policy changes can lower the natural rate.

Right-wing policy prescriptions include cutting unemployment benefits (which would supposedly discourage idleness) and repealing the minimum wage; liberal prescriptions include education, job training, and employer subsidies; and more radical ones include price controls and a more centralized wage bargaining system. But these complexities are lost when a certain unemployment rate becomes "naturalized." Instead, the debate merely turns on what should be the Fed's trigger point for shutting down the economy.

And the Wall Street/Fed consensus is that that point has already been reached, which is why the central bank tightened policy four times in the first half of 1994—tightenings that were applauded in a *New York Times* editorial about "The Fed's Prudent Course."[15] If the natural rate is 6.2 percent, then the 6.0 percent rate of June 19, 1994, was too low, meaning that one-third of a million people now working should be disemployed, to bring the jobless count to just over eight million.

Some liberal economists believe eight million is too high and that the real figure is closer to seven million. *New York Times* reporter Louis Uchitelle summoned Robert Solow of the Massachusetts Institute of Technology (MIT) to make this argument in the April 24, 1994, edition. This seems to be the limit of debate in the paper of record—which is more natural, seven million or eight million people out of work? Left completely out of the picture are the unofficially unemployed—the nearly nine million people who'd like full-time work but can only find part-time slots, or who'd like to work but have given up the search as hopeless, or who wouldn't know where to park the kids if they could find a job.

But who cares so much about inflation anyway? And what do people really mean by the word inflation? Ordinary people think of inflation as a rise in their cost of living—the ever-widening gap between what they earn for an hour's work and what they must spend to survive. But that's not what it means to Wall Street.

Wall Street thinks of inflation in at least two important senses. One is a general rise in the price level that erodes the value of their stock in trade, money. And the other is a rise in the wage level that might increase labor's share of national income at the expense of business and finance. The real reason a low unemployment rate is to be feared is that it increases the bargaining power of labor—a crime against nature!

In a May 22, 1994, *New York Times* story, Thomas L. Friedman obscured this conflict by claiming that "it is not only the J.P. Morgans of Wall Street who worry about inflation. So do the record numbers of Main Street Americans who are invested in the bond and stock markets through their pension funds or mutual funds.... More people expect that a tight-money policy will safeguard their investments."

But 60 percent of workers aren't covered by pension plans, and, according to the Fed's 1989 Survey of Consumer Finances, only 19 percent held stocks and 4 percent held bonds, either directly or through mutual funds.[16] For all but the very rich, jobs are far more important than investments. The *New York Times*'s Main Street is a misleadingly posh thoroughfare.

Commenting on classical theories of a natural rate of interest, a concept that inspired Milton Friedman's natural rate of unemployment, John Maynard Keynes noted that concepts like this are merely covers for preserving the status quo, and the status quo should be something "we have no predominant interest in."[17] But, of course, many powerful people have a passionate interest in a status quo of weak labor and falling real wages. Turning to nature is a neat cover for such an agenda, and well-paid team players that they are, *New York Times* journalists are happy to do their part.

Notes

1. *New York Times,* July 29, 1988.
2. *New York Times,* February 5, 1990.
3. *New York Times,* October 10, 1989.
4. *Washington Post,* October 22, 1990.
5. Andrew Tobias, "Money Angles: Give Greed Another Chance," *Time,* November 26, 1990, p. 74.
6. New York *Daily News,* October 22, 1990.
7. *New York Times,* October 19, 1990.
8. *New York Times,* October 12, 1990.
9. *New York Times,* October 12, 1990.
10. John L. Hess, "Social Security, the Candidates and the Media," *Extra!,* January/February 1988, p. 4.
11. CNBC, July 11, 1994.
12. Stuart Weiner, "New Estimates of the Natural Rate of Unemployment," Federal Reserve Bank of Kansas City *Economic Review,* 4th quarter 1993, p. 53.
13. *New York Times,* May 29, 1994.
14. Weiner, "New Estimates."
15. *New York Times,* May 18, 1994.
16. Arthur Kennickell and Janis Schek Marquez, "Changes in Family Finances from 1983–1989, Evidence from the Survey of Consumer Finances," *Federal Reserve Bulletin,* January 1992, p. 1.
17. John Maynard Keynes, *The Collected Works of John Maynard Keynes,* Vol. 14, Donald Moggridge, ed. (London: Macmillan, 1973), pp. 242–243.

PART FIVE

Beyond Clinton

15 Contracting the American Spectrum: The '94 Election

Wines's World:
The Tie-Dyed Clinton

November/December 1994

THE FRONT PAGE of the *New York Times*'s "Week in Review" section is a platform that both reflects and helps set the conventional wisdom. Michael Wines, one of the *Times*'s top political reporters, used that space on September 11, 1994, to amplify the claims by "Mr. Clinton's loyal critics in Congress and Democratic research circles . . . that only a basic change of direction will revive his political fortunes."

Wines's unnamed sources called on Clinton to "govern from the center." "They fear that his handling of many major issues has enabled Republicans to persuade the public he is the sort of tie-dyed, union-label liberal that voters shun," Wines wrote. "They argue that the only way to erase that stain is to pursue policies that can attract moderate Republicans as well as Democrats."

You may be wondering just which policies "stain" Clinton as a "tie-dyed, union-label liberal." After all, Clinton's major legislative victories—like NAFTA, the crime bill, and deficit reduction—were in support of centrist or conservative policies. His administration's major initiative, health care reform, was founded on the industry-friendly "managed competition" model rather than on the progressive single-payer plan. When Clinton has taken a controversial progressive position—as with recognition of gay civil rights in the military, his economic stimulus program, or the nomination of Lani Guinier as assistant attorney general—he's retreated briskly.

Wines acknowledged some of these things, but discounted them. Even though Clinton has pushed "centrist legislation," he "has won most of his legislative victories with few Republican votes, preferring to roll his opponents with the same coalition of unions, elderly and other beneficiaries of Federal protection that almost elected Hubert Humphrey."

Maybe that's what happened in Wines's world. In the real world, Clinton got his budget passed by dropping provisions that various industries objected to, like the energy tax and grazing-fee hikes. He got NAFTA passed by including all sorts of breaks for business interests; more Republicans than Democrats ended up voting for the pact. To get the crime bill over, Clinton wound up trimming the social programs that were supposed to balance the "law and order" provisions like increased death penalties.

Ironically, most of these concessions were made to satisfy conservative Democrats—the "loyal critics in Congress" who were quoted constantly in the press, complaining that Clinton didn't "govern from the center." The Clinton administration generally followed the center-right agenda of the "New Democrats," which was supposed to bring voters back to the Democratic Party; since that didn't happen, the press seemed intent on writing off the administration—regardless of the evidence—as another failure for the left.

Want to Cast an Informed Vote for Congress? Don't Look to Major Dailies

January/February 1995

DAN SHADOAN

"THE FIT BETWEEN the country's information needs and its information media has become disastrously disjointed," Ben Bagdikian wrote in *The Media Monopoly*, describing the multitude of local political districts encompassed within the market of a single daily newspaper.¹

While it may be unrealistic to expect a major metropolitan newspaper to fully cover every school board race and township supervisor contest within its circulation, it's not too much to ask that U.S. congressional races be given serious attention. The House of Representatives is among the most powerful institutions in the country, and each of its members is chosen locally. If voters can't get independent information on these races from their local papers, they are unlikely to get it from any other news source.

However, a survey of the leading papers in three major cities revealed an almost total lack of coverage of the races in most congressional districts in their readership areas. Unless the race in your district was marked by scandal, had no incumbent, or was deemed a "close race" in the journalists' foggy crystal balls, you were likely to get no information that could guide your ballot choice from these papers.

FAIR surveyed campaign coverage in the *New York Times*, *Chicago Tribune*, and *Los Angeles Times* from the beginning of 1994 until election day, November 8, 1994. The papers were monitored to see what coverage was given to congressional races in the papers' central city and suburban congressional districts.[2]

One measure of how newspapers covered the congressional election was how many articles were devoted to each individual district's race. The *New York Times* ran twenty-seven separate articles on the twenty New York districts surveyed—an average of 1.35 articles per district, over more than ten months. Eleven of the twenty races were never the subject of a single article. Some of these races were featured in "round-up" articles that covered two to five races each, but overall the *New York Times*'s coverage of congressional races was clearly weaker than that of the other papers.

The *Los Angeles Times*'s reporting was a slight improvement, with forty-nine articles on twenty-three districts, or 2.13 articles per district. But excluding the two districts (24, 46) that garnered more than ten articles each, only sixteen articles remained on the other twenty-one districts—0.76 articles per district. Again, eleven districts received no full-length stories during the campaign.

The only paper to carry at least one article on every district's race was the *Chicago Tribune*. (It's a sad comment when a paper deserves praise simply for finding each congressional district in its city worthy of at least one article.) With the fewest number of districts (13), it printed ninety-seven single-district articles, by far the most, at 7.46 per district. Excluding the three districts (5, 8, 11) with more than ten articles, the average of 3.0 was still more than double the *New York Times*'s average for all races.

How was the little coverage that existed distributed? As with presidential campaigns, races that involved scandal were a big draw. The most-covered race in the *Chicago Tribune* was that of the Fifth District, in which much-indicted Representative Dan Rostenkowski struggled in vain to retain his seat. Illinois's Second District was the subject of seven articles—even though the Democratic incumbent, Mel Reynolds, had no opponent—due to Reynolds's alleged affair with a teenage campaign worker and a probe of his campaign finances.

Incumbent Republican Robert Dornan's mudslinging contest with Democratic challenger Mike Farber in California's Forty-sixth District made it the second-most-covered race in the *Los Angeles Times*. The eleven articles often focused on the "character issue," centering on Farber's accusations of Dornan's spousal abuse and Dornan's libel suit against Farber.

At the opposite end of the coverage scale were urban districts with nonwhite majorities. An average of 1.6 articles were devoted to each minority district—about half the typical amount of coverage. Of twenty such districts in the three metropolitan areas, eleven had no articles at all written about them.

Two-thirds of coverage of minority constituencies was given to three districts: that of scandal-plagued Reynolds, who had no opponent; Dornan's, which surprisingly has a Latino majority; and New York's Seventeenth District, where salsa star Willie Colon ran unsuccessfully for the Democratic nomination. Without these "high-profile" districts, the average for races involving nonwhite constituencies fell to 0.45 articles per district.

The papers of record also flocked to districts in which they foresaw tight races. The *Los Angeles Times*, for example, gave heavy coverage to Republican Rich Sybert's challenge to Democratic incumbent Tony Beilenson, which ended up being decided by a margin of only 2 percent.

But the papers weren't usually so good at guessing which races would be close. No New York race got as much coverage in the *New York Times* as that of the Fourteenth District, which includes Manhattan's affluent Upper East Side. In its seven stories, the paper stressed the tightness of the race between Carolyn Maloney, the Democratic incumbent, and Charles Millard, the Republican challenger. On election day, Maloney easily defeated Millard, 63 percent to 36 percent.

Meanwhile, in New York's First District, incumbent George Hochbrueckner—like Maloney, a freshman Democrat—was unseated by Republican Michael Forbes. There were no articles in the *New York Times* that focused on this district.

The *Chicago Tribune* ran twenty-three stories on the Eighth District in Illinois, a well-off suburban district, also stressing the possibility that Republican incumbent Philip Crane might be unseated. He actually got 65 percent of the vote. A closer race in the Third District, where Democratic Representative William Lipinski was reelected with 54 percent of the vote, was the subject of only three stories in the *Tribune*.

An open seat—there were only two in the three metropolitan areas—was an obvious draw for the papers. In Illinois, Democrat Frank Giglio and Republican Gerald Weller competed for the open Eleventh District, and the *Chicago Tribune* devoted seventeen articles to the race.

The *New York Times* ran five stories on New York's Nineteenth District, a suburban district north of the city, where Hamilton Fish, Jr., was trying to win the open seat that had been held by his father and his grandfather before him. These stories actually contained information about Fish's policy positions, a rare feature in campaign coverage—although the paper seemed most interested in the familial drama of Fish abandoning his ancestors' Republicanism for the Democratic Party.

Despite the often-repeated conventional wisdom about the public's "anti-incumbent mood," the practice of focusing attention on open seats and "close" races handicapped most challengers and reinforced advantages of incumbents—including greater fund-raising ability and name recognition from coverage of congressional activities.

Across the nation, the media reported on the public's disenchantment with politics as usual. "In this year of the anti-incumbent, almost any Washington connection beyond a trip with the kids to the Lincoln Memorial is being considered a potential weapon to be used against congressional candidates," wrote Melinda Henneberger in the *New York Times*.[3] With a little help from the media, however, most incumbents could and did overcome this mood.

FAIR tallied election articles that mentioned candidates' names. In the three papers, incumbent candidates' names appeared an average of 14.02 times, major-party challengers came up 5.39 times, and third-party candidates 2.1 times. Given this advantage, it's easy to see why the election was viewed as a disaster for incumbents when "only" 91 percent of them won their races nationwide.

If coverage of major party challengers was insufficient, especially in urban ethnic neighborhoods and in "safe" districts, it was virtually nonexistent for third-party candidates—except for frequent musings on Ross Perot's various plans to support local candidates. A few former Republicans running on right-wing tickets got scattered mentions—particularly David Levy, the incumbent in New York's Fourth District, who ran (unsuccessfully) as a Conservative after losing the Republican primary.

Peace and Freedom, American Independent, and Libertarian candidates across the Los Angeles area received little mention in the *Los Angeles Times*. The most substantive attention given to a third-party candidate in any race occurred when the *New York Times* ran a letter to the editor by Thomas Leighton—who was running as a TBA (Take Back America) Green in the Fourteenth District.

If an election is no more than a horse race, then the press could do its job merely by covering the front-runner (assuming that the press can accurately guess who that is). But if it is truly an exercise in democracy, with candidates trying not only to win but also to bring ideas to a public dialogue, then covering long-shot challengers and third-party candidates is essential to broaden the debate.

The willingness of these three major papers to neglect all but the flashiest election races has serious implications for a democratic system of government, which is reliant on knowledgeable constituencies. Representatives in the House are the most direct link between citizens and the federal government. When metropolitan newspapers fail to give voters the information they need to cast an informed ballot, they help to sever that link.

Drafting Students into the "War on Immigration": Channel One's Anti-Immigrant Propaganda Has a Captive Audience

January/February 1995

KIM DETERLINE

CALIFORNIA'S PROPOSITION 187, voted into law in November 1994, denies access to education, nonemergency health care, and other social services to illegal immigrants. Many of those affected are students, as were many of the leading opponents to the measure, with youth in Los Angeles, San Francisco, and other cities organizing walkouts and demonstrations.

Although youth are infrequent consumers of traditional news from papers and TV, there is one form of media that many students are exposed to whether they want it or not: *Channel One*, the in-school satellite TV news and advertising program that junior high and high school students in California and across the country are forced to watch.

Channel One's viewers are literally a captive audience: Schools who accept the program are contractually bound to show it to students, to keep the screen uncovered and maintain the volume at a prescribed level. Unlike other material presented to students, *Channel One* circumvents any traditional curriculum review process, to be fed directly to young people as an accurate rendering of current events.[4]

In October 1994, as the debate over Proposition 187 heated up, *Channel One* showed a four-part series on illegal immigration.[5] The framing of the story illustrated common media myths about illegal immigration. The series focused almost exclusively on Mexican immigrants, implying that Mexico is overwhelmingly responsible for the immigration "problem." Given the series' focus, one would think that illegal immigrants were sneaking across the border, overrunning the country, and exploiting social services. None of these presumptions is true.

Less than 1.5 percent of the U.S. population is undocumented, according to the U.S. Census. The percentage of the population that is foreign-born is half what it was at the turn of the century. Undocumented immigrants are ineligible for almost all public benefits, including unemployment and Social Security, even though they pay into these programs through payroll taxes. According to Urban Institute research, only about one-quarter of immigrants are undocumented; most of those do not sneak across the border, but instead enter legally and stay after their visas expire—and only one-third of them come from Mexico.[6]

The *Channel One* segments reflected a military mentality toward immigration: The first segment led with the question of whether the United States had "lost control of its borders"; the second took viewers along on an Immigration and Naturalization Service (INS) raid of a Texas factory; the third segment started off with U.S. border patrol agents describing "Operation Gatekeeper." Not until the fourth segment, which featured interviews with immigrants, was the story framed by anyone besides anti-immigration advocates or agencies.

Channel One reporters led with inflammatory language and war imagery, promising "a trip to the front lines in the war on illegal immigration" and a look at "ground zero in what some people are calling the war against illegal immigration."

Use of anti-immigrant rhetoric in nonattributed quotes also slanted reporting. One of the opening comments from *Channel One* reporter Tracy Smith was: "It's been said that the U.S. has lost control of its borders. Despite high-tech fences and armed guards on patrol, illegal immigrants just keep on coming." Smith later introduced an interview with a Proposition 187 supporter by declaring, "Some people even say illegal immigration will be the end of America as we know it."

A televised INS raid of a factory in Texas displayed blatant double standards and questionable journalistic practices. The cameras carefully avoided showing the faces of the INS agents "to protect their identities." Yet *Channel One* showed no qualms about airing the faces of the factory workers accused of being undocumented. In coverage reminiscent of the TV show *Cops,* reporters behaved more like deputized INS agents than like journalists, as cameras accompanied officers running through the woods, hunting down individual fleeing workers.

Much of the reporting seemed to encourage viewers to stereotype people based on ethnicity or place of residence. "Half of the millions of illegal immigrants live here in this state, a lot of them in neighborhoods like this one," one reporter declared, standing in a park populated by Latinos. "In this neighborhood, most of the people are recent arrivals who don't speak much English," another announced. Demonstrating the same stereotyping that such coverage is likely to encourage, a *Channel One* journalist pointed out a group of Latino men talking to someone in a car as an example of illegal immigrants looking for work—without offering any evidence that the men were undocumented.

Sources determine from whose point of view the story is told and shape the parameters of debate. In every segment but the last, anti-immigration sources outnumbered immigrants or immigrant rights advocates. In the first segment, five anti-immigration advocates were quoted before the single dissenting source appeared. The last segment was introduced, "Today, the view from the other side.

The immigrants' story from the immigrants themselves." The "other" side are immigrants, implying that the "U.S. side" is the anti-immigration position.

When advocates for one side appear first, outnumber their opponents, and receive more air time, their points of view will set the terms of the debate. Those who appear after the terms of debate are set usually end up answering their opponents' points rather than making their own.

Much of the discussion in the *Channel One* series centered around the point of view of border guards and INS agents, interviewed at length, often without being balanced by critical sources. Left out was any mention of the harassment by border guards of legal immigrants and citizens of Latino descent, long documented by such organizations as the American Friends Service Committee's Immigration Law Enforcement Monitoring Project.

In the third segment, Ronald Prince, a sponsor of Proposition 187, blamed illegal immigrants for California's economic problems: "If we do not do something and do it quickly we will not have a state government in California. We are losing our public education sector, we are losing our health care sector, we are losing our welfare system and a lot of this is attributable to illegal aliens."

If immigrant advocates had been setting the terms of the debate, they might have argued that it was Proposition 13, a 1978 law that has drastically limited property tax revenues, that has hurt California's schools and other social services. They also might have pointed out, as the Urban Institute's Michael Fix and Jeffrey Passel did in a *Houston Chronicle* op-ed piece, that illegal immigrants are not eligible for welfare and that unauthorized use is "so low as to be undetectable."[7]

In the same segment, which focused on Proposition 187, *Channel One* cited as definitive California Governor Pete Wilson's estimates of how much illegal immigrants cost the state. A significant part of the series revolved around the question of whether immigrants were costing the United States "too much." In fact, claims of immigrants bankrupting the country have been challenged in such studies as the Urban Institute's *Immigration and Immigrants: Setting the Record Straight*, which showed that when both legal and illegal immigrants are counted, noncitizens contribute billions more dollars a year to the economy than they take out in services.[8]

The study found that while immigrants do use more services on the state level than they pay in state taxes, this is also true of native citizens. Each resident normally uses more state services than he or she pays in taxes, with the difference being made up by business taxes. When it allowed these misleading statements to go unchallenged, *Channel One* contributed to a political climate in which officeholders scapegoated immigrants for general economic problems.

Because it forces students to watch commercials in schools—disproportionately students in low-income communities[9]—*Channel One* itself is controversial. Opponents such as Unplug, an Oakland-based national youth organization against commercialism in schools, assist students in fighting what they see as the selling of poor students to corporations.

This controversy, and the fact that students, parents, and teachers in different cities have staged walkouts and demonstrations to get *Channel One* itself out of schools, makes *Channel One* particularly vulnerable to media criticism. In the fourth part of the immigration series, a reporter mentioned a student letter protesting *Channel One*'s "dehumanizing" portrayals of Latinos.

Later in the month, *Channel One* aired a somewhat more balanced segment on a student demonstration against Proposition 187. Reporter Rawley Valverde acknowledged, "Many students from *Channel One* schools complained about how the media has covered immigration, including *Channel One*'s reports."[10]

"Move to the Right": Pundits' Tried-and-Failed Advice

January/February 1995

JIM NAURECKAS

WHEN ASKED what advice she had for Bill Clinton on election night 1994, ABC commentator Cokie Roberts snapped: "Move to the right, which is the advice that somebody should have given him a long time ago."[11]

Although most pundits used the more euphemistic "move to the center," Roberts's prescription was constantly being offered by media spin doctors. One of the most prominent was Al From, leader of the Democratic Leadership Council (DLC), a corporate-backed group of "New Democrats" who have long argued that moving to the right is the key to winning elections.

Is it? "New Democrats," if anything, did worse in the 1994 election than plain old Democrats. The DLC's chair, Representative Dave McCurdy (D.–Okla.), got only 40 percent of the vote in his bid for the Senate. Senator Jim Sasser (D.–Tenn.), a DLC leading light, won only 42 percent in his reelection drive. The DLC's Representative Jim Cooper (D.–Tenn.), best known for his "bipartisan" health care reform plan, managed only 39 percent.[12]

Another prominent DLC member—a past president of the group—wasn't up for reelection, but President Bill Clinton would have to be considered one of the election's big losers. Although he campaigned as an "agent of change" who would reverse trickle-down policies, in office, Clinton overwhelmingly followed the DLC recipe for success. He offered centrist or conservative proposals on issues like crime, welfare, deficit reduction, and trade. On health care, he avoided a single-payer approach pushed by progressives in favor of a complex, expensive, insurance industry–friendly plan.

But commentators insisted—without providing evidence—that Clinton had abandoned the New Democratic faith. "Elected as a New Democrat, he stumbled during his first two years in office largely because he proposed Big Government solutions, like his health care plan, to a populace that thought it had already rejected them," said *Time*'s Michael Duffy in a preelection article.[13] *Newsweek*'s postelection cover story by Howard Fineman referred to "the New Democrat centrist themes he ran on in 1992 (and mostly forgot about after he was elected)."[14]

The denunciation of the centrist Clinton as an out-of-touch leftist is an old pattern, one that *Extra!* pointed out after Clinton was heralded in 1992 as the candidate who would finally wean the Democratic Party away from "Mondale/Dukakis liberalism." Before their electoral defeats, both Walter Mondale and Michael Dukakis had been hailed by media pundits as moderate candidates who would take back the party from the left.[15]

If it wasn't a Clinton shift to the left that led to the Republican victory, what was it? The biggest difference between 1994 and 1992 was not the country's opinion of Clinton, but who in the electorate was motivated to vote. A survey taken by Gallup for CNN and *USA Today* (neither of which did much with the results) suggests that if all eligible voters had come out, the results would have been far different: Those who turned out were significantly wealthier, whiter, and more Republican than those who stayed home. And those who voted in 1994 were much more affluent and more conservative than the voters in 1992—as a lonely letter to the editor in the *New York Times* pointed out.[16]

What's keeping the Democrats home? Many news outlets found it a great puzzle that Clinton wasn't getting more of a boost from the "booming" economy. "Democrats Getting No Lift From a Rising Economy," a front-page *New York Times* piece marveled.[17] Just the day before, that same front page had announced still more good news: "Statistics Reveal Bulk of New Jobs Pay Over Average," the headline declared.[18]

If you read that article, however, the news wasn't all that great. Reporter Sylvia Nasar's big story was that most new jobs were in high-paying *categories,* a statistic that means little: The fact that managers as a group make a lot of money doesn't mean that being an assistant manager at McDonald's is going to make you rich.

The real news was buried in a graph that accompanied the story. While the salaries of managers and supervisors—who make up about one-fourth of the American work force—have climbed, real wages for the other 75 percent of U.S. workers have fallen every year from 1987 to 1993 and were basically flat in 1994.

This reality, hidden behind economic happy-talk in so much news coverage, goes a long way toward explaining both the conservatives' anger and the Democrats' apathy. Clinton's party has done little to address the economic stagnation plaguing working people and minorities; at the very beginning of his administration, he abandoned the modest economic stimulus program that he successfully ran on. That was part of the post–1992 election "move to the center" that pundits like Cokie Roberts had encouraged him to make.

Notes

1. Ben H. Bagdikian, *The Media Monopoly* (Boston: Beacon Press, 1992).

2. The districts included were New York's Districts 1–20, Illinois's Districts 1–11 and 13–14, and California's Districts 23–39, 41–43 and 45–47.

3. *New York Times*, October 23, 1994.

4. See John Murray, "TV in the Classroom: News or Nikes?" *Extra!*, September/October 1991, p. 6.

5. *Channel One*, October 4–7, 1994.

6. *Houston Chronicle*, August 14, 1994.

7. *Houston Chronicle* op-ed piece, August 14, 1994. See also U.S. Department of Justice, Immigration and Naturalization Service, *Report on the Legalized Alien Population* (Washington, D.C.: Government Printing Office, 1992).

8. Michael Fix and Jeffrey Passel, *Immigration and Immigrants: Setting the Record Straight* (Washington, D.C.: Urban Institute, 1994).

9. Robin Templeton, "Who's Failing Whom?: Media Coverage of Public Education," *Extra!*, March/April 1994, p. 16.

10. *Channel One*, October 18, 1994.

11. *ABC World News Tonight*, November 8, 1994.

12. The poor electoral showing of the leading "move to the right" advocates was barely mentioned in mainstream press commentary. It was discussed in a December 19, 1994, *New Republic* article (John Judis, "The New Democrat Delusion," p. 14); a November 19, 1994, letter to the editor in the Minneapolis *Star Tribune* was virtually the only mention in the daily press.

13. Michael Duffy, "Alone in the Middle," *Time*, November 14, 1994, p. 52.

14. Howard Fineman, "Revenge of the Right," *Newsweek*, November 21, 1994, p. 37.

15. Jim Naureckas, "Conventional Wisdom: How the Press Rewrites Democratic Party History Every Four Years," *Extra!*, September 1992, p. 11. See Chapter 5 of this volume.

16. *New York Times*, November 25, 1994.

17. *New York Times*, October 18, 1994.

18. *New York Times*, October 17, 1994.

Appendix:
The Media's Corporate Connections

Media corporations, like other corporations, are controlled by boards of directors. These individuals, selected by the stockholders, are ultimately responsible for deciding who runs the news operations that these corporations own. Many of these corporate directors are also on the board of other corporations, forming what are called "interlocking directorates." A survey of the interlocks of some leading media corporations reveals that the people who control the nation's news are in many cases the same people who run the country's largest corporations.

Capital Cities/ABC

(ABC TV and radio networks, *Kansas City Star*, etc.)
Interlocks with:
Avon
Berkshire Hathaway (investments, insurance)
Cigna (insurance)
Coca-Cola
Consolidated Rail
General Housewares
Gillette
IBM
ITT
Johnson & Johnson
Melville (retail)
Rohm & Haas (chemicals)
Sheraton
Texaco
Hartford (insurance)
Union Pacific

CBS, Incorporated

(CBS TV and radio networks)
Interlocks with:
AT&T
Automatic Data Processing

Bulova (watches)
Chase Manhattan (banking)
CNA Financial Corporation (insurance)
Continental Grain
Cummins Engine
Getty Oil
Hasbro (toys)
Loews (hotels, insurance, tobacco)
Pathogenesis (pharmaceuticals)
Rite Aid (drug stores)

General Electric Corporation

(NBC, CNBC, etc.)
Interlocks with:
American Stock Exchange
Baxter (pharmaceuticals)
Bristol-Meyers Squibb (pharmaceuticals)
Citicorp (banking)
Champion (paper products)
Chemical Bank
Chubb (insurance)
CPC International (food processing)
Exxon
General Mills
Goodyear
Home Life Insurance
Illinois Tool Works
Merck (pharmaceuticals)
Olin Corporation (arms)
PepsiCo
Quaker Oats
Roadway Services (freight)
Stanley Works (tools)
U.S. Air
USX (steel, oil)

The New York Times Corporation

(*New York Times, Boston Globe*, etc.)
Interlocks with:
Amax (natural resources)
Bristol-Meyers Squibb (pharmaceuticals)
CS First Boston (banking)
Federal Reserve Bank of New York
Kelso & Company (banking)

New York Life Insurance
PepsiCo
Phelps Dodge
Santa Fe Pacific
The Colonial Fund

Dow Jones and Company, Incorporated

(*Wall Street Journal, Barron's*, etc.)
Interlocks with:
Alcatel Alsthom (telecommunications)
American Express
Amoco
Bankers Trust
Brooklyn Union Gas
Chemical Bank
Chubb (insurance)
Continental (insurance)
Corning (glass)
Dayton Hudson (retail)
Eli Lilly (pharmaceuticals)
Federal Reserve Bank of New York
Ford
Hallmark Cards
ITT
ITT Hartford Insurance
ITT Sheraton
J. C. Penney
New York Stock Exchange
Revlon
RJR Nabisco (tobacco, food processing)
Ryder System (truck leasing)
Sara Lee
Shell Oil
Tri-Continental (investments)
Union Carbide (chemicals)
Xerox

Washington Post Company

(*Washington Post*, Minneapolis *Star Tribune, Newsweek*, etc.)
Interlocks with:
Bank of New York
Bowater (paper)
Coca-Cola
H. J. Heinz (food processing)

IBM
J. P. Morgan (banking)
McDonald's
Morgan Guaranty Trust (banking)
National Service Industries (cleaning)
New York Stock Exchange
Union Pacific (rail)

Time Warner, Incorporated

(*Time, Fortune, People, Sports Illustrated*, etc.)
Interlocks with:
American Security Systems
AON (insurance)
AT&T
Chase Manhattan (banking)
Colgate Palmolive
Dayton Hudson (retail)
Firestone Tire & Rubber
Freeport-McMoran (natural resources)
Fuji Xerox
G. D. Searle (pharmaceuticals)
Inland Steel
Morgan Guaranty Trust (banking)
New York Stock Exchange
Rank Xerox
Ryder System (truck rentals)
Springs Industries (bedding)
Toys "R" Us
Turner Broadcasting Systems

Source: *Standard and Poor's Register of Corporations, Standard and Poor's Directors and Executives*

About the Book and Editors

Why did major news outlets virtually ignore the only cost-effective plan for universal health care coverage—even though polls showed the plan had majority support? Why did leading journalists go out of their way to attack Bill Clinton's rivals in the 1992 Democratic primary—while focusing unprecedented attention on Clinton's personal life? Why do establishment media consider falling unemployment to be *bad* news?

In the tradition of I.F. Stone and George Seldes, the contributors to *The FAIR Reader* probe the often mysterious connections between press and politics in the 1990s. The essays are filled with startling information about the critical issues of our time—from the Gulf War and the Clarence Thomas hearings to the debates over health care reform and NAFTA—documenting the deceptive, one-sided mainstream reporting that leaves the public in the dark.

Particular attention is paid to the election of 1992 and the Clinton administration, showing how the media promoted, undercut, and finally shaped Clinton to fit a media agenda. the book demonstrates that systematic media bias poses a threat to the democratic process and the free flow of information to the U.S. citizenry.

FAIR, founded in 1986, is the national media watch group dedicated to the principle that independent, aggressive, and critical media are essential to an informed democracy. In the nine years since FAIR was launched, it has gained national recognition for its well-documented studies of media bias, its challenge to powerful media figures like Rush Limbaugh, and its award-winning journal of media criticism and politics, *Extra!*.

The FAIR Reader collects *Extra!*'s most incisive reporting on journalism and politics in the '90s. It will be invaluable to anyone interested in decoding the media agenda behind the daily news.

Jim Naureckas is the editor of *Extra!*, the magazine of FAIR. A graduate of Libertyville High School and Stanford University, he got his first job in journalism covering the Iran-contra scandal for *In These Times*. He is the coauthor of *The Way Things Aren't: Rush Limbaugh's Reign of Error* (New Press).

Janine Jackson is FAIR's research director and the cohost of FAIR's syndicated radio show *CounterSpin*. She writes a monthly column on labor and media for the Labor Resource Center at Queens College. Jackson graduated from Sarah Lawrence College and the New School for Social Research.

About the Contributors

Dean Baker is an economist at the Washington, D.C.–based Economic Policy Institute.

Dorothee Benz is director of communications for the Garment Workers' Union (ILGWU) Local 23–25 in New York City.

Veena Cabreros-Sud, formerly the co-coordinator of FAIR's Women and Media Project, is director of marketing and distribution for Third World Newsreel.

John Canham-Clyne is director of research for Public Citizen's Congress Watch.

Steve Cobble is a political consultant based in Albuquerque, New Mexico, who worked on Jesse Jackson's 1988 presidential campaign.

Jeff Cohen is executive director of FAIR and coauthor of *Through the Media Looking-Glass* (Common Courage) and *The Way Things Aren't: Rush Limbaugh's Reign of Error* (New Press).

Mark Cook has reported on Central America for *Undercurrents* radio and other media outlets.

Kim Deterline, formerly the activist director of FAIR, heads the media activist group We Interrupt This Message.

Tiffany Devitt is the publisher of *Extra!*.

Robert Dreyfuss is a Washington, D.C. writer and media relations specialist who has worked with Physicians for a National Health Program and Ralph Nader's Public Citizen.

Laura Flanders is coordinator of FAIR's Women and Media Project and the executive producer and host of *CounterSpin*.

William Gibson is professor of sociology at California State University at Long Beach and the author of *The Perfect War: Technowar in Vietnam* (Atlantic Monthly Press) and *Warrior Dreams: Paramilitary Culture in Post-Vietnam America* (Hill & Wang).

Patrice Greanville is an economist and former editor of *Cyrano's Journal,* a mass-consciousness review.

Doug Henwood is the editor of *Left Business Observer* and the author of *Wall Street* (Verso).

John Hess, a contributor to the *New York Observer,* worked for the *New York Times* from 1954 to 1978.

Sam Husseini is FAIR's activist coordinator.

About the Contributors

Farah Kathwari is a former FAIR intern.

Justin Lewis is associate professor in the Department of Communication at the University of Massachusetts at Amherst and the director of the Center for the Study of Communication.

Mike Males is a graduate student in social ecology at the University of California at Irvine.

Joshua Meyrowitz is professor of communications at the University of New Hampshire and the author of *No Sense of Place: The Impact of Electronic Media on Social Behavior* (Oxford).

Michael Morgan is associate professor in the Department of Communication at the University of Massachussetts at Amherst.

Renu Nahata is the former administrative director of FAIR.

Rob Richie is national director of the Center for Voting and Democracy, a Washington, D.C., group that researches and publicizes alternatives to winner-take-all voting systems.

Dan Shadoan is FAIR's shipping and sales coordinator.

Lawrence Soley teaches at Marquette University's College of Communications and is the author of *The News Shapers: The Sources Who Explain the News* (Praeger).

Norman Solomon is a syndicated columnist and the coauthor of *Unreliable Sources* (Lyle Stuart) and *Through the Media Looking Glass* (Common Courage).

John Summa, a writer with a Ph.D. in economics, currently teaches economic development at North-South University in Dhaka, Bangladesh.

Index

ABC, 129, 162, 169, 175
   Gulf War, 19, 29, 33, 35, 36, 46
   1992 elections, 81, 94–95, 95, 98, 109
   Panama invasion, 12, 17
   welfare, 190, 191, 192
   See also specific programs
Accuracy in Media (AIM), 41
ACTPN. *See* Advisory Committee on Trade Policy and Negotiations
Adams, Brock, 116
ADM. *See* Archer-Daniels-Midland
Advisory Committee on Trade Policy and Negotiations (ACTPN), 148
AEI. *See* American Enterprise Institute
Aetna, 161–162
AFDC (Aid to Families with Dependent Children). *See* Welfare
AFL-CIO, 153
AGE. *See* Americans for Generational Equity
Agnew, Spiro, 93
Agran, Larry, 55, 56
AIDS, 196, 197, 218
Aid to Families with Dependent Children (AFDC). *See* Welfare
Ailes, Roger, 114, 140
AIM. *See* Accuracy in Media
Ajami, Fouad, 34–35
Albright, Madeleine, 182
Alliance for Managed Competition, 168
Almanac of American Politics, The, 106
Alter, Jonathan, 38, 69, 190–191
Altman, Roger, 124
AMA. *See* American Medical Association
American Enterprise Institute (AEI), 23, 80, 122, 187
American Medical Association (AMA), 196, 200
American Petroleum Institute, 83
Americans for Generational Equity (AGE), 220
American Spectator, 98
America Tonight, 34–35
Amnesty International, 20
Amoco, 172
Andreas, Dwayne, 98
Antifeminism, 194–195
AP. *See* Associated Press
Apple, R. W. "Johnny," 20, 24, 47(n5), 134, 179
   1992 elections, 58, 65, 66–67, 72, 109
Applebome, Peter, 59
Arab-American Anti-Discrimination Committee, 39
Archer-Daniels-Midland (ADM), 98
ARCO, 82, 83, 98
Ardito Barletta, Nicolas, 15
Aristide, Jean-Bertrand, 177–178

Arledge, Roone, 28
Armey, Dick, 163
Armitage, Richard, 21
Arnett, Peter, 16
Aspell, Tom, 33, 46
Aspin, Les, 125
Associated Press (AP), 26, 176, 195–196
Atlantic, 71, 74(n77), 80
Auerbach, Stuart, 146
Ayres, B. Drummond, 84

Babcock, Charles, 59
Bacon, Kenneth H., 146, 147
Bagdikian, Ben, 228
Bailey, Douglas, 78
Baird, Zoe, 130–132
Baker, James, 25
Baltimore Sun, 106
Balz, Dan, 64
Barnes, Fred, 28, 141, 177
Barnet, Richard, 25
Barone, Michael, 210–211
Barron's, 5
Barry, Robert, 82
Bazell, Robert, 28
Beckel, Bob, 78
Behr, Peter, 154
Bell, Jeffrey, 130
Bell Curve, The: Intelligence and Class Structure in American Life (Herrnstein & Murray), 74(n77)
Benagh, James, 218
Bentsen, Lloyd, 85, 86, 124, 129
Bergman, George, 182
Black, Charles, 78
Blackwell, James, 33
Blakemore, Bill, 38
Blandon, José, 14
Blanton, Tom, 8
Blystone, Richard, 33
BNL bank scandal, 137
Bode, Ken, 67
Boggs, Thomas, 82
Bolick, Clint, 133
Bond, Rich, 86
Boomer, Walter, 41
Boskin, Michael, 5
Boston Globe, 13, 62, 84, 105, 106, 193
Bowen, Jerry, 36
Boxer, Barbara, 109, 110, 111
Bradley, Bill, 103–104, 105
Bradsher, Keith, 221–222
Braun, Carol Moseley, 109, 111
Braver, Rita, 17, 22

246

Bread for the World, 173
Brinkley, David, 46, 98, 129
Brock, William, 130
Broder, David, 84, 85, 103, 107
    1992 elections, 58, 65, 81, 82
Brokaw, Tom, 12–13, 112, 173
    Gulf War, 29, 32, 36, 37, 40
Brookings Institution, 23, 80, 81, 124
Brown, Jerry, 68–69, 74(n61), 113, 149
    and Democratic convention, 81, 82
    and horse race coverage, 55, 58, 59, 67
    and Whitewater, 137, 138, 139
Brown, Ron, 82, 124, 154
Browne, Malcolm, 30
Brownstein, Ronald, 59, 65
Buchanan, Patrick, 24, 59, 64, 74(n61), 129, 151
Buckley, Kevin, 14
Buckley, William, 220
Burkhalter, Holly, 173
Burrelle's Broadcast Database, 78, 80
Bush, Barbara, 113
Bush, George, 3–4, 85, 89–90
    Iran-contra scandal, 8–9, 68, 96
    and 1992 elections, xv, 59, 68, 78, 94–95, 137
Bush, Neil, 137
Bush administration, 30, 91, 137, 159, 193. *See also*
    Gulf War; Panama invasion

Cain, Bob, 161
California Center for Health Statistics, 196–197
California Department of Justice, 197
Capital Cities/ABC, 34
Capital Gang, 70, 83, 128
Capra, Tom, 32
Carter, Hodding, 29
Carville, James, 78
Casey, William, 39
Cavanaugh, John, 146
CBS, 26, 28, 42, 43, 46, 141–142
    Gulf War civilian deaths, 37, 38, 39
    Gulf War sources, 33, 34–35, 36
    Haiti, 179, 181
    1992 elections, 67, 78, 97, 98, 108, 115–116
    Panama invasion, 11, 12, 16, 17, 22
    Somalia, 174, 175, 176
Cedras, Raoul, 179
Center for Constitutional Rights, 31
Center for Immigrants Rights, 131
Center for Investigative Reporting, 98
Center for Responsive Politics, 91
Center for Strategic and International Studies, 23
Center for the Study of American Women and
    Politics, 111
Center on Budget and Policy Priorities, 192
Centers for Disease Control, 197
Central Broadcasting Service. *See* CBS
Centrism, xvi
Chafee, John, 162, 168
Chancellor, John, 44, 95, 129
Channel One, 232–235
Charen, Mona, 83, 128, 180
Chase, Rebecca, 192
Chemical Bank, 82
Cheney, Dick, 182
Cherubin, Pierre, 178–179
Chevron, 172

Chicago Tribune, 8, 19–20, 81, 104, 141, 164
    1988 elections, 84, 86
    1994 elections, 229–231
China, 88, 153–154
Chomsky, Noam, xv, 24
Christian Coalition, 97
Christian Science Monitor, 20, 25, 85, 129–130
Chung, Connie, 98
Cigna, 161–162
Citizens for Tax Justice, 128
Citizens Trade Campaign, 149
Citizen Trade Watch, 147
Clarke, Torie, 94
Cleveland *Plain Dealer*, 190
Clinton administration
    Baird/Wood controversy, 130–132
    cabinet appointments, 123–125
    campaign promises, 121–123, 129–130
    corporate support, 122–123
    economic plan, 128–129
    and economy, 128–129, 221
    gay issues, 126–127
    Guinier nomination, 132–134
    Haiti, 177–182
    military spending, 128–129
    1994 elections, 235–236
    Somalia, 171–177, 183(nn 8, 29)
    teenager stereotypes, 196, 197
    and welfare, 188, 189, 193
    Whitewater scandal, 137–141
    See also Health care reform; North American Free
        Trade Agreement
Clinton, Bill
    corporate support for, xvii, 122–123
    and Iraq, 51(n177)
    and 1992 convention coverage, 82
    and 1992 horse race coverage, xv, 58, 59, 66–67,
        68, 69, 73(n46)
    personal scandal coverage, xv, xvii, 62–63, 88, 96,
        116, 137, 141–142
    and Sister Souljah, 107–108, 117(n21)
    voter knowledge, 88–89, 90–91, 92
    See also Clinton administration
Clinton, Hillary Rodham, 112–115, 138, 139,
    161–162
Clymer, Adam, 162, 163, 164
CNN
    and Buchanan, 70
    Clinton administration, 122
    Clinton economic plan, 128, 129
    gay issues, 127
    Gulf War, 33, 35
    health care reform, 161
    1992 elections, 67, 70, 80, 83, 97
    Panama invasion, 13, 16
    Romania, 12
Cobain, Kurt, 201
Cochran, John, 82
Cockburn, Alexander, 25
Cockburn, Patrick, 38
Cohen, Richard, 138, 214
Cole, Johnetta, 124
Colon, Willie, 230
Common Cause, 122, 220
Common Cause Magazine, 159
Compton, Ann, 29, 94, 95

Conduct Unbecoming (Shilts), 126–127
Conoco, 172
Constant, Emmanuel, 181
Coontz, Stephanie, 188
Cooper, Jim, 162–163, 164, 169, 235
Cooper, Kenneth J., 64–65
Cordesman, Anthony, 32–33, 46
Corn, David, 124, 164
Corporate advertising, xvi, xviii, 167
  and Gulf War, 42
Corporate agenda, xvi, xvii–xviii. *See also specific topics*
Corporate media ownership, xvi
  and campaign funding, 98
  and defense industry, 34
  See also specific topics
Crane, Philip, 230
Crichton, Sarah, 194–195
Crime, xviii, 205–215
  and civil rights, 212–213, 215(n8)
  and racial issues, 205–206, 208–209, 212, 213–215
Cronkite, Walter, 29
Crossfire, 70, 74(n61)
  Clinton administration, 127, 129
  gay issues, 127
Cruz, Rogelio, 15
C-SPAN, 15
Cuba embargo, 98, 124
Cullum, Lee, 33

Dallas Times Herald, 33
D'Amato, Alfonse, 139
Danforth, John, 7
Davis, Gray, 111
Deaver, Michael, 30
Decter, Midge, 23
Dellums, Ron, 125, 127
Democratic Leadership Council (DLC), 82–83, 235
DeParle, Jason, 219
Detroit Free Press, 31
de Waal, Alex, 174
Dionne, E. J., 24
DiVall, Linda, 78
Dixon, Alan, 109
DLC. *See* Democratic Leadership Council
Dollars and Sense, 148, 164
Donahue, 25
Donahue, Thomas, 153
Donaldson, Sam
  Gulf War, 19
  Panama invasion, 11
"Doonesbury," 3
Dorgan, Byron, 151
Dornan, Robert, 229, 230
Dow Chemical, 83
Dowd, Maureen, 59, 68, 142
Downey, Tom, 167–169
Duffy, Michael, 236
Dugan, Michael, 33
Duggan, Dennis, 212, 215(n8)
Dukakis, Michael, 67, 84, 86, 124, 236
Duke, David, 59, 70, 71–72, 214
Duvalier, Jean Claude ("Baby Doc"), 82, 124, 180

Earth in the Balance (Gore), 97
Eastland, Terry, 7

Economic Policy Institute, 147
Economic Report of the President, 5
Economist, 145, 146
Economy, 4–6, 9(n9), 128–129, 221–224. *See also* North American Free Trade Agreement; *specific topics*
Edmonds, Patricia, 111
Edsall, Thomas B., 59, 82, 84, 107
Edwards, Lynda, 99
EEOC. *See* Equal Employment Opportunity Commission
Ehrenreich, Barbara, 114
Eisner, Peter, 13
Eizenstadt, Stu, 124
Elderly people, xvii, 218–220
Electronic Workers, 152
Eleta, Carlos, 15
Eller, Jeff, 176–177
Endara, Guillermo, 14–15
Equal Employment Opportunity Commission (EEOC), 6
Evans, Rowland, 106, 125, 129
Everts, Rob, 167

Face the Nation, 141–142
FAIR. *See* Fairness & Accuracy in Reporting
Fairness & Accuracy in Reporting (FAIR), xvi, 6, 7, 32, 42, 63
Fair Trade Campaign, 147, 148
Farber, Mike, 229
Farnsworth, Clyde H., 145–146
Farrah Aidid, Mohamed, 175, 176
Farrell, John Aloysius, 105
Fedarko, Kevin, 200
Feder, Judith, 158
Feinsilber, Mike, 26
Feinstein, Dianne, 109, 110, 111
Ferguson, Thomas, xvii, 83
Ferraro, Geraldine, 109, 110, 112
Fields, Suzanne, 109
Fineman, Howard, 236
Fineman, Mark, 172
Fish, Hamilton, Jr., 230
Fisk, Robert, 31
Fitzwater, Marlin, 94
Fix, Michael, 234
Flint, Anthony, 105
Flowers, Gennifer, 62, 88
Forbes, Michael, 230
Ford, Guillermo "Billy," 15
Fortune magazine, 217
Foster, Vince, 139–141
Francis, Fred, 12
Franco, Francisco, 70
François, Michel, 178
Frankel, Max, 19, 62–63
Freedom House, 21
Friedman, Milton, 222
Friedman, Thomas, 26, 122, 154, 223
From, Al, 235
Frontline, 98

Gallup, 42–43
Garment, Suzanne, 80
Gartner, Michael, 32
GATT. *See* General Agreement on Tariffs and Trade

Gay issues, xv, 97, 126–127
GE. *See* General Electric
Gelb, Leslie, 41, 44
Gender issues, xvii, 23
   Baird/Wood controversy, 130–131
   female candidates, 108–112, 117(n31)
   1992 elections, 108–116
   See also Sexual harassment
General Agreement on Tariffs and Trade (GATT), 154
General Dynamics, 220
General Electric (GE), 34, 82, 128, 129
Georgia Pacific, 83
Gergen, David, 69, 80, 95, 134
Germond, Jack, 70, 179
Gershman, John, 146
Gerstner, Louis, 123
Gerth, Jeff, 137–138, 143(n2)
Gilpin, Kenneth N., 221
Gingrich, Newt, xviii
Glaspie, April, 27, 48(n51)
Glassman, James K., 154–155
Glodt, David, 98
Goldberg, Bernard, 217–218
Golden, Tim, 148
Goodman, Ellen, 192–193
Goodman, Walter, 65
Good Morning America, 70, 98, 190
Gordon, Michael, 26
Gore, Al, 82, 95, 97, 98
Government news management, 32–34, 41, 46, 50(n144)
Gralnick, Jeff, 176, 183(n29)
Gramm, Phil, 139, 163
Greenberg, Stan, 78
Greenfield, Jeff, 139, 140
Greenfield, Meg, 24, 35, 151
Greenwood, Bill, 162
Greer, Frank, 78
Gregg, Donald, 9
Greider, William, 82, 146, 147, 151
Grenada invasion, xv, 22, 30
Guinier, Lani, 132–134
Gulf War, 19–46
   aftermath of, 43–45
   Bush lionization, xv, 19–20, 95
   civilian deaths, 37–39
   government news management, 32–34, 41, 46, 50(n144)
   Hussein demonization, 20–21, 25, 29–30, 40
   media enthusiasm for, 25–26, 28–29, 46
   media-government identification, 19–20, 22–23, 29
   media pro-Iraq accusations, 27–28
   media self-analysis, 41–42
   negotiations rejection, 25, 26–27, 40–41
   and Panama invasion, 22, 24
   public opinion polls, 42–43
   and recession, 5
   sources, 23–25, 34–37
   terrorism theme, 39–40
   U.S. 1993 Iraq bombing (1993), 45–46
   U.S. motivations, 21–22
   and U.S. support for Iraq, 27, 48(n51)

Haass, Richard, 45
Hacker, Andrew, 105
Haiti, 82, 177–182
Hamburger, Tom, 159
Harkin, Tom, 58, 60, 64, 67, 73(n46)
Harris, Ron, 200
Harrison, Lawrence, 131
Hart, Peter, 78
Harvard Civil Rights Civil Liberties Law Review, 133
Hate crimes, 39
Health care reform, xv, xvii, 83, 157–169, 221
   conflicts of interest, 167–169
   Hillary Clinton role, 161–162, 169(n13)
Health Insurance Association of America (HIAA), 161–162, 164, 167
Healy, Melissa, 15
Heinl, Robert, 180
Henneberger, Melinda, 231
Herman, Edward, xv
Herrnstein, Richard J., 74(n77)
Hersh, Seymour, 51(n177)
Hertsgaard, Mark, xv
Hertzberg, Hendrik, 21, 68
Hess, Stephen, 80, 130
HIAA. *See* Health Insurance Association of America
Hickman, Harrison, 78
Hill, Anita. *See* Hill-Thomas hearings
Hill, Earlene, 194
Hill-Thomas hearings, 6–7, 110, 141, 142
Himmelstein, David, 162, 164
Hinds, Michael deCourcy, 5
Hitchens, Christopher, 29
Hoagland, Jim, 26
Hochbrueckner, George, 230
Holocaust revisionism, 71
Holtzman, Elizabeth, 109
Homelessness, 217–218
Honeywell, 34
Horton, Willie, 3
House, Karen Elliot, 40
Houston Chronicle, 234
Human Rights Watch, 173, 179
Hume, Brit, 95
Hunt, Al, 128
Hunter-Gault, Charlayne, 173
Hussein, Saddam, 20–21, 25, 29–30, 40. *See also* Gulf War

Ifill, Gwen, 65
IMF. *See* International Monetary Fund
Immigration, xvii, 130–132, 232–235
Immigration and Immigrants: Setting the Record Straight (Urban Institute), 234
Immigration Reform and Control Act (IRCA), 131
Imus, Don, 140
INFACT, 34
Ingwerson, Marshall, 129–130
Institute for International Economics, 147
Institute for Policy Studies, 23, 25
International Monetary Fund (IMF), 173–174
International Physicians for the Prevention of Nuclear War, 35
International Public Affairs Consultants (IPAC), 7
In These Times, 83, 164
Inventing Reality (Parenti), xv
IPAC. *See* International Public Affairs Consultants
Iran-contra scandal, 8–9, 88, 96
Iran-Iraq War, 20, 47(n17)

Iraq. *See* Gulf War; Iran-Iraq War
IRCA. *See* Immigration Reform and Control Act
Ireland, Doug, 129
Irvine, Reed, 41
ITT, 220

Jackson, Brooks, 97
Jackson, Jesse, 67, 81, 82, 84
    crime, 213–215
    and Sister Souljah, 107, 108, 117(n21)
    and Wilder, 106–107
Jackson, Michael, 199
Japanese American Citizens League, 131
Jehl, Douglas, 31
Jenkins, Brian, 40
Jennings, Peter, 14, 33, 81, 173, 191
Johnson Smick International, 140
Joint Center for Political and Economic Studies, 205
Joint Economic Committee of Congress, 6
Jones, Paula, 141–142
Jong, Erica, 130
Jordan, Mary, 64
Jordan, Robert, 106
Jordan, Vernon, 123
Journal of the American Medical Association, 164
Judis, John, 83

Kagay, Michael, 60
Kalb, Bernard, 41
Kamarck, Elaine Ciulla, 83
Kantor, Mickey, 78, 82, 122, 154
Kasem, Casey, 24
Kasriel, Paul, 221
Kassebaum, Nancy, 163
Kempton, Murray, 172
Kent, Arthur, 33
Kernisan, Louis, 180
Kerrey, Bob, 58, 64–65
Kerrison, Ray, 133, 142
Kerry, John F., 103–105
Keyes, William, 7
Keynes, John Maynard, 223
KGTV, 167
Kinsley, Michael, 70, 74(n61), 97, 127, 129, 150–151, 165
Kipper, Judith, 35, 40–41
Kirkpatrick, Jeane, 24
Klein, Joe, 80, 141–142, 174, 188
Knoll, Erwin, 24
KNSD, 167
Kolbert, Elizabeth, 58, 59
Kondracke, Morton, 46, 179
Koppel, Ted, 45, 139, 140, 169, 182
    Gulf War, 22, 23, 28, 37, 39
    Panama invasion, 13, 14, 15, 24
Koss, Mary, 194
Krauss, Clifford, 14
Krauthammer, Charles, 189
Krulwich, Robert, 34
Kummel, Eve, 152
Kurtz, Howard, 43, 60, 62, 151
Kuwait. *See* Gulf War

Ladies' Garment Workers, 152
Laurie, Jim, 45, 175
Lauter, David, 60

Ledbetter, James, 181
Lee, Gary, 159
Lee, Martin, xv, 37
Legal Times, 168, 169
Lehrer, Jim, 22–23, 29, 46, 82. *See also MacNeil/Lehrer NewsHour*
Leighton, Thomas, 231
Leo, John, 105
Levine, Irving R., 221
Levy, David, 231
Lewis, Ann, 78
Lewis, Anthony, 85–86, 130, 151–152, 219
Lewis, Neil, 7
"Liberal bias" complaints, xv, xvi, 86, 89
    and NAFTA, 149–150, 151–152
    and voter knowledge, 89, 93
Limbaugh, Rush, 139–141, 142
Lincoln Review, 7
Lipman, Samuel, 217
Liscio, John, 5
London *Independent*, 31, 38
London *Observer*, 26
Los Angeles Council on Child Abuse and Neglect, 199
Los Angeles riots, 109, 193
Los Angeles Times, 9, 15, 60, 80, 83, 113
    gay issues, 126–127
    gender issues, 113
    Gulf War, 31, 42
    1988 elections, 84, 86
    1992 horse race coverage, 56, 58, 59–60
    1994 elections, 229–231
    non-substantive 1992 election coverage, 64, 65
    personal scandal coverage, 62, 63
    Somalia, 172, 174
    and teenager stereotypes, 197, 198, 199, 200
Lott, Trent, 28
Loughlin, Mary Anne, 13
Luce, Thomas, 78
Luttwak, Edward, 24

MacNeil/Lehrer NewsHour, 8, 80, 173
    Gulf War, 23–24, 33, 41–42
    health care reform, 162, 163, 164, 166
    1992 elections, 69, 80
    Panama invasion, 13, 47(n32)
MacNeil, Robert, 8, 23, 166. *See also MacNeil/Lehrer NewsHour*
Madison Guaranty S&L, 137, 138
Magnet, Myron, 217
Mahdi Mohamed, Ali, 175
Mahe, Eddie, 78
Malek, Fred, 78
Malone, Julia, 98
Maloney, Carolyn, 230
Managed competition. *See* Health care reform
Mandel, Ruth, 111–112
Mann, Thomas, 78, 80
Manufacturing Consent (Herman & Chomsky), xv
Maraniss, David, 64
Maren, Michael, 174
Margolick, David, 134
Margolis, Jon, 84
Marshall, Jonathan, 14–15
Martin Marietta, 82, 83
Massachusetts Mutual, 220

Matalin, Mary, 94
McCain, John, 32
McConnell, Scott, 212–213
McCurdy, Dave, 235
McDermott, Jim, 162, 165
McDonnell, Ellen, 169
McDougal, James, 137, 138
McFate, Katherine, 205
McGrory, Mary, 141
McInturff, William, 78
McLarty, Thomas, 124
McLaughlin Group, 46, 70, 106, 177
  Gulf War, 33, 46
  Haiti, 177–178, 179
McLaughlin, John, 106, 129, 142, 177–178, 179. *See also McLaughlin Group*
McQueen, Michael, 205
McWethy, John, 17, 46, 161
Mead, Lawrence, 193
Media-government identification
  and Gulf War, 19–20, 22–23, 29
  and Panama invasion, 13–14, 47(n32)
Media Monopoly, The (Bagdikian), 228
Media self-analysis, 41–42, 57, 62–63, 77, 93
Meet the Press, 85, 152
Menendez brothers, 199
Merck, 168
Merrilles, Craig, 148
Metropolitan Life Insurance Company, 161–162, 220
Meyerson, Morton, 78
Michigan Law review, 133
"Middle-class tax cut," 65
Mikva, Abner, 7
Military spending, 33, 91, 128–129
Millard, Charles, 230
Miller, Dennis, 32
Miller, George, 163
Milwaukee Sentinel, 188
Minerbrook, Scott, 210
Minneapolis *Star Tribune*, 81, 159, 164
Mondale, Walter, 84, 85–86, 236
Monning, Bill, 35
Moorer, Thomas, 41
Morning After, The (Roiphe), 194
Morning Edition, 167–169, 182
Morton, Bruce, 38
Moynihan, Patrick, 220
Murdoch, Rupert, xvi
Murphy, Dennis, 38
Murray, Alan, 151
Murray, Charles, 74(n77), 187–188, 189
Myers, Lisa, 69

Nader, Ralph, 25
NAFTA. *See* North American Free Trade Agreement
Nairn, Allan, 180, 181
"Nannygate," 130–132
Nasar, Sylvia, 5, 236
Nation, The, 29, 83, 124, 172
National Association of Private Psychiatric Hospitals, 195–196
National Association of State Boards of Education, 196
National Bureau of Economic Research, 9(n.9)
National Center for Health Statistics, 196–197

National Center on Child Abuse and Neglect, 198
National Commission on Children, 198
National Council for Research on Women, 142
National Crime Victimization Survey (NCVS), 207–208, 211
National Institute of Ecology (Mexico), 147
National Institute of Justice, 198
National Journal, 80
National Organization for Women (NOW), 142
National Public Radio (NPR), 167–168, 175
  Haiti, 180, 181
  health care reform, 83, 164
Nazism, 71
NBC, 34, 129, 181, 189, 206, 221
  Gulf War, 20, 32, 33, 35, 40, 44
  1988 elections, 77, 85
  1992 elections, 69, 81, 82, 95, 112
  Panama invasion, 12–13, 13, 28
  Somalia, 176, 183(n29)
NCVS. *See* National Crime Victimization Survey
Neighbor to Neighbor, 166–167
Nelson, Lars-Erik, 219
Neuharth, Al, 110
Neuschler, Ed, 164
New Criterion, 217
New England Journal of Medicine, 46, 164
Newhouse, Neil, 78
New Politics of Poverty, The: The Nonworking Poor in America (Mead), 193
New Republic, The, 20–21, 68, 105, 141, 165
Newsday, 13, 16, 112
Newsweek, 125, 149, 174, 213, 236
  Gulf War, 21, 24, 35, 36, 38
  Haiti, 177, 178, 179
  1992 elections, 56, 69, 70, 80, 114
  sexual harassment, 141–142, 194–195
  teenager stereotypes, 197, 198, 201
  welfare, 188, 189, 190–191
New York *Daily News*, 176, 219
New Yorker, 51(n177), 180
New York Newsday, 7, 177, 200, 219
  crime, 214, 215(n8)
  Gulf War, 26, 27, 29, 41, 45
  1992 elections, 109, 113, 114, 115
New York Observer, 212
New York Post, 133, 140, 142, 174, 176
  crime, 205–206, 212–213
  1992 elections, 67, 73(n44), 108
New York Times, 36, 39, 43, 44, 80, 97, 123
  Baird/Wood controversy, 130–132
  Clinton cabinet, 124
  crime, 214
  economy, 5, 221–222, 223
  elderly people, 219
  gay issues, 126, 127
  gender issues, 109, 110, 111, 114, 115
  Guinier nomination, 132–133, 134
  Gulf War censorship, 30
  Gulf War enthusiasm, 26, 27
  Gulf War negotiations, 40, 41
  Haiti, 179, 181
  health care reform, 157–158, 159, 160, 161, 162, 163, 164, 165–166
  homelessness, 217–218
  Iran-Contra scandal, 9
  media-government identification, 19, 20, 21, 24

NAFTA, 132, 145–146, 147, 148, 149–150, 151–153, 154, 155
  1984 elections, 84, 85
  1992 alternative candidates, 68, 69
  1992 Buchanan candidacy, 72
  1992 election polls, 60
  1992 elections, 56, 80
  1992 horse race coverage, 58, 59–60, 67
  1994 elections, 227–228, 229–231, 236
  non-substantive 1992 election coverage, 64, 65, 66
  Panama invasion, 14, 15, 24, 47(n5)
  personal scandal coverage, 62–63, 66–67
  racial issues, 103, 104, 105, 107, 108, 132–133
  sexual harassment, 7, 142
  Somalia, 172, 173, 174
  U.S. 1993 Iraq bombing, 45
  welfare, 189, 193
  Whitewater, 138
Nicaragua, 14, 181
Nicaragua Solidarity Network, 181
Nightline, 12, 13, 15, 70, 115
  Clinton administration, 125, 139, 140, 169, 182
  Gulf War, 22, 23–24, 28, 40
  1984 elections, 83–86
  1988 elections, 3, 30, 67, 77, 83–86
  1992 elections, 55–72, 61, 77–99
  alternative candidates, 55–56, 67, 68–69, 74(n61)
  Buchanan candidacy, 59, 64, 70–72
  and campaign funding, 98
  candidate coverage demands, 98
  candidate false claims, 97
  conventions, 81–86
  gender issues in, 108–115, 117(n31)
  horse race coverage, xv, 58–60, 66–67, 68–69, 77–80, 90
  and Iran-Contra scandal, 8, 9
  media self-analysis, 57
  non-substantive coverage, 58–59, 63–66, 94–95, 96
  personal scandal coverage, xv, 62–63, 66–67, 96, 115–116, 137
  polls, 60, 62, 78, 79
  and racial issues, 103–108
  voter knowledge, 87–94
  Wilder candidacy, 56, 106–107
  1994 elections, 227–236, 237(n12)
  lack of coverage, 228–231
  Proposition 187, 232–235
Nissen, Beth, 12
Nixon, RichardBush, 3
NLDEF. *See* NOW Legal Defense and Education Fund
Noriega, Manuel, 11, 14. *See also* Panama invasion
North American Free Trade Agreement (NAFTA), 132, 145–155
  and "liberal bias" complaints, 149–150, 151–152
  public opposition to, xvii
North, Oliver, 7, 8, 14, 178
Novak, Robert, 83, 125, 128, 129
NOW. *See* National Organization for Women
NOW Legal Defense and Education Fund (NLDEF), 142
Nunn, Sam, 127

Oakland Tribune, 14–15
Oliphant, Pat, 20

Omaar, Rakiya, 174
On Bended Knee (Hertsgaard), xv
Orin, Deborah, 73(n44)
Ornstein, Norman, 80, 122
Osgood, Charles, 28
Ostrow, Ronald J., 64

Page, Clarence, 141
Panama invasion, xv, 11–17, 47(n5), 177
  and Gulf War, 22, 24
  justification for, 14–15
  and media-government identification, 13–14, 47(n32)
  Panamanian casualties, 12–13
  Panamanian public opinion reports, 11–12
Panetta, Leon, 124
Pangozzi, Amy, 131
Parenti, Michael, xv
Parker, Jay, 7
Passel, Jeffrey, 234
Passell, Peter, 155
Pate, Tony, 207
Patterson, James, 193
Pauling, Sharon, 173
PBS, 82, 95, 98
Peck, Edward, 35
Perle, Richard, 8
Perot, Ross, 78, 82, 149, 231
Peyser, Andrea, 174
Philadelphia Inquirer, 147, 158
Phillips, Kevin, 80, 81
Phillips, Leslie, 111
Phillips, Mark, 37, 115–116
Pinkston, Randall, 46
Pinochet, Augusto, 70
Pizzy, Alan, 174
Police Foundation, 207
Political analysts, 78, 79
Polls, 60, 62, 78, 79
Portland *Oregonian*, 108
Powell, Colin, 44, 126
Priest, Dana, 158, 162
PrimeTime Live, 11
Prince, Ronald, 234
Procter & Gamble, 166–167
Progressive, The, 24, 146
Proposition 187 (California), 232–235
ProQuest, 148
Prudential, 161–162
Psychology Today, 196

Quayle, Dan, 78, 88, 89, 93, 97
Quinn, Sally, 122

Rabinowitz, Dorothy, 41
Racial issues, xvii, 71, 74(n77), 222, 230
  and crime, 205–206, 208–209, 212, 213–215
  Guinier nomination, 132–134
  and Gulf War, 20, 39, 40–41
  and immigration, 232–235
  media sources, 23, 24
  and 1992 elections, 103–108
  and welfare, 191, 192, 193
Ralston Purina, 7
Rand Corporation, 34, 40
Rangel, Charles, 124

Rape in America, 198
Rather, Dan, 98, 108, 179
    Gulf War, 28, 39, 40, 46
    Panama invasion, 12, 13, 14
    Somalia, 173, 175, 176
Reagan administration, 30, 47(n17), 91, 191. *See also* Iran-contra scandal
Reagan, Michael, 127
Reilly, Jack, 98
Republican National Committee, 42
Reuters, 15
Reynolds, Mel, 229, 230
Richards, Ann, 112
Richter, Paul, 64
Riegle, Don, 150
Right from the Beginning (Buchanan), 70
Right Turn (Ferguson & Rogers), xvii
Ringle, Ken, 181–182
Risen, James, 65
Rivlin, Alice, 124
RJR Nabisco, 123
Roberts, Cokie, 29, 35, 109, 235, 236
Roberts, Sam, 104, 214
Roberts, Steven V., 122
Rockefeller, Jay, 163
Rockwell, 220
Rodriguez, Felix, 8
Rogers, Joel, xvii
Roiphe, Anne, 212
Roiphe, Katie, 194
Rollin, Betty, 189
Rolling Stone, 82, 146, 151
Rollins, Ed, 78
Romania, 12–13
Roosevelt, Theodore, 3–4
Rose, Judd, 11
Rosenbaum, David E., 131
Rosenberg, Howard, 36
Rosenfeld, Stephen, 72
Rosenstiel, Thomas, 60
Rosenthal, A. M., 20, 103, 212
Rosenthal, Andrew, 59
Rostenkowski, Dan, 229
Rowen, Hobart, 149, 155
Royce, Knut, 27
Royko, Mike, 214
Rubin, Robert, 124
Ruddy, Chris, 140
Russert, Tim, 77, 81

S&L scandal, 124
Sabato, Larry, 116
Sachs, Susan, 41
Safire, William, 34, 72, 142
Said, Edward, 24
Salinas de Gortari, Carlos, 147, 148
Salisbury, Harrison, 41
Samuelson, Robert, 163
Sand, Leonard, 217
San Francisco Chronicle, 36
Sasser, Jim, 235
Saturday Night Live, 32
Schmitt, Eric, 127
Schneider, William, 80, 84, 86
Schwarzkopf, H. Norman, 29
Sciolino, Elaine, 173, 174

Seidman, William, 124
Sessions, William, 40
Sexism. *See* Gender issues; Sexual harassment
Sexual harassment, 141–142, 194–195
    Hill-Thomas hearings, 6–7, 110, 141, 142
    and 1992 elections, 115–116
Shalala, Donna, 125, 196
Shields, Mark, 70, 128
Shilts, Randy, 126–127
Shultz, George, 15
Siad Barre, Mohamed, 173, 176
Siegel, Mark, 116
Silverado S&L, 137
Simon, Bob, 46
Simon, Paul, 7
Sister Souljah, 107–108, 117(n21)
60 Minutes, 22, 25, 113
Smith, Jack, 191
Smith, Tracy, 233
Solomon, Norman, xv
Solow, Robert, 223
Somalia, 171–177, 183(n8)
Sources, 127, 130, 139
    Gulf War, 23–25, 34–37
    NAFTA, 147, 149–150, 153–154
    1992 elections, 78–80
    See also Washington pundits
South Africa, 7, 70
"Special interests," 82, 85, 153
    and Clinton administration, 121, 122, 124
    voter knowledge, 92–93
Spin doctors, 30, 78, 79, 107
Squier, Robert, 16, 78
Squires, James, 78
Stahl, Lesley, 25, 34–35
Star, The, 62
Star Wars, 33
Stephanopoulos, George, 128
Stewart, Jim, 28, 46
St. John, Spenser, 181–182
St. Petersburg Times, 127
Stringer, Howard, 30–31
Sullivan, Kathleen, 12
Survey of Consumer Finances, 223
Swoboda, Frank, 59
Sybert, Rich, 230

Talan, Jamie, 200
Teenager stereotypes, 195–201
Teen pregnancy, 187–191, 196
Teeter, Robert, 78
Texaco, 34
This Week with David Brinkley, 98, 190, 191, 192
Thomas, Clarence. *See* Hill-Thomas hearings
Threlkeld, Richard, 97
Tierney, John, 57, 62
Time magazine, 146, 178, 190, 219
    Gulf War, 34, 42
    Somalia, 173, 174, 175
    and teenager stereotypes, 197, 198, 200
Tobacco Institute, 83
Today show, 28, 32
Tomasky, Michael, 107
Toner, Robin, 58, 60, 63
Toronto Globe and Mail, 12, 16
Travelers, 161–162

Traylor, Daniel, 142
Trudeau, Garry, 3
Truman, Harry, 37
TRW, 220
Tsongas, Paul, 58, 60, 65, 67, 68

Uchitelle, Louis, 223
Unemployment, 5, 9(n9), 221–224
Uniform Crime Reports, 199, 207, 211
United Air Lines, 82
United Healthcare Corporation, 168
U.S. Agency for International Development, 173–174
U.S. League of Savings Institutions, 220
U.S. News & World Report, 44–45, 105, 122, 197, 198
   crime, 206, 207–211, 213, 214
   NAFTA, 147, 148
   1992 elections, 80, 114
   welfare, 192, 193
U.S. Steel, 220
Unplug, 234
Unreliable Sources (Lee & Solomon), xv
Urban Institute, 189, 234
Urschel, Joe, 142
USA Today, 125, 154, 164, 187
   1992 elections, 68, 109, 110, 111
US Healthcare, 169
Utley, Garrick, 38

Valverde, Rawley, 235
Vietnam War, 16
Village Voice, 48(n51), 98, 107, 129, 174, 181
Vincent, Billie, 39
Vital Statistics of the United States, 199

Waas, Murray, 48(n51)
Wallace, Chris, 85
Waller, Littleton W. T., 180
Wall Street Journal, 5, 133, 187–188, 189, 205
   Gulf War, 21, 40, 41
   NAFTA, 146, 147, 151
Walters, Barbara, 22, 27
Warren, James, 81
Washington Monthly, 164
Washington Post, 60, 72, 80, 81, 82, 97
   China, 153–154
   Clinton administration, 122, 123, 133, 138
   crime, 213, 214
   elderly people, 219
   Gulf War, 24, 27, 32, 35, 41, 43, 44
   Haiti, 178–179, 181–182
   health care reform, 157, 158, 159, 161, 162, 163
   Iran-Contra scandal, 9
   NAFTA, 146, 149–150, 151, 154–155
   1988 elections, 84, 85
   1992 horse race coverage, 58, 59, 60
   non-substantive 1992 election coverage, 64–65, 94–95
   personal scandal coverage, 63
   racial issues, 103, 106, 107
   Somalia, 172
   teenager stereotypes, 195
   welfare, 188
Washington pundits, 78, 79, 80–81. *See also* Sources; specific people
Washington Times, 111
Wattenberg, Ben, 80
Weber, Vin, 167–169
Weekly News Update on the Americas, 181
Weil, Andrew, 175
Weinberger, Caspar, 88
Weiner, Stuart, 222
Weisskopf, Michael, 64
Welfare, xviii, 187–193
   and teen pregnancy, 187–191
   voter knowledge, 91, 92, 100(n60)
Wessel, David, 5
Weymouth, Lally, 133, 134
WHDH, 166–167
Whitewater scandal, 137–141
Whitman, David, 192
Wicker, Tom, 219
Wilder, Douglas, 56, 106–107
Wilkins, Roger, 105
Will, George, 33, 84, 106, 129, 133, 134, 192
Williams, Juan, 81, 106
Willis, Brad, 31
Wilson, Pete, 234
Wines, Michael, 227–228
WLIB, 205
Wofford, Harris, 158
Wood, Kimba, 130–132
Woodruff, Judy, 13, 47(n32)
Woolhandler, Steffie, 163, 164, 166
World Policy Institute, 23
Wynette, Tammy, 113

Yeakel, Lynn, 110–111

Zahn, Paula, 78
Zimbabwe, 173–174

११ १२ १३ १४